Cashless Investing
in Real Estate

CASHLESS INVESTING IN REAL ESTATE

Jack Cummings

Playboy Press   New York

Manufactured in the United States of America.
FIRST EDITION.
Playboy Press/A Division of PEI Books, Inc.

Library of Congress Cataloging in Publication Data

Cummings, Jack, 1940–
    Cashless investing in real estate.

    1. Real estate investment. I. Title.
HD1382.5.C85   332.63′24   81–82782
ISBN 0–87223–749–4   AACR2

To Robert Lynwood Cummings
and
Anne Marie Cummings,
two kids who are growing up in a wonderful age
filled with opportunities.

Acknowledgments

Any book is a labor of love and hate, hours of work when the body is tired, weeks of depression when nothing springs out of the mind's fountain, and then the mixed emotion of its final completion and realization that it's over, but what next? Yet there are those who make it work: Nancy Parsegian who got it all started, and Charlotte Anne Winkle who knows it will work.

Contents

APPENDIX

Cashless Investing

in Real Estate

1

Real-Estate Investing:

What You Need to Succeed

ON JANUARY 15, 1984, the purchasing power of the U.S. dollar is expected to be approximately 25% of its 1967 buying power—a dollar will be worth 25¢. Inflation is going bananas, and more and more people are becoming desperate at the fear they will simply run out of economic rope. Gasoline will hit $5.00 a gallon in Europe— and before long, $3.50 a gallon in the U.S.A. What will you do? Where will you turn?

Fortunately, there is a very simple answer. You will invest in real estate, beginning right now.

Before we discuss the prerequisites for successful real-estate investing, let's review what you *don't* need to be a success.

A *college degree* absolutely is not required. Look at history— some of the wealthiest and most successful men and women in the world didn't graduate from college; many didn't even finish high school. Some professions, of course, require such higher education, and many high-paid professionals are also successful real-estate investors. But you can do it with or without college. In fact, too much of the wrong kind of education can stand in the way of success here. I've seen C.P.A. types, bankers, and lawyers analyze and plan and think about doing something so long that some dumb guy with a dream and some guts took the opportunity by the horns and made a bundle of money before the thinkers knew what had happened.

Knowledge of the real-estate industry must be a requirement, then, right? Wrong. You can be a success in real-estate investing without a lot of fancy knowledge of real-estate finance, or appraising, or management, or trends, or law, or accounting. Those areas are important elements of the business, but you can *hire* that expertise when and if you need it. Fancy learning is great if you are in the business. As an investor, you should stick to the basics and learn the "tricks" of making deals work.

If a college degree isn't needed, and in-depth knowledge isn't a prerequisite, do you have to be a *right age?* I almost said no to this one, too. But age is a product of time, and there is a right time for everyone to buy real estate. That time, for you and me, is always *now*.

Success comes to people of all ages in real estate. I have known young men and women who were just starting out and were achieving major successes. At the same time, I have known people who shunned real estate for years while working at nine-to-five jobs. When they took a little of their cash and finally bought some real estate, what happened? Past their prime of life, they discovered a way to an independent life free of financial worry beyond their wildest dreams—through real-estate investing.

Your age, then, is not important when it comes to buying real estate. But it *is* a factor in your real-estate-investment planning. The young can establish a buying plan whose goals differ from those of their elders. Success and financial independence are achieved when you feel you have attained them in accordance with your established goals.

What about being a male or a female? And let's not forget your ethnic origin, or the language you speak. These make a difference to your ability to be successful, don't they?

Again, no. There is no requirement that you must be male, white, and have a Royal British background. Today, there is no real basis for viewing these elements as barriers to success in real estate. Yesterdays are long past in this field; today—as you, whoever you are, will know upon completion of this book—*you* control your destiny, no one else.

At last we come to money. *Money*, then, is the one thing you *must* have in order to invest in real estate, right? Does everyone agree money is the one thing needed to buy real estate?

I get to say an emphatic *NO!* Money isn't a prerequisite to investing in real estate. Not a lot of money! Not *any* money!

Other books have shown investors how to develop new and creative ways to build their fortunes into larger fortunes. But what about all the people who are still wondering where they are going to find the money to pay the rent at the end of the month? What about the young couple struggling to make it in this world of rising costs? Can you imagine the problems the elderly have in trying to match 1960 or 1980 retirement incomes with the out-of-proportion 1986 costs they are going to be faced with?

Out of every 400 persons living in the United States as of the writing of this book, about one is a millionaire. That is more than double what it was just a few years back, and is an impressive statistic. But what about the other 399 people? Are you one of those?

If you are, then it is time you started getting smart. Smart—not brilliant. Smart—not a college degree. Smart, as in money. You can do this by learning just *three* secrets about getting money and keeping it.

- The first is: You will never keep anything you didn't attain through a goal.
- The second is: The best way to have wealth to keep is through real estate.
- The third is: Anyone can buy real estate.

Let's look at the first one. You can luck into anything, but never count on luck. By establishing a sound goal and a well-devised plan, you will get—and keep—the things you want.

People who go about their lives without goals are never truly aware when they have gained something worth keeping (this means more than money or tangible things). They overlook opportunities, as they don't recognize the sound of its knock. They trust in luck, and, for the most part, are losers. Only if you have a goal and work for that goal will you be a lasting success at anything.

5

Therefore, your admission into the ranks of successful real-estate investors must be preceded by your development of a goal, and then a plan by which you will work for that goal. To begin at something as worthy as making a fortune, surely you can start off on the right foot!

Of course, there is a missing link to this so far. It takes more than just a goal or just a plan. It must be a goal that *you* can attain and measure. A goal that has no specific and well-defined moment of attainment is not a good goal. "I want to be wealthy beyond my wildest expectations" is hardly a correct goal, for you would never truly attain it. Your concept of wealth will constantly rise as your achievements rise. As you attain both successes and failures, you will look ahead and no longer feel the same needs, or, for that matter, desires. I know that I need specific goals to reach out for. When they are in my grasp, I set new goals, higher than the first.

The plan you set must be a good plan to fit your goal. For planning to be effective, you must have clear goals. This will enable you to keep your plans simple and direct.

The third essential element is action. The most worthy goal, the best plan, and the greatest intentions won't make you anything unless you act on them. Action, then, is the key. It is far better to act on a mediocre plan than not to act on the best plan devised.

The second secret you should learn is that wealth today is quickly obtained through real-estate investments.

There are countless reasons why real estate is the number one wealth builder if you know how to use it and to invest in it. Yet all the reasons I could give you would only add embellishment to one basic fact: that real estate is an immovable necessity.

Food, clothing, and shelter. These are the three basic things that modern man must have in both quantity and quality to live in comfort. And each of the three—food, clothing, and shelter—comes from real estate. Real estate is the foundation for all the food we eat, the clothing we wear, and the shelter in which we live. Because real estate is immobile, we live where the real estate is that provides these necessities.

It is our need for real estate, its limited quantity, and its immobility that cause wide differences in value and make real-estate investing a science of variables. Understand the relationship between these three factors and you will succeed.

All of this sounds basic, I know, but that's how simple it is to successfully invest in real estate. All you need is that basic understanding, a goal, a plan, and then action. It requires guts, that inside feeling that comes as you make a decision that might shape your life, your future, your financial independence.

Some of you will move cautiously into the realm of real-estate ownership. Many of you will never buy. The nonowners will rationalize their inability to buy real estate, but the reason is their failure to develop goals or plans. Millions and millions of people will never own real estate because they either don't know how simple it is or they fear the consequences of their own actions. You, on the other hand, are ahead of that game. You can buy. You can own. Do you want to?

But what about cash? Doesn't it take cash to buy?

The title of this book is *Cashless Investing in Real Estate*. This cashless-investing concept isn't new to me, nor to any of the thousands of investors who have built fortunes using these techniques. Investing without the use of your own cash is one of the most basic principles of economics. In fact, let's call it Jack's Number One Law of Economics: *Never use your own cash if you can make more money using someone else's money.*

To be able to use the multitude of techniques I will give you in this book, you must understand the full significance of this statement: When you find a situation where you can earn a greater return by borrowing money than by using your own cash, then borrow the money.

Let me apply this to a simple transaction.

Charles has $50,000 of cash he can invest. He finds a duplex priced at $50,000. It is completely rented at a net rent (after all expenses) of $7,000 per year. This is a return of 14% on his money.

On the other hand, he could put $5,000 down on the duplex and borrow the balance from the seller (or another lender) at 12% interest over a 30-year term. The payment on this mortgage would be $5,553 per year. This means Charlie would take in $7,000 and pay out (on the mortgage) $5,553 per year. This would leave him with $1,447—a return of 28% on the investment of $5,000. If Charles buys ten properties like this, using all of the $50,000, his benefit will be far greater than buying one for all cash. But even if Charlie pur-

TABLE 1

The Effects of 12% Inflation on Cash and Property over 10 Years

Start of Year	The Cash at 12% Inflation	The Duplex
1	$100.00	$ 50,000.00
2	$112.00	$ 56,000.00(end of 1st year)
3	$125.44	$ 62,720.00(end of 2nd year)
4	$140.50	$ 70,246.40(end of 3rd year)
5	$157.35	$ 78,675.96(end of 4th year)
6	$176.23	$ 88,117.08(end of 5th year)
7	$197.37	$ 98,691.13(end of 6th year)
8	$221.06	$110,534.07(end of 7th year)
9	$247.59	$123,798.15(end of 8th year)
10	$277.30	$138,653.92(end of 9th year)

chases only the one duplex, saving the other $45,000 cash for another deal, it's wiser than an all-cash transaction.

Now this looks easy, and it is. But there is something much more important and very often overlooked. Inflation. That evil thing that the young worry about and the old cringe from. Inflation is a bad thing—unless you know its secret and how to make it work for you.

Let's assume that over the next few years the rate of inflation will stay at its present 12% per year. This means that what costs $100 now will cost $112 next year, and $125.44 the year after, and $140.50 by the end of the third year (12% compounding each year.) This is the effect of inflation alone; it is not a function of the normal supply-and-demand effect in a healthy market where there is no inflation. It is a sure thing.

The duplex Charles buys will react to this inflation just as everything else does. It will go up in value each year by the same 12% inflation, as shown in table 1.

The totals in table 1 might look like a lot, but they are just the effect of a 12% inflation. What cost $50,000 in 1982 can be expected to cost $123,798.15 ten years later at a 12% annual inflation rate. This is a 277.39% increase in the original value. Each year it will take more cash to have the same buying power of the first year's $100. By the start of the tenth year, you will need $277.30 to buy what you could have bought for $100 the first year.

The problem is, inflation has been well above this 12% rate in past and more recent history, and who knows what it will be in the future? Some societies experience 50% or 70% and more inflation each year.

The way to counteract the effect of inflation is to buy real estate. In fact, the way to take advantage of inflation is to buy real estate on terms.

Let's take a look at the duplex Charlie bought for $50,000 with $5,000 down and a $45,000 mortgage at 12% interest. If Charlie sells the duplex at the end of the first year, the new value *due to inflation alone* will be $56,000. He will owe a balance of $44,818.40 on the mortgage (of the $5,553 total payment Charlie made to the lender for the first year, $5,371.40 was interest and $181.60 was principal reduction of the mortgage). If we deduct the amount owed on the mortgage from the price he receives for the duplex, you can see that Charlie's equity (the value after deducting mortgages owed) is now $11,181.60, as shown below:

New value	$56,000.00
Less existing financing	−$44,818.40
Equity at end of the 1st year	$11,181.60

As Charlie invested $5,000 at the start of the year and his equity is now $11,181.60, the increase of $6,181.60 is a 123.6% yield on the invested capital.

Try to get that kind of a return from your local savings-and-loan. You can't.

What you are witnessing is the incredible multiple effect inflation has in real estate. As values rise because of inflation, it is the whole value of a property that increases, but a major part of the original investment—the mortgage—is "fixed" and does not increase. Therefore the investment equity jumps up tremendously. This is why, even in times of inflation, real estate is an exceptional buy.

The logic is easy to follow, but many people who understand it fail to use it. The key to battling inflation is in using the purchasing technique that meets your specific need. This book provides a number of techniques that turn the secrets of investing into simple, clearly understood axioms. When you finish reading, you should have gained the confidence to invest in real estate and the edge to success.

2

How Risky Is It?

I HAD a long phone conversation with one of the real-estate licensing officials from California about the techniques of investing in real estate with little or no money down. The occasion of the conversation was a review of the certification of a seminar of mine within California as a part of its continuing-education courses for the real-estate profession.

It seemed that this official—who, by the way, was holding up certification of the seminar—objected to a number of things I had included in the seminar. The strongest objection was against a technique called "pyramiding." I quote her viewpoint: "Pyramiding is one of those sexy ways to entice people into deals where they can lose their shirt."

That was about the nicest thing she had to say about pyramiding, and she went on to knock other creative aspects of my program. Softening somewhat to my verbal caressing, she ended by saying—and I paraphrase—"If you want to get approved by this state, Mr. Cummings, you *will* do exactly as I am suggesting."

What she suggested was: Tell everyone about the risks of investing techniques that promise a lot for nothing; tell the brokers and salesmen not to use flamboyant techniques, because they are risky; tell the investors to be careful and avoid high-flying concepts.

Now, I can't find fault with her point of view, but I do find fault with the philosophy that creative investing is risky. The fact is that flamboyant can be worthwhile, and anyone who understands (I mean truly understands) real estate and motivations of people will know that money—and in particular *your* money—is one of the least necessary commodities in buying real estate. Money only aids in the *selection process*. What is risky is *not* to own real estate.

Therefore I will continue to espouse the virtues of buying real estate—but on the chance some of you readers may have doubts about the real-estate market as a place for your money, let me give this word of caution (and let this woman rest her case):

There is nothing sure in life. Not the next real-estate deal you might make, not the ground you sleep over, not the food you eat. There has never been a stock sold that could not have gone down as easily as it went up, nor an ounce of gold traded where someone didn't lose. Even in the most ambitious market for the least risky item of all (whatever that is), there will be risk. Even putting your cash in the bank, or tying it up in government bonds or something like that, is risky, because it locks you into something that may itself go down in value.

Real estate is filled with risk. It is connected to people, and *they* will try to beat you if time doesn't. Real estate is people-inspired: If they want it, its value goes up; if they won't sell it, the price offered goes up; and if they still say no and the buyers begin to look elsewhere, the value goes down here and up there. People determine what real estate is worth by being willing and able to buy. People can and do create value and they can and do decrease value.

Your real estate is a mixture of rights given by people and limited by people. You will never get *all* the rights to land. Some of these rights have been taken away in the name of "betterment." Or it might be that the previous sellers didn't sell you everything—they kept some mineral rights, or an easement across the property to other property, or they kept 50% of the water flowing through the river on the land, and so on. Subdivisions, in an attempt to keep values up, require (in the deed) that homes of a certain size be built and that they conform to certain styles and the like. Cities impose a vast multitude of ordinances that restrict your free use of *your land*. They tell you where to put a building, how much grass to plant, what trees you can cut, and what you have to plant. They tell you if you can build, and they can keep you from building, make you tear down or close your building because they don't like your attitude about safety and the like. Indeed, if they want, they can make your life miserable to the point where you wonder why you ever bought a piece of land or got involved with that thing called "real estate."

States and the quasi-official agencies that come with them fight among themselves and with governing committees and lawmaking bodies to make things even worse. Why, even *God* wouldn't have been able to create heaven and earth if he'd had to go through the red tape that is strangling the housing industry in this country.

If I sound cynical about the state of the real-estate market, don't despair. Despite all these headaches, even though it can be very frustrating to watch a group of untrained, appointed, retired citizens from all walks of life sit in judgment (on zoning boards, boards of adjustment and variance, on commissions, as councilmen, etc.) on the rights you should no longer have, the rewards of investing in real estate are still there. But don't turn one more page of this book if you expect to find an easy way to build your wealth. While it is true that you can become a millionaire—if that is what you want—it won't be easy. It will take a lot of hard work and some risk to be sure.

A word about risk!

Buying real estate through the use of other people's money is not flamboyant, wild, sexy, or risky. I say this with clear understanding that this is a bit of a paradox. The word "risk" is relative: What is risky to you might be child's play to another. Working within your comfort level is one of the keys to being a success in anything. What is needed is a method for you to expand your investment techniques so that you will be comfortable with real estate. The level of comfort will vary for different readers, and will also change as time goes on. As you begin to utilize the techniques I will be giving you, you will find that your concept of "risk" will be greatly different from what it is today.

Buying real estate with other people's money doesn't mean that you must risk more, nor does it mean the seller must risk more. This will be relative to the deal and to the person. This book discusses *forty* different techniques of investing. Some of them are oriented to the seller's side of the deal, others to the buyer's side. It will be very helpful to know both sides of the technique, since, as a buyer, you will someday be a seller.

Each technique will be presented in detail as to what it is and how it is used, and will be illustrated with an example devised for simplicity and clarity. I want you to see the technique in action because most investment books are too theoretical to be applied in real situations. This book is for you to *use*. I will not bore you with unnecessary technical details—that would be like trying to explain exactly how an electronic calculator works, or to explain the mechanical apparatus of a typewriter. You don't need to know that part to make the tool work for you.

Over the past dozen years, I have found that my reflections on the training of real-estate salesmen and the education of real-estate investors have changed. In my younger years, I was obsessed with explaining the details, the reasons why this or that worked. I've since come to feel that all that blah-blah-blah is best left for the purist who won't do anything without understanding why it works. Let's move on to what does work and how you can make it work for you.

3

Setting Goals

A FEW OF YOU have no doubt read Robert J. Ringer's book, *Winning Through Intimidation*. Some of you may have taken his words to heart, so much so in fact that you believe the entire real-estate profession and market to be filled with nasty people out to cut each other's throat (to get, or to avoid paying, a commission).

Fortunately the real-estate profession is not entirely as Mr. Ringer portrayed it. His attitude simply illustrates my conviction that you attract those of the same attitude that you possess: Negative therefore attracts negative, positive attracts positive, contrary to what electromagnetic forces would dictate.

Winning, when it comes to real-estate investing, is a multifaceted event. There is no exact point when you can say you won or the other person lost. Winning, in fact, is not really defined in relation to another person's losing. There is no point in saying, "I won, the seller lost," or, "I won, the buyer lost."

The reason for this must be carefully understood if you plan on playing the game of real estate with the idea of winning.

The Game of Real Estate: Who Are the Players?

Let's choose up sides. Team A consists of you and whomever you can get to aid you in your fight to win. Team B? It consists of all the players against you. Here's their roster:

1. Income taxes
2. Sales taxes
3. Social-security contributions
4. Real-estate taxes
5. Devalued currency
6. Inflation (unless you get it over on your side)
7. Higher cost of living
8. Lower purchasing power of the dollar
9. Supply-and-demand cycles
10. Rising medical costs
11. Rising insurance costs
12. Rising fuel costs
13. Rising unemployment
14. Tougher job competition
15. The multitude of new taxes yet to be devised
16. Growing government power
17. Reduced personal powers and freedoms
18. Those who do not follow the golden rule
19. Governmental giveaways that sap you to death
20. And so on and so on. . . .

You can see that it's an unequal match—unless you know the weaknesses of Team B's players. Most players on Team A find that it's easier to submit early. The towel can be thrown in at any time, the game comes to a halt, and Team A simply shines the boots of Team B's players for the rest of its life.

Or Team A wins.

That's right—against seemingly impossible odds, Team A can win, and without having to resort to Ringer's Intimidation. You see, Ringer had it all wrong. He picked out the wrong enemy to fight, and, like the dog growling at the shadow in the dark, thought that a brave front would win out. Of course, if there was nothing in the shadow, or the shadow was just a pussycat, then the growl would work—either to bolster the growler's self-confidence or to frighten

15

the pussycat away. But you can't count on intimidation. Not in the great big world where there are bigger shadows caused by bigger and meaner people than you will be. Be positive and attract positive people. Avoid negative anything.

"Look, son," the gunfighter said, patting the six-shooter strapped to his side, "no matter how fast you are, there is bound to be some hot gun out there trying to prove he is faster."

"Golly."

Know the rules of the game.

If you are going to win, you have to know the rules. Once you know who the players are and how to distinguish them from the good guys out there trying to help you, the next thing you must keep in mind is exactly what game you are playing.

Does that sound like a stupid statement? Well, hold on. If you play basketball, the higher the score, the better, right? On the other hand, golf is just the other way—a lower score is great. The problem is that in real estate you have more choices than just a higher or lower score.

Select the goals you want to reach, then play the correct game to reach those goals.

In the next chapters you are going to feast on 40 specific techniques for buying real estate. Most of these techniques will be adaptable to any kind of real estate, while some are specifically oriented to certain kinds of real estate. There are, however, six elements that you must recognize as goals to attain. They are in fact your key to the weakness of those players on Team B.

Let's take a short look at these elements.

- *Appreciation*
- *Tax Shelter*
- *Equity Buildup*
- *Cash Flow*
- *Inflation Fighter*
- *Personal Satisfaction*

In my book *Successful Real Estate Investing for the Single Person* (published by Playboy in 1981), I explored each of these elements in detail, and the material that follows is excerpted from the book. Even if you have read it before, it is well worth reading again.

Equity Buildup

When a part of the purchase price is covered by a mortgage, you will have a predictable annual equity buildup as you pay down the mortgage balance.

If you bought a $50,000 home and put $10,000 down, you would have a mortgage of $40,000 to pay off. As you reduced the amount you owed, the value to you of the property would grow. This occurs even if the value of the property itself doesn't increase at all. When, ten years down the road, you have reduced the mortgage to $30,000, your equity is now at least $20,000—double the original equity. In this example, a $50,000 home is purchased with a first mortgage of $40,000 at 10% for 30 years, monthly payment (principal and interest) is $351.

As you can see in table 2, the amount of principal reduction of a mortgage increases as the mortgage matures. While the monthly payment itself doesn't change over the thirty years, the amount applied to interest is greater in the first years. In table 2, the end of the first five years shows a principal reduction of only $1,358, while the last five years pays off $16,517.

Appreciation

Appreciation is a highly sought-after element of investing in anything. You don't buy diamonds or gold or real estate hoping it will go down in value. You want it to appreciate.

TABLE 2
Equity Buildup Through Mortgage Reduction

End of Year	Balance Owed on Mortgage	Equity Buildup
0	$40,000	$ 0
1	39,773	227
5	38,642	1,358
10	36,373	3,627
15	32,651	7,349
20	26,557	13,443
25	16,517	23,483
30	0	40,000

TABLE 3
Equity Buildup Through Appreciation

End of Year	Assumed Value	Balance Owed on Mortgage	Equity
0	$ 50,000	$40,000	$ 10,000*
1	52,500	39,773	12,727
5	62,500	38,642	23,858
10	75,000	36,373	38,627
15	87,500	32,651	54,849
20	100,000	26,557	73,443
25	112,500	16,517	95,983
30	125,000	0	$125,000

* Down payment

But this is one of the magic factors that cannot be predicted with any exactness. Some land goes up in value very rapidly, creating very large gains, yet what some investors never seem to grasp is that the value of the property doesn't have to double for you to double your investment; in fact, small gains in the appreciation can double or even quadruple your equity.

Again, the price of the home is $50,000, with a 30-year mortgage of $40,000 at 10%. The second column is based on a simple 5%-per-year increase in value.

Table 3 shows how this works. If this property were a house that you rented to one of your friends and the rent just covered expenses and mortgage payments, so that you just broke even, you could retire $115,000 richer than when you started. This is a benefit you don't get by paying rent—and the mortgage payments came out of someone else's pocket.

It is possible, of course, for the market value of a property to decline, and then reduction of the mortgage may not increase equity. However, reduction in value rarely occurs if you have followed the simplest investment techniques. In a depression, of course, real estate holds on better than most investments, because it is a necessity.

Tax Shelter

You have heard of people—often doctors and other professionals—buying into tax shelters. You may have bought into one yourself. There used to be lots of different kinds—movies, books, cattle, oil, art expeditions, charities, and, of course, real estate, to name just a few. One by one the IRS has been knocking them off, until the only one left that makes any sense is real estate.

The Economic Tax Act of 1981 had a major impact on the earlier ideas of tax shelter and use of depreciation tables. In essence, the old laws and rules of "depreciation" were thrown out the window, and the Accelerated Cost Recovery System (ACRS) replaced the depreciation concept. While no longer depreciation in classic terms, the end result of this 1981 law was to enable an investor to "depreciate" the cost of the investment over a shorter life and in more simplified terms than before. The law was designed to encourage investment by allowing the investor to recover the investment in the form of an artificial deduction from income.

The IRS devised new tables for the Recovery System which enable an investor to "depreciate" the cost of real-property improvement in 15 years at an accelerated rate which is about 175% of straight line in the beginning on a declining basis.

For example, investments made between 1981 and 1984 would have the following percent of recovery allowed:

15-YEAR RECOVERY %

Year	Percent of Value to Be Recovered
1	10*
2	10
3	9
4	8
5	7
6	7
7–10	6
11–15	6

* Based on the pro-rata months owned the first year.

There are other tables for some shorter-life items in a building, such as personal property. Some items—like autos and light trucks—have a maximum recovery of 25% the first year, 38% the second, and 37% the third. A review of these new laws with your C.P.A. would be desirable.

A tax shelter is a trade-off and conversion of ordinary income to income taxed at lower, long-term-capital-gains rates. Over the years, as you depreciate a property, you reduce your book value in it. This

19

book value is called your "basis." This is important to know when you refer to tax-shelter deals, because if there is no ultimate conversion of ordinary income into capital gains, the tax shelter may not be a very good one.

When you sell a property, the gain is the amount of money you get above your basis. Remember, basis is not the price you paid for a property. Take a good look at how basis is determined:

1. Start with the price you paid.
2. Add any closing costs which are part of the acquisition of the property.
3. Add any capital improvements while you own the property (buildings, repairs of a capital nature which you do not take as expenses for the year).
4. Add expenses such as taxes and interest which you have not taken as a deduction from earned income.
5. Subtotal the amount to this point.
6. Subtract from the subtotal all depreciation you have taken while you have owned the property.
7. What's left is your basis.

You can see that the only deduction in arriving at basis is, in fact, depreciation or ACR. Because depreciation is your tax shelter, and what you are sheltering is ordinary income, when you sell, the amount of the capital gain (assuming that the income qualified as a long-term capital gain) which is above your basis will include this depreciation.

Also, because you can pick your own time to sell, you can convert and move the income from one year to another. Sometimes you postpone the conversion until well down the road, to when your ordinary income-tax rates will be much lower (in retirement, for example).

Keep in mind that the best tax shelter is one that shelters most of its own income. Several years ago syndicates were putting together deals that gave investors a lot of instant shelter but no long-range conversion. Properties were being front-loaded with heavy mortgages that not only were nonamortizing but actually led to the principal balance being built up. The pro forma (a projected analysis) of the income properties was often overstated, and deal after deal got into trouble. Many tax-shelter deals failed because the property was so heavily mortgaged that the income could not support the expenses, and there was no other benefit to balance the loss of income.

When it comes to income-producing property, take advantage of the kind of tax shelter that most benefits you. The fast tax shelter through fast ACR may not be the answer to your problem. You might do better to remember that for most people the best shelter is a new source of income with which to pay the tax. In selecting a property, you have to look at *all* of the magic factors of real estate.

Remember also: Whenever you can get Uncle Sam to kick in and pay part of your investment, take advantage of this.

Cash Flow

If someone pays you for the use of some of your real estate, you may have cash flow. Cash flow is the money you have in your hand at the end of each month (or year) as a direct result of your real-estate investment. In essence, cash flow is the bottom line. It's what's left when you begin with gross income and deduct actual expenses and mortgage payments.

For example, assume you own a duplex and you rent out one side for $400 per month. You live in the other side with a friend, who pays you $175 per month for that privilege. Your gross income would be $575 per month, or $6,900 per year. Your upkeep and expenses for the duplex might run you $1,500 or more; let's say you can pay your real-estate tax, keep up the yard, and maintain the property in good repair for $1,850 per year. Assume your total mortgage payment of principal, interest, and insurance ran you $375 per month, or $4,500 per year. With this information we look at the cash-flow analysis:

Gross income		$6,900
Less:		
Expenses	$1,850	
Mortgage	4,500	
		6,350
Cash flow		$ 550

While $550 may not seem like an enormous amount of money, in addition to the cash flow you are (1) living free, (2) building equity,

(3) seeing your investment appreciate, and (4) sheltering not only income from the investment but perhaps other income as well.

When you progress in your investment capability, you will see that there are many properties that will score highly on the four magic factors of real estate discussed thus far.

Inflation Fighter

Take another look at the three basic necessities of man—food, clothing, and shelter. These three items have many similarities. Each is subject to the supply-and-demand rules that regulate their values. Each involves the input of raw materials and the manipulation of people to create the finished product. Each item can be bought, held, used, traded, and to some degree used up.

The first two, food and clothing, are needed in a steady flow. Who would say, "I've bought all the food I'll ever need" or "Well, I don't have to buy any more clothes" (unless he said this on the fast way down from the Empire State Building)?

Because it's impractical to stockpile a lifetime supply of food and clothing, you will constantly be at the mercy of inflation when you go out to buy these two necessities. The food or clothes you buy today will certainly cost more five years from now to replace. Yet a five-year-old loaf of bread is worthless, and a five-year-old suit of clothes is next to worthless. If you don't consume these two necessities, you may not have any value at all. (There are exceptions, of course. I understand that some furs, if kept in like-new condition, are more valuable because of inflation. Also, it is possible to store some food stocks that will reach maturity at an increased price over a period of years, such as wine and fine brandy.)

Real estate is an absolute item. It simply *exists*, and it exists in a certain location. If this sounds like double-talk, don't be misled. Real estate is valuable not because of the space it occupies on this earth but because of its location in relation to other locations.

A given duplex will vary in value depending entirely on which of a thousand different places it happens to occupy in the United States. It is possible to set this duplex on land that costs the same in different locations and still end up with different values, simply because location is what you pay for.

Because all real estate does begin with land, and because land, and its location, will largely determine ultimate value, real estate is not only unique but is also the only true inflation fighter.

This fifth magic factor of real estate is a combination of all, or most, of the first four. It is important for you to recognize that all of the first four factors will not always occur in all real-estate transactions. Investment in vacant land, for example, will not necessarily produce cash flow. By itself, this is no reason to avoid purchasing vacant land. What is needed is some counterbalance. There must be the promise, at least, of a greater benefit from one or more of the other factors.

Personal Satisfaction

There's a modern approach to investing in real estate, or at least in some kinds of real estate: "If you like it and you can afford it, then buy it." The concept here is that there will be times when you just *want* to own whatever it is. There may be no logical economic reason: The cash flow may be nonexistent, there may be no hope of appreciation, and the only tax shelter might be the loss you take when you have to give it away.

People react emotionally when buying other commodities, don't they? How about those fancy cars, or expensive designer clothes, or dinner at the most expensive spots in town? Emotion is a real factor when you buy something you can use.

Don't let your analytic mind get you so bogged down with the economics of an investment that you overlook this most important aspect of all. Do you like what you are proposing to buy? If not, then you should ask yourself the next question: "Am I forced to buy something I don't like because there is nothing around I can afford that I do like?" If the answer to this last question is yes, then you simply need to work hard at building your portfolio so you will eventually be able to afford what you like.

You will find that no single real-estate investment will accomplish all six of these elements. There is a trade-off between them and your goals. Some properties appreciate more than they develop cash flow, or tax shelter. Some properties don't appreciate but are magnificent moneymakers. Your winning in this game means playing toward the correct factor. If you need a tax shelter, buying property for appreciation is not getting you closer to winning the game. It might even cause you to lose.

One Man's Tea Is Another's Champagne

Warren G. Harding, one of the nation's foremost real-estate exchangers, paraphrases, "I never saw a piece of real estate I didn't like." He goes on to say, in his famous Acres of Diamonds seminars, that all real estate is good; it has a use, a purpose that is determined not just by the real estate but by the person using it.

Some people sell because their needs, as determined by one of the six elements mentioned, are no longer being met. A buyer of vacant land for appreciation might now need tax shelter. He has land still appreciating; he sells the land and buys another kind of property.

This change of events has created a market for real estate not out of fear that the value of the first property was going down, but out of a new need that could no longer be satisfied by that property.

When Is It Time to Buy or Time to Sell?

I've been asked this question a thousand times: When do you sell real estate?

As I've never been good at soothsaying, the best answer is to sell or exchange the moment the property no longer satisfies a need that another property will—unless you anticipate (or hope) that an event soon to occur will make a major change in either your situation or that of the real estate.

Let me explain. I own a tract of land that I feel is worth at this moment around $850,000. I have part of it leased for enough to cover my annual expenses and pay a few dollars into the till. I bought the property for its potential appreciation, paying only $42,000 in total about six years ago. Appreciate it did. Now I need cash flow and some tax shelter to offset that.

However, I don't want to sell—for two reasons. First, the capital-gains taxes would take away a great portion of my reinvestment capital. Second, the city is about to build a new major highway that will join with the road this property fronts on not more than 200 yards away. The impact of this new road could (a) cause the property to double or triple in value in two or three years, and (b) give me a potential tenant for a building or buildings I can build to generate both cash flow and tax shelter.

My trends are clearly in my sights. But sometimes the solutions are not so obvious.

Remember that whatever you buy will reach a point where it no longer is economically desirable to you.

This is the relative point of real estate. From your point of view, everything will reach an economic disposition time. Now, that doesn't mean you *have* to sell or exchange that property for something else. The sixth factor, the emotion factor, might cause you to say, "To hell with economics—I can afford this, so I'll keep it." There is nothing wrong with this kind of thinking, as long as you are rational about it—as long as you recognize the reason you make that statement.

As you move on now into the world of *doing*, keep this in mind. The techniques you are learning work two ways: They are buyer's *and* seller's methods. You can use them wisely to buy, and you can use them to sell. It will all begin to unfurl on the next page.

4

Split-Fund Your Way

into the Deal

SPLIT-FUNDING is the first of the many techniques you will find
in this book. It is not by any means the best, nor the most important—unless it does the job for you at the moment you need it to. In
fact, that's the way it is with all the techniques in this book. They
are tools for you to use—simply that. Like picking up the right
wrench for that stubborn nut and bolt, the right technique to select
will be the one that will do your bidding and clear the smoothest
passage toward your goals. Some of these techniques are apt to
be usable from your point of view but not acceptable to the other
side of the transaction. If he balks and won't sell (or buy, if roles
are reversed), you must find a technique that will work for you
both.

The key to using these methods is to be flexible. Above all, understand that some people will be governed by inertia—they won't
want to do anything that isn't exactly as their advisers have told
them it should be or as it presently is. If you don't present them

with a simple contract with easy-to-understand, conventional terms of cash to the existing mortgage, they won't understand it. It is possible to be so creative that you frighten the pants off your sellers.

When you come across one of these "set in their ways" types, or a seller or buyer who relies on the counsel of the greatest advisers of them all—the bartenders and hairdressers of America—you'll find that being creative confuses them. In fact, you might have to let them read this book to understand that creative financing and creative concepts can be beneficial to all parties as long as goals are attained or placed in closer proximity.

Getting Ready to Dive with These Techniques

Each of the following chapters, beginning with this one, will follow similar formats. There will be a technique offered and briefly described. Then there will be an example showing the use of this technique. Following the example, I will discuss some of the finer points of the technique, giving you some of the elements that may be of special importance in the negotiations of contracts using the method.

In outline form, each chapter will look like this:

A. TECHNIQUE 1.
    1. Definition
    2. Example
        a) Case-study example
        b) Fine points of negotiations using the method
        c) Viewpoints (when deemed important)
    3. Pitfalls

Okay, this is the way each technique will be presented. Naturally, some will be longer and more complicated than others, but each will follow this basic outline. Your review of these techniques will therefore become a simple matter as you will know exactly where to look within the chapter to find the points you wish to refresh yourself on later as you begin to use these methods to build your own fortunes investing in real estate.

Let's start.

Technique Number One: *The Split Fund*

Split-fund the deal so you can take care of a major part of the cash down out of income from the property.

The split-fund down-payment technique is a simple use of mathematics in creating an illusion that often works to put deals together with little actual up-front cash. The illusion occurs when the buyer offers to meet the seller's down-payment amount but spreads the total down payment over more than one installment. The illusion is that the payment is being agreed to, but in reality it isn't. Sellers can use this technique equally well to create an illusion that the down payment is much less than it will be in reality.

What happens in this method that can create these two different points of view is simply the splitting of what would be the total down payment into more than one amount, then requiring these separate amounts to be paid over a short time. If the buyer had only $10,000 in cash at the moment, but the seller wanted $20,000 cash down, the buyer, in using this technique, would agree to pay the $20,000, but on the basis of $10,000 now and the balance of $10,000 at another time. This second payment might be very close in time, say a few months, or more distant in time.

This second payment is not a mortgage, however, and will differ from other techniques where the seller holds financing in the amount of the balance. In fact, there could be mortgages held by the seller in this transaction which would not be a part of this split-funding.

Sellers might offer the property for sale on the basis of $10,000 down and the other $10,000 six months later for tax reasons (such as moving payments into two different years) or simply to help sell the property.

EXAMPLE: Charlie was interested in buying a small, seasonal apartment building in Vero Beach, Florida. He found a nice five-unit property that the owner was willing to sell at a bargain price (for the area) of $150,000. There was an existing mortgage of $85,000 on the property. This left an equity (total value less mortgages) of $65,000. The seller was willing to hold $30,000 in paper, which would be a second mortgage in this case, and wanted $35,000 cash down.

28

Charlie had $15,000 that he was willing to invest at this moment without taking a risk of reducing his operating capital and reserve for opportunities.

However, Charlie knew that as the tourist season was just a month away, he could count on a lot of income from this property, as well as from his other investments, and therefore he could reasonably pay the seller more cash later on, after closing.

So Charlie offered this:

To assume the existing mortgage of	$85,000
To give the seller a second mortgage of	30,000
To pay the down payment wanted of	35,000
Total purchase price	$150,000

Charlie showed the seller the offer, which, on the face of the agreement, was as I've just outlined. On the second page of the agreement, in the details of the terms, Charlie spelled out the format of the down payment. Charlie said he would pay:

$15,000 cash at the closing
$10,000 cash at the end of 6 months
$10,000 cash at the end of 18 months

These payments had nothing to do with the second mortgage and did not provide for interest on the two $10,000 payments.

The seller examined the offer and, after some deliberation, made this counter:

$15,000 cash at closing—just as offered
$15,000 cash at the end of 6 months
$5,000 cash at the end of 12 months

Charlie accepted this counter as it gave him the time he needed to get the total cash needed. The extra tax shelter from the five units would aid Charlie in some respect, but the extra income from the five units would be the main factor in generating the needed cash.

The fine points of using the split-fund down-payment deal will depend on the situation, of course. Knowing as much as you can about the income potential, and the timing of that potential, will be crucial in using the revenue from the property to cover some or all of the delayed down-payment portion. If the property has a seasonal income that is very high during parts of the year, then this can be put to use.

Watching your own tax liability during the year of the purchase can also aid you, as you might get sufficient shelter in the year of the purchase to warrant buying now when you might have been inclined to wait until you had more cash to invest. At the same time, as a seller, you might want to spread the cash over two years to lessen a tax liability, while at the same time avoid including this delayed portion in a long-term mortgage.

The Seller's Look at the Split Fund

While the split-fund transaction is usually thought of as a buyer's tool, the seller can very effectively use the technique to entice buyers into the marketplace where a more conventional kind of transaction frightens them away. Naturally the primary goal of the seller must be met by the use of this tool, and if that goal is the "move" of the property, then the sale generated by its use is the proper result.

Sellers who are highly motivated to sell will find the split-fund transaction an ideal way to get a reasonable up-front cash payment and still not have to wait out a long-term mortgage for the rest of their equity. In Charlie's deal, the seller might have decided the best way to move the property was to offer it at only $15,000 cash down. An advertisement at this cash down might have attracted someone (Charlie?) who, once hooked on the deal, wouldn't mind the two additional payments of $10,000 each to meet the total $35,000 entrance money.

This entrance money, or, as it is often termed abroad, "key money," is treated separately from the mortgages, when in reality it might be secured by a mortgage to give the seller protection and assurance of its eventual payment.

The Buyer's Look at the Split Fund

If you are a buyer attempting to get the most leverage and benefit out of your cash, then the split fund is just another tool you can use to that end. Builders and developers who know they will be going through a refinance in a year or so can use this technique to great advantage (and so can you) as they know that when the second or third split-funded payment is due, they will be refinancing the total transaction anyway. A condo-conversion of a rental apartment building works nicely with this kind of financing of the down payment, since the second payment can often be met just out of sales of the condos, or at least out of the new financing placed on the property.

This technique can be used in every kind of transaction where there is a down payment, to reduce the up-front cash; and if you use it with no interest on the split-funded payment, then you can reduce your overall interest cost. Keep in mind that the government will impute interest at a nominal rate (the rate changes, so see a current bulletin or check with your accountant for the current imputed IRS interest rate). The current 1981 imputed rate was dropped to 7%. This means the IRS will assume you added 7% interest into the price and will recompute the transaction in that light. If the amounts are small and the time short, the interest imputed may not have any effect on the transaction from your point of view. However, large amounts for long durations can have a major effect on the seller. His accountant will tell him all about that.

Pitfalls

From the Seller's Side of the Deal

I just mentioned one—the 7% imputed interest in a non-interest-bearing transaction on the split-funded part of the deal. As long as you are aware of this, it won't make any difference. In fact, sellers often take that into account and let the split fund run without interest. After all, it might not be more than a few hundred dollars, and even if it is more, it will be before-taxes money. Remember, even 7% interest on $10,000 is only $700, and if you are in a 50% tax bracket that cost is now down to $350. In a large transaction, that shouldn't break the deal for the seller, but it might be enough of an incentive for the buyer to come and look at your property.

The biggest pitfall, of course, is the seller's not getting sufficient cash to secure the deal. This will depend on a multitude of circumstances—the market, how badly the seller needs to sell, the conventional financing market, the competition, and, of course, the will and nature of the buyers. Are there any? Do they have cash? If there is one who does, perhaps you should hang on to him.

From the Buyer's Point of View

Can you meet the split-funded payment? And even if you can, if you are enticed into the deal because you can afford the low down payment but nothing more, then you will have a short-lived ownership unless the values go up and you make a killing in a resale. Mind you, a lot of buyers do exactly that, with the luck of the Irish or whatever on their side. I have seen many not so lucky, however, so plan your finances so you don't get caught with the Irish on the other side of the deal.

5

The Fried-Chicken
Down Payment

BARTER is one of the oldest methods of exchange. I can just imagine the cavemen offering each other their scraps of meager existence: a dead fish for some rotten bananas; a hunk of lizard for some bird eggs; a pretty rock for a few hours of rolling around in the hay. Each item given was taken by the other and something of equal value or interest passed back to the first party. Barter. It was and is a most interesting way to make transactions work. All kinds of transactions, by the way, and not just real estate.

Isabel runs a small backyard business, more a hobby than a vocation. She has a green thumb, so she grows exotic and rare tropical fruit trees and shrubs. Her product, then, is plants. In a barter, she can offer these plants as a down payment on something. Perhaps the developer of a condominium, contacted well before any other arrangements are made, might be delighted to let Isabel use $10,000 or more of her plants as a down payment on one of his condominiums. The developer would use the plants within the project (or another project) as landscaping or decoration.

Barter of a product is slightly different from the other forms of barter I will illustrate. In this situation we are dealing with the actual plants—not a craft or trade such as doing landscaping or planning the landscaping, which are services and not products.

EXAMPLE: Charlie is a book publisher, so his product is books. All kinds of books. Now, while this might seem to be a difficult product to barter for real estate, the trick is to find a user for the books. The owner of a bookstore would be good a choice, of course. Now, second question: Does the bookstore owner have real estate for sale? And if he does, will he take the books as a partial down payment?

If he does have real estate for sale, and takes the books, the story is over and the deal made. However, it usually doesn't work that way in real life. The bookstore owner doesn't have what Charlie wants. As is often the case with barter, you must become creative. This means that you must keep the user of your barter item in the back of your mind while you go out to find what you want.

Charlie finds a nice vacant lot he would like to buy for an investment. It is offered fairly at $50,000. Charlie has $20,000 worth of books (at retail value) that he wants to unload. He would take $7,000 for them at a bulk sale, so he offers them to the owner of the lot at that price as the down payment, owing the lot owner the balance of $43,000 on terms satisfactory to the seller.

The lot owner balks at the offer of the product, but Charlie then points out (through his broker) that there is a bookstore owner who will take the books off the lot owner's hands, either on consignment for resale at $10,000 or at a discount of $5,000 cash. The owner now has a choice: He can take a chance of picking up $3,000 by putting the books with the bookstore owner on consignment (if they sell, he gets paid; if not, the books are his), or he can take the instant cash of $5,000. If you were the owner of a lot interested in converting your equity into some cash and a mortgage at good terms, what choice would you make?

On the other hand, Charlie could just as easily have been a jeweler, able to pick up gemstones at a bargain rate and, with a few hours in his well-equipped workshop, turn out magnificent and expensive jewelry. This kind of product will easily be passed off in a transaction, assuming it is genuine and priced competitively. I've never seen a million-dollar transaction where the seller wouldn't have been able to absorb a $30,000 piece of jewelry if there was some motivation to make it work out that way. (The broker who might lose out on a nice commission could be just the guy to end up with the 30-grand ring.)

It is not difficult to get builders to take building materials, or get land developers to take machines used in land development. The true test of your creative ability to use barter will be in finding *the user for your product*, then making that person an instrumental part of the deal, as either the main principal or a third-party taker, to make the transaction work.

There are ten questions every seller should ask in a barter transaction:

1. Is the value of the product being offered fairly assessed?
2. If it isn't, then can one be set, or is the buyer way out of line?
3. Do you have a use for the product?
4. Can the product be easily sold to a user?
5. Must you take a discount to sell it, and how much?
6. Do the rest of the terms meet with your approval?
7. Will the broker take all or part of the product?
8. Will the broker hold off his or her commission until all or part of the product is sold or further exchanged?
9. Can you exchange the product with someone else for something you would like or would take?
10. Is this the only way you can see a deal being made?

The answers to these questions don't require any discussion on my part other than to say you will have a good understanding of the pros and cons of the deal once you have gone into each of them. Mind you, even if the first nine answers are unsatisfactory, the deal might still be good if the answer to question 10 is that barter is in fact the only way you can make the deal. Need is the strongest motivator of all.

Some sellers actually seek barter as a way of moving their real estate. Some property-rich (also called "property-poor") people find themselves with a lot of real estate, little cash, and in need of material items. I've seen such people barter for boats, airplanes, machinery, and almost any other product you can think of. They decide on a product, then find an owner of that product or a manufacturer of the product, and make a deal.

Some landowners use vacant land as money. They buy large tracts of land at a low price, subdivide it into lots now worth ten times the original price, and use these inexpensive lots in nearly every transaction they make. Buy a $20,000 car and give the car dealer one lot worth $5,000 and $15,000 in cash. Buy a $150,000 home and give the seller $10,000 worth of lots and some more cash down. That's the idea. Can you see other applications?

Buyers will best use this tool if they do some homework on their sellers. In essence, find sellers who are inclined to use your product.

Pitfalls

From the Seller's Side of the Deal

While barter can be exciting and can open a lot of markets for you, there is a lot of junk out there ready to fall into your lap if you aren't careful. Always have the offered product appraised if you are not sure of its real value; never take the word of the other party nor appraisals he offers you. He may be honest, but there is a natural tendency to bolster one's own product and to overlook the fact that values don't always remain the same. Get an opinion you feel comfortable with, and try to get it from the most qualified person available for the product at hand. You might be offered a real bargain, and you don't want to miss the opportunity.

From the Buyer's Side

As an investor giving up a product, are you getting full value for your product? Or has the seller simply absorbed your product into the overinflated price he was asking for his real estate? This is a real hazard, so you must know values. One of the best ways to assure you aren't being underpaid for your product is to negotiate without the product first, if you can. This is difficult in many situations, so you may have to offer to barter with the idea of starting low and working up the ladder to make the best deal possible.

Barter is a great way to go—and if your "sales" market is off, it might be the only way to go.

6

The Glue Deal

A "GLUE DEAL" is a transaction in which the status of the buyer is the main ingredient of the deal. In this kind of deal, the position, reputation, or influence of the buyer is generally more important than cash. There are many reasons why the buyer is in such a position, and it is important not to jump to the conclusion that only the famous or the most respected in their professions will fall into this category. In real estate, the localized situation might create an environment where simply owning the adjoining property would put the would-be buyer into a glue deal. Sellers of certain kinds of property would be well advised to seek out "glue people" in hopes of making a deal with them to quickly dispose of their property, thereby solving their problems or meeting their goals.

Many real-estate investors seek to become "glue people" and never attain that stature. It's not absolutely necessary, but should you select some specialty in real estate that would make you worth more than cash, you will find that deals will seek you out—transactions in which you can buy without using cash, only your good and special name.

Joe used his talent in making himself a "glue person."

Joe had been in real estate for many years, and over that time had put together about a dozen highly successful real-estate syndicates. These group purchases of investments were the product of several elements. First, Joe's interest in finding good investment properties that he and his father could jointly invest in. Second, the realization that, if he found many good investments and spread his capital around, he could take advantage of a reduced risk by having more baskets in which to place his eggs. The third element was the fact that, by having some co-investors, he was able to buy larger properties than he and his father might have considered for themselves alone.

As word got around that Joe was successful at this kind of real-estate transaction, sellers began to seek Joe out to "market" their property. They were in essence giving Joe free options on their land or property so he could get his act together and form a syndicate. For Joe, this was ideal, as he could now spend the time necessary to check out the real estate properly, and then form the syndicate, knowing that he wasn't risking the usual front money to tie up the property.

This is the easiest form of specialization for a new or expanding investor to develop. When you have completed several group deals like Joe's, you will be on your way to becoming both wealthy and well known. (There will be more about syndication in chapter 39.)

Louis is the Shopping-Center King in his area, and it pays off. His specialty is developing shopping centers, and there are many people like him around the country. Some are more nationally known, like Farber, or Debartolo; others are just local guys who have a good reputation for building strip or local centers. If you were a seller of a good site for one of these centers, you might find that offering your site to one of the local "glue people" would entice him into an ultimate buyout of your site.

You will get a higher price, by the way, if you offer a buyer good terms. And when it comes to developmental property, "good terms" don't necessarily mean long-term mortgages at low interest. A developer wants to know that the site he is buying is ready to go and that there aren't any hidden charges in the deal. Taking a tract of raw land and turning it into a shopping center or condominium apartment building is a hard task filled with countless nickel-and-dime costs that come about as the land is brought to the point where it is ready to go. The best terms you could offer a builder might simply be some time—time for the builder to examine what these costs might actually be, or to even begin the process *prior to his having to give you some up-front cash.*

I'd sell Len Farber one of my vacant tracts today without one thin dime down if he would proceed with the development of a regional shopping mall—and if the circumstances were right, so would you.

The Seller's Viewpoint

I believe the glue deal is better as a seller's tool. To use it to best advantage, you should first attempt to ascertain what kind of use the property should be put to, and then find the specialist for that use—the best "glue person" for you. If the property is already developed, you might need to find a ready user, or an investor to simply replace you as holder of the property. The glue person might be the user, or a known investor who has a lot of cash or property. By not asking for cash, but simply the security of the cash in the form of mortgages against other property, you can make almost any qualified person a "glue person."

The other side of this is the buyer coming into a deal and telling you, "Hey, look, I'm a real top banana and I'm the best and/or only guy to make this deal. I'm your 'glue person.' " Personally, I've heard this line so much that I discount it about 98% of the time. Indeed, so skeptical are many sellers that it may be hard for a buyer to convince the seller that he is a "glue person" unless this fact can be tactfully conveyed by a wise broker.

The Buyer's Viewpoint

The buyer's viewpoint is one of mixed emotions. The form of the transaction is excellent if you can develop the situation toward property you want to acquire. On the other hand, if you have gained some specialty, then you will have opportunity knocking at *your* door. When it does, you will have a motivated seller who has sought you out to make that glue deal. Don't look at these kinds of opportunities as desperation or trash deals. Real opportunity can come out of this kind of situation, and you should be willing to look into the deal to see whether it fits your goal pattern and whether you can take advantage of the opportunity.

Pitfalls (from Both Sides of the Deal)

Sellers, beware of false profits. "Not all is as it seems" is not just a saying, it is a fact. As I have just said, I feel the glue deal is a better seller's tool than a buyer's tool, but that doesn't mean sellers aren't at risk. Any transaction that allows a buyer to get in without much, or any, up-front cash and/or risk adds to the risk of the seller. It doesn't matter how big the "glue person" is, prudence dictates that all sellers protect themselves to the utmost in *all* transactions; and when there is little or no cash in the deal, protect yourselves to the maximum in as many areas as possible.

Nothing beats cash as a form of protection when it comes to making deals. But not all buyers have cash, and some who do may not want what you are trying to sell (or won't pay your price and you won't drop down to theirs).

Of course, before you can weigh the risk against the gains, you must understand exactly what it is you are risking. If you are simply risking time, by holding your property off the market while the buyer goes through a series of determined, or yet to be determined, steps to ascertain the value or the development potential of your property, that is one thing. However, if you are passing title to a corporation that is about to go into bankruptcy, then you are risking more than time.

Sellers can protect themselves relatively securely by retaining title to their property until they get that ultimate cash up front. This means giving options rather than closing on the no-cash or little-cash deal. Time then becomes the major element of risk, and if there are no other ready buyers, that risk may be acceptable.

Check out your buyers in every glue deal. Never rely on what they say about themselves. I believe this is one of those instances where what others say about the person is more important. Question the tradespeople they deal with, look primarily for their record of performance. Do they pay on time? Are they successful in all their projects?

41

Buyers, look out for the Trojan Horse.

If you are one of those "glue people," then my most sincere congratulations. But watch out for all those deals you have thrown at you. Devote some time to examining each deal. This might be done by one of your staff members if you are that large, or you yourself might take a few moments each day or each week to look over the transactions that come to you.

One way to make that task easier is to make a checklist of all the specific things you want to know about each deal. When you get a call or inquiry, send the person this checklist. This compels them to give you the kind of data you want in the form you are comfortable with. It can take hours just looking at a presentation to find the simplest data because you aren't sure where it is. I've examined countless presentations that no doubt had taken a lot of time to prepare but were thoroughly confusing to me. Not because the presentation lacked data, but because it contained too much data. I had to wade through too much unimportant data to get the meat of the deal. I and other investors will simply glance over these deals. We might miss out by not being able to accept your knock of opportunity—but then, so might you.

7

The Paper-Cup Deal

THE "PAPER-CUP DEAL" involves using mortgages you hold as collateral for a loan. This type of transaction can generate ready cash in situations where, for one reason or another, you don't want to "sell" the notes or mortgages you are holding. In essence you take a note (which may be secured by real estate or some other collateral, or may be unsecured and backed by someone's signature alone) and borrow money using this note as collateral for your loan.

EXAMPLE: Charles was a buyer and seller of real estate and frequently took back mortgages and notes when he sold his properties. These notes and mortgages varied in interest rates and term of years—depending on their maturity, Charles's need to sell the property in question, and of course the general market conditions at the time of each sale.

Charles had a rather interesting situation come up where he needed some ready cash to take advantage of that "opportunity knocking at his door." He was able to get most of the money he needed by cashing in some certificates of deposits that were due. But he was short about $10,000 to make the deal, and nothing he attempted in the way of creative dealmaking seemed to work. The seller wouldn't back down on his demand for that extra $10,000 in cash.

None of the notes and mortgages Charles had were "small enough" to sell, even at a discount to generate only $10,000. And anyway, Charles didn't want to sell the notes at the discount the current market for money would demand if there was an alternative.

You see, Charles knew all the makers of the notes well (after all, he had sold them real estate), and he knew that in each case there was a chance the note would be paid off prior to the due date. This payment of notes is not uncommon. As a matter of fact, it is usual in real-estate loans. The average loan lasts around seven to nine years, no matter how long the term of the mortgage. However, when you discount a note that has 15 years remaining on its term, the buyer of the note won't take into account the potential early payment. The early payment thus becomes a great bonus in discounted mortgages. (More on this later.)

Not wanting to take a discount when the notes stood a great chance of being prepaid, Charlie hit on another idea. What he did was select one note that had about a $25,000 balance. He took this note to the maker's bank, introduced himself to the commercial-loan officer, and proposed that the bank lend him $10,000 which Charles would sign personally for and, in addition, place as collateral for the loan the note in the amount of $25,000.

The bank knew the maker of the loan, of course, and knew that in the event Charles defaulted on the loan of $10,000 they would have the entire $25,000 note in their hands as security.

Charles received his cash without having to sell any of the notes.

Do Your Homework When You Borrow Against Notes

Whenever you attempt to borrow on notes, or when you plan to attempt to sell them, make sure you approach the maker's banks first. You will note I said *banks*. It's possible that the maker of the note has more than one bank. You would know of at least one simply from the checks you have been receiving on the mortgage payments. Another source of information on other banks is the maker himself.

When you sell real estate and hold mortgages, it's a good idea to have a financial statement from the buyer. If you are holding a large sum of paper in the deal, you might even require annual updates of the financial statement. This statement should be simple to fill out and can follow the kinds most savings-and-loans associations use. What you are looking for are (1) bank references and (2) businesses the buyer deals with. There are other things that might be helpful, of course; but with banks and other businesses he deals with, you have two potential lenders against this note.

By doing your homework early, prior to a sale, you will have the data you might need at your fingertips when you need it.

Fine Points to Know When You Borrow Against Notes

There are several things that are useful to know about this tool.

First, you need not pledge the entire note and mortgage. It is possible, for example, to pledge only the first $25,000 of a $100,000 note. This way, if you default for some unforeseen reason, you won't lose the entire note.

Second, you should develop a position of strength when you negotiate any loan. If you are offering to pay a reasonable interest rate, and the note you are willing to pledge as collateral has some seasoning (a history of prompt payments), your deal should be attractive to the lender. Loan officers, however, do have a way of making borrowers feel uncomfortable. Don't be arrogant, but don't be intimidated either.

The third point to borrowing against notes is to do it when the situation warrants it. I've seen many prospective buyers sit on their assets and let good buys slip past them because they didn't want to borrow money. The simple fact is this: If you are collecting on money you loaned out (via a note and mortgage you are holding from a sale of real estate), why not get some cash out of the note through a loan and let the note pay off your loan?

EXAMPLE: Frank owes me $30,000 on a mortgage and pays me $500 each month. I want $10,000 to buy something, so I borrow the ten grand and give the lender the note from Frank as collateral. I pay the lender $250 per month until it's paid up, but who pays it? Me or Frank? All I do is take $250 out of the $500 and I am still ahead $250 while I am paying off the ten grand.

45

Viewpoints

The Seller

The seller is getting cash, so he looks on this transaction as a simple matter of holding firm and getting his cash. The wise seller, however, will help buyers think of this possibility. After all, you will find buyers who aren't aware that they can borrow on notes they are holding. A smart seller won't let a qualified buyer get out of his grip.

The Buyer

Once the buyer understands the concept of making the best use of the money he has and the money owed to him, he is on his way to making more deals through creative efforts. Generating cash when you need it is an important aspect of dealing in real estate, or other investments. Holding notes and mortgages in the sale of real estate is a matter of eventuality: If you buy and sell enough, you will sometime hold a mortgage. Using this future cash as collateral for cash you need *now* is not only okay but prudent—if the deal you have coming up is indeed a good deal.

The Lender

The lender might be a bank, of course, but don't overlook private sources. Lenders are businessmen looking for the most secure deal or the greatest yield at the lowest risk. You are offering them a business transaction, and the note is their security.

Pitfalls

From the seller's side: none.

Buyers, on the other hand, will find any source of borrowed cash an additional risk.

When you borrow, you risk. This risk might be acceptable, but the loan becomes another obligation—you will have to pay back or accept the consequences. In this case, you lose the note or a major portion of it if you fail to meet your obligation. It is not infrequent for a buyer to "bite off more than he can chew." The heavy leveraging and overextending of debt in some real-estate purchases can spell disaster. If there is a reversal in your economic well-being, you could be courting bankruptcy.

The investor who never accepts risk, however, never gains.

8

Scrip: The Legal Money *You* Print

THERE ARE three basic forms of scrip that you can use to buy real estate, or for that matter, anything covered in this book. Because each of the three forms utilizes the same type of negotiable instrument, I will treat the three in detail in this chapter and then describe the finer points of two of them in chapters 9 and 10.

Scrip is a form of money. It has a long history of use and is frequently found within large companies as a type of negotiable paper that employees can use to redeem against the company store. Scrip, in the context in which I use it, is a promise in written form that clearly binds the "banker" to honor the value of the paper against specific claims of the holder. These claims may have some restrictions on them, and the obligation may have a beginning date as well as a termination date. This written form can be anything from a "gift certificate" to a formalized legal document spelling out the complete terms of the obligation.

Scrip is either *written* against something the "banker" has—such as a service or tangible items—or *charged* against the service or items of others. The latter form has two variations: If you don't have a service or item to use, you can buy those services from someone else, using your "soft paper," or you can sell those services or items at a discount (commission).

EXAMPLE: Charles runs a fast-food spaghetti house named Joe and Rose's. It is doing very well, and Charles wants to open up several more outlets, maybe start a franchise or something. However, like a lot of restaurateurs, Charles has all of his money tied up in his one restaurant.

So he decides to do the next-best thing. He will start buying sites so that, when he does have enough capital, he will be on the way with the right locations. Instead of paying top dollar for locations that are presently the hottest, he will buy locations that he believes will be hot a few years from now.

Charles locates a site that he falls in love with because he knows the area will be ideal for a restaurant in a few years. New roads are being built, and the single-family and multifamily homes being constructed are naturals for a good fast-food spaghetti joint. The site belongs to the owner of the local Ford dealership (a fact that will work out nicely for Charles, as you will see) and is most reasonably priced at $55,000. The seller will take back some paper, but he wants at least $15,000 cash up front. The $40,000 balance can be paid off over ten years at 10% interest.

Charles has only $5,000 in cash, so he has his broker draw up the following offer:

Cash at closing	$5,000
Scrip	15,000
Seller-held first mortgage payable over seven years with an interest-only payment at 10% each year, then full payment of outstanding balance ...	35,000.00
Total offer:	$55,000.00

The above-mentioned scrip is redeemable at Joe and Rose's restaurant in meals, wine, and spirits (not to include service or tax). There is no termination date on the redemption of this scrip, but it is limited to $1,000 per night.

49

Charles's offer differs in several respects from the terms the seller is requesting. First of all, he is offering only $5,000 in cash, but $15,000 in scrip. He has lowered the mortgage term to seven years, but he is asking for interest-only payments. These elements of the offer are to catch the attention of the seller, and at the same time to give Charles some negotiating room.

The seller, as I have already mentioned, owns a sizable company with many employees, and therefore will have ample opportunity to use up the scrip: He can offer top salesmen, executives, buyers, and so on free dinners and drinks as a premium—and he solves his problem of unloading the site.

Charles is able and willing to cut the amount of scrip by any amount the seller wishes and add that sum to the mortgage. Of course, to balance this, Charles would ask for longer terms or even a reduced interest rate.

There are many fine points in scrip deals.

The key to using scrip is to use it whenever you can. If you are a businessman with service or inventory that can be used by the owner of a property that you are buying, you should attempt to use some scrip as a part of the deal.

If Charles had been the owner of a hardware store, he would have made his offer to buy giving scrip against his merchandise.

Don't jump to the conclusion that you have to own a fast-food joint or hardware store, however. The next two chapters will show you how to make these exciting scrip deals without owning the shop yourself.

Presenting the Offer

The finesse of the offer is often the most crucial part of a scrip deal. If your broker or salesman making the offer is skittish about the method of purchase, you will be doomed from the start. A short pep talk with the salesman on the advantages of the scrip to the seller might be in order. The most important thing, however, is for the broker, salesman, or lawyer who might be an intermediary in the deal to let the seller make up his own mind.

A few tips to those presenting the offer:

1. Have some details on the "banker" of the service or merchandise handy when the offer is presented. "Here is a brochure on Charles's resort in Martinique, at which he is offering you, as a part of the down payment, two weeks each summer for forty-five years. . . ."
2. Show or indicate how the seller can "unload" the scrip if he should choose not to use it up himself. He can use it as cash the next time he buys, or give it as premiums, etc.
3. Point out the benefits to the seller of achieving his goal to get rid of the property.

The Seller's Viewpoint in All Forms of Scrip Transactions

The seller gets scrip in all three of the scrip transactions covered in this book. He needs to closely examine the "nature of the promise" to be sure the future draw against services will, in fact, be honored. Once the quality of the promise is assured, the seller needs to review the factors of use. Can the seller use the merchandise or service offered? If not, or only partially, then can the seller spin off the balance of the offered item?

If the seller can get rid of the scrip, the scrip then was cash to the buyer and cash to the seller.

The most dangerous aspect of scrip from a seller's point of view is *disuse.* If there are great delays in using the scrip, the end product can disappear: Restaurants go out of business, hotels are converted to apartments, etc. Also, as the paper has no interest accruing to it, the longer the seller holds on to the promise, the less valuable it becomes. Therefore, if the paper promise is good and the service or merchandise valuable, the seller should make every attempt to either use it or spin it off quickly.

The Buyer's Viewpoint

When you offer someone your merchandise or service at face value as a part of your offer to buy their property, but they only have a future delivery of the service or merchandise, you have a *double* profit in the transaction.

51

First of all, in essence, you have gotten an *interest-free loan* from the seller: He gave you cash (which you used in the purchase of his property) and you told him to come in and eat it up in spaghetti, or to take merchandise or whatever. Each time he comes in, however, you not only reduce what you owe him, you also profit from the fact that he spends the paper money you gave him *at your place of business.*

You have a built-in profit in your goods or services. Every time you sell your goods or service at face value, you make a profit. If that profit is 20%, for example, and you are able to use $10,000 worth of scrip against your own product, then it really costs you $8,000—and then only if it is redeemed on the day you make the deal. The longer the delay, the more you gain from the interest buildup you earn on the money.

There may also be another benefit to you: In many businesses, the very act of doing business is beneficial.

Pitfalls

From the Seller's Side

There are several pitfalls that sellers should watch out for when taking scrip as a part of any real-estate transaction. I've already discussed the obvious necessity of being sure the document (the scrip itself) is properly executed and that it covers, for example, the potential sale of the business from which the promised merchandise or service is to be drawn. A new owner of Charlie's spaghetti restaurant may not take kindly to a party of 500 people who, having eaten and drunk their fill, smile and hand over a letter signed by Charles giving $15,000 of scrip against the bill.

The scrip itself should be freely transferable to have maximum value to the seller receiving it. You don't want to sell your property to someone and take $50,000 of nontransferable scrip from a Ford dealership unless you plan on owning several cars yourself. Instead, you would take the scrip in smaller denominations and use them to trade into other items or property.

Be very careful of the time limitation on scrip. I once took some scrip for accommodations at a hotel owned by one of my clients for a fee he owed me. The "due bill," as this kind of scrip is frequently called, had a five-year duration. I still find it amazing how fast those five years went by. At the end of the term, over half of the due bill was unused. Bad planning on my part, but I kept putting off full use of the scrip, and thus lost the value. Don't let this happen to you.

Scrip, by the way, is the same as cash when it comes to the IRS and taxes. Do not be tempted to "forget" the amount of paper money you receive in a transaction. Keep in mind that the buyer is reporting having "paid" you that amount, and that if you get caught, the IRS will make things very hot for you. They *won't* take the scrip, by the way, for payment of taxes owed (or for payment of the penalty either).

From the Buyer's Side

There are some special pitfalls for buyers who give scrip on their own goods or services.

Let's say you have just given Brad $15,000 of scrip that he can use anytime in the future to buy anything in your inventory. So far you have made a good deal. However, before you can turn around, there is an increase in the wholesale price of your merchandise and your cost almost doubles. The result: You have promised to give up $15,000 of merchandise that now costs you $18,600. Further cost increases can eat up your investment in a hurry.

Investors using scrip must take into account the potential increase in their cost of goods. If the profit margin is good and the benefits of paying no interest on scrip cover the potential price increase, then you will come out fine. If the cost of your merchandise is very volatile, then be careful.

It is a good idea to try to put some restrictions on the use of scrip by the seller. Setting a maximum on the return of scrip during a week, or month, can help stop a heavy run against the business during a peak time of normal business. A restriction on transferability is not good for the seller, but he might accept exempting your steady clients, at least, from transfer.

The toughest pitfall of them all, however, is the inability to cover the drawdown of the scrip. Some buyers give scrip with all good intentions of being able to cover the value when the time comes. Plan for the eventual draw on the scrip, and don't get caught short.

Chapters 9 and 10 will cover two additional forms of scrip: scrip you buy from someone else (soft paper) and scrip you "buy" on a commission and trade at full value. As I have covered many of the viewpoints and pitfalls of scrip transactions in general, and fairly completely from the seller's side, these two subsequent chapters will look only at the two variations of scrip transactions and a view from the buyer's side.

9

Watered Scrip

"WATERED SCRIP" is scrip you buy from someone else on soft terms. To get the most out of the discussion of this kind of scrip, you will need to review chapter 8, which discussed the basic concepts of scrip transactions. In chapter 8, you saw that the use of scrip (paper money, which you print and use against your own merchandise or service) is an exciting way of generating more business for yourself while you are buying property without using the kind of cash printed by Uncle Sam. However, not every buyer has a business or service against which he can write paper money. In fact, most buyers find themselves without either a service or merchandise that is of interest to the sellers of available real estate.

Fortunately, the concept of scrip is so flexible that it is not important or necessary for you to use your own scrip. Indeed, as I will show you in this chapter and in chapter 10, you can get scrip from others and use that as your paper money. Moreover, you can "buy" this paper money from other people without spending cash of your own.

Because scrip is manufactured "money" that anyone who has a service or merchandise can create, these same people can "sell" their scrip to you. This sale will probably have to be initiated by you, since most people don't know of this form of transaction—or, if they do know about it, they fail to see how it can benefit them (which gives you another edge).

The purchase of scrip can take several forms. This chapter deals with one way of buying scrip from others, while chapter 10 deals with a separate method of dealing in the scrip of others.

Buying Scrip on Soft Terms

"Give me scrip in the amount of $10,000, which can be spent in your furniture store, and I'll give you a first mortgage on my snake farm. The mortgage pays out in three years at 7½% interest."

Or . . . "Give me $5,000 of scrip good at your spaghetti house and I'll give you a second mortgage on my home over 18 months at 9%."

Or . . . "Give me $5,000 of scrip against new or used cars off your lot in exchange for this lot east of Naples, Florida."

In each case I've given you something for your scrip. You might get a mortgage or a vacant lot, but you have an item that will convert to money or is in itself real estate. You give up, at some future date, furniture, spaghetti, or a car. Each of these items of merchandise is a profit item to you, and trading them for scrip is additional business that you might not have had otherwise. The cost to the "banker" is zero. No risk at all.

On the other hand, the buyer of the scrip is going to use this scrip as a part of another transaction.

I might take the $10,000 dollars of scrip from the furniture-store owner and use it as a down payment on a condominium from a condo developer. He can use the scrip at the furniture store as he buys furniture for his apartments, so it is cash to him.

I might take the $5,000 of scrip from the spaghetti house and offer it along with the $5,000 from the car dealer as all or part of a down payment to another property owner.

In each instance I am giving the seller of the real estate something more tangible to them than the concept of additional debt. Obviously, if I had been able to give the mortgages or lot east of Naples directly to the sellers of the real estate I wanted to buy, I'd have done that. In fact, I more than likely tried to do exactly that, but failed.

You will find that the same seller who took the $10,000 in scrip at the furniture store would have balked at the $10,000 mortgage on the snake farm. The seller of the condo didn't want to hold a mortgage; he would, however, take the furniture. It is all a matter of need. He didn't need the mortgage. He could use the furniture.

The seller of the furniture, on the other hand, has a nice profit in the furniture and can use the extra business the scrip brings in. Taking the mortgage isn't a problem for a merchant who is making a profit on the sale.

Some sellers simply don't like the thought of a buyer getting in for "no cash down." This fact works against the buyer trying to pyramid or exchange mortgages on a direct one-on-one basis. But by doing some homework, the buyer can find the kind of scrip the seller would be able to use, and then "buy" the scrip on terms favorable to the investor. Once you are in possession of the right kind of scrip, the real-estate transaction can be made. Obviously, you don't want to go out and "buy" $10,000 worth of scrip in a fast-food item or some other merchandise or service you have no need for yourself unless you are sure the seller of the real estate you want is going to take it. Therefore, you must set up the scrip deal but not close on it until your real-estate transaction is finalized.

Dealing with the Bankers of the Scrip

Dealing with the merchants and professionals in their scrip can be difficult if you don't come right to the point with the person capable of making the decisions you want. It will do you no good to spend hours trying to convince a clerk of your plan—you must talk with the owner. Go right to the top and spell it out very clearly. Let them read the three chapters on scrip in this book; you might open their eyes to a mountain of new business that they can generate for themselves. Explain some of the details, but keep the investment secret. You don't want to be too generous with your plan, as you are going to use their scrip to make your deal.

Bankers of scrip reading this chapter should note that you must exercise every effort to secure your scrip. If you know the person with whom you are dealing, then you can rely on your past history of business dealings to a great degree. However, always insist that the notes, mortgages, or whatever you receive for your scrip is well documented and bona fide.

Real-estate investors seeking to buy scrip should be prepared to follow the above requirements. The concept of dealing with scrip is more than buying with little or less of your own cash; it is a matter of moving the transaction to a close the best way possible. There will be times when the introduction of scrip—". . . and in addition to all the other aspects of this offer, I'll give you $5,000 of scrip good at Magic Carpet Travel Agency for any trip around the world or to any place in the world you'd like to go . . ."—is a bit of magic that can make the hardest seller melt a little. Of course, the better you have done your homework, the better you can select that item to do the trick you want.

The "Viewpoints" and "Pitfalls" are much the same as those discussed in the preceding chapter. The added dimension of a third party "banking" the scrip can in some instances increase the security to the seller of the real estate, but this factor will depend on the actual case at hand. The general warning to all sellers of real estate is to make sure the scrip you are taking is valid at the establishment on which it is drawn.

One pitfall for the investor using third-party scrip: You give the spaghetti-house owner your mortgage for his scrip, which you then use to buy some real estate—only to find later that the spaghetti-house owner refuses to honor the scrip.

Because of this, all investors buying scrip on any terms must assure themselves that the scrip is indeed good and that there are some teeth in the contract to back up the other guy's promise.

These pitfalls can be taken care of reasonably well, and the advantages of using scrip can well outweigh the disadvantages mentioned.

10

Commissioned Scrip

"COMMISSIONED SCRIP" is third-party scrip that you redeem at a discount but trade at full value. This third method of using scrip differs from the first two, discussed in chapters 8 and 9, only in the way the scrip is obtained.

Due to the fact that the viewpoint of the seller will be identical to those already covered, I will skip that part of the detailed analysis and home in on the main part of this technique.

As I mentioned in chapter 9, most of the scrip transactions that you will be able to effect will be with scrip from third parties, because sellers will naturally be more willing to take scrip that can be used to purchase items or services they can use. This fact reduces the amount of scrip you can use from your own business, but it does not reduce the availability of scrip transactions. Some simple homework can give you clues that will open up the toughest deal by enabling you to offer that hard-nosed seller the right terms.

Buying Scrip on the Delay at a Discount

Assume for a moment that you own a travel agency. Your commissions vary according to the kind of trip sold and the carrier used. One of the top commissions paid travel agencies comes from wholesalers such as Cartan, Gateway, and others. These companies package tours, which agencies then sell. The agency's pay rate increases as the volume of business increases. It rises to the point where the total commission might be double the beginning rate, and, best of all, the rate at the high end is sometimes retroactive to the first sale.

Selling travel requires no inventory stocking for the travel agent; unlike a shopkeeper, the travel agency does not normally "buy" the travel. With this in mind, I enter the picture. I want to buy a property owned by a Mr. Ronald, and I discover that Mr. Ronald enjoys traveling. (I learn this by asking his secretary if he likes to travel.) As part of my offer to buy his property, I might include an offer of $10,000 of scrip that can be used for any travel presented by "the following Tour companies"—and I attach to the offer several brochures featuring the travel offerings of the companies. Brochures from such companies as Gateway and others are often very beautiful and their presentations are enticing. The fact that my offer includes, in addition to all its other aspects, a *carte blanche* selection from any travel offered in the several booklets will melt the hardest heart.

Now, what I have left out here is the fact that I went to *you* first (remember, you own the travel agency). I offered to become your outside agent for the year, or longer, during which time I was going to sell, if nothing else, a package of $10,000 worth of one or more trips from the selected tour companies. For doing this, I want from you a "commission" of 5%.

Using the third-party scrip at a discount gives the investor the advantage of a zero loan plus return.

After making this deal with you, I now "sell" the scrip to Mr. Ronald. I give him the other parts of my deal, of course, but until he picks out his travel program, I haven't paid any of the $10,000 needed to redeem the scrip. In fact, when he comes into the travel agency, I only have to pay $9,500.

I can earn 15% or so on the $10,000 I would have paid Mr. Ronald when I had bought the property. In addition, I will receive another 5% from the travel agency when I buy the travel for Mr.

Ronald. This 20% reduction is much better than paying a high interest, isn't it?

Look around your neighborhood and talk to some merchants to find some you can work with.

Sit down over a cup of coffee with some merchants in your area and tell them of your plan to help build their business by increasing their volume of sales. If you can't get to first base with the merchants, then let them read this book, or at least the three chapters on scrip. It could change their lives.

Pitfalls in Third-Party Scrip Bought at a Discount

In this format, you don't actually pay for the scrip until it is redeemed. This causes several problems, some for you and some for the "banker."

From your point of view, the most important thing about having scrip like this is that you can pay for it at a discount. Keep in mind, though, that you must get your deal with the "banker" in writing. You don't want to find yourself charged with a penalty on the scrip because of a misunderstanding about the 5% fee. Have it clear that until the scrip is turned in you don't have to pay anything. Make sure that the "contract" is good for the specific items covered and that it will be redeemed by the merchant once cleared by you.

The "banker" in the deal must of course be sure that you will pay once the scrip is redeemed. The best way to assure this is for the scrip to state that the redemption is to be covered by you when turned in to the store or merchant. Just add a simple clause on the scrip, such as: "Any merchandise [or service] against which this scrip is to be used for payment will be delivered to the bearer of the scrip within five days of presentation at [merchant's store], and upon monetary redemption by [your name]."

A Quick Review of the Three Scrip Transactions

1. *Scrip you write against your own services or merchandise.* Excellent if the seller will take it. It gives you the advantage of making a profit from the "sale" of your own service or merchandise, as well as giving

you an interest-free loan. Don't hesitate to use this technique anytime you can. All the seller will do if he doesn't like the idea is eliminate it from the offer. Then again, he might take some of the service and offer the broker the balance as part of the commission.

2. *Scrip you buy from someone else at soft paper.* This kind of scrip can sometimes be bought at a big discount. In fact, you might "buy" scrip from one person at a big discount using scrip you get from a third person at a discount. For example, Charles owns a restaurant. I offer him $10,000 worth of scrip he can redeem at Magic Carpet Travel Agency for cruises or whatever. I have a commission due me on the $10,000 of 5%, so that will only cost me $9,500 when Charles turns in the scrip. But because he gets the travel money now, he sells me scrip at his restaurant at a big discount. He gives me $15,000 worth of spaghetti dinners in scrip. I have made a great deal if I can get someone to take the spaghetti off of my hands.

3. *Scrip you redeem at a discount but trade at full value.* This is the last technique, covered in this chapter, and it opens a vast world of potential scrip deals. "Seek and ye shall find."

11

The Commission
Down Payment

FOR SOME INVESTORS, the real-estate agent's commission is a compelling reason to have an active real-estate license. Real-estate commissions, after all, can add up; and if you are pinching every penny, then the salesman's split, which might be yours in the deal, can aid in making the transaction work for you.

When a buyer of real estate is a broker or salesman, he or she can, under the right procedure, participate in the real-estate commission that would be due if the property were listed so as to include such a commission. The proper procedure might depend on the state, but, speaking from an ethics point of view, all real-estate salesmen participating in the sale and commission should make sure they have carefully and duly notified the *seller* of that fact.

An example of such an event would be one where I, as a broker, entered into a purchase of a property listed with another office. It would be natural for me to be interested in buying a prime property that was on the market. Assuming that I had already shown or presented the property to several of my clients and knew that none of those clients was interested in the property, I would proceed to make my move.

First, I would simply draw a usual form offer spelling out that I wanted to buy the property and indicating the terms of the offer. I would) have a paragraph that said something like this: "It is herein noted that Jack Cummings, principal broker with Cummings Realty, Inc., is a licensed real-estate broker within the state of Florida and is buying this property for his own account, and that other licensed brokers or salesmen within the state of Florida, or outside the state, may participate in the purchase either now or in the future. This fact does not waive any rights that Cummings Realty, Inc., has in participating in the realty fee or commission due as per the MLS (or other listing form) with Try County Reality, Inc."

It is true that I frequently make offers *sans* commission—in other words, I make my offers net to the seller, leaving out my participation in the fee. But at the same time, I would deduct it from the amount of my offer. The end result is basically the same. I get the benefit of what commission I would have obtained, but the other broker (if any) can attempt to get this full commission. Usually the seller recognizes that I would have been able to claim half the fee, so he adjusts the co-broker's fee accordingly at the final accounting.

If the commission was 6% of the total price (a fairly common percentage across the country for single-family homes, though commissions can range from 4% to 8% for such improved property and higher for vacant land), the salesman in the deal, after splits with his office and the co-broker office, could expect to have from 1½% to 2% of the price returned to him at the closing.

If I were buying a $180,000 property at 6%, the total commission would be $10,800. If there were another broker (the listor) involved, then my office would get $5,400 or half of the split. As a salesman with my own firm, I would then be entitled to at least half of that (depending on my performance plateau) or $2,700.

If I were paying 10% down, or $18,000, I would have reduced my cash down to only $15,300. And you can see that if I received 100% of the commission, I would have reduced the cash down to only $7,200.

Fine Points of Using Commissions to Reduce Your Cash In

Not all deals are made through outright purchases. Indeed, it is not unusual for a deal to be made via an IRC 1031 or other form exchange. In these events, the frequent custom is to "pool and split" the commissions between brokers. In essence, all the sellers in the deal will owe a commission on the property they are contributing to the exchange. If I were exchanging one of my properties for something else, I would potentially owe a commission myself into this pool. If the commission from my side of the exchange is larger than that from the other side, then there is no benefit to me in "pooling and splitting." In these situations, I will do a YKYIKM. This is called a "Yook-kem," and means simply, You Keep Yours—I Keep Mine. In short, if there is a fee from each side of the deal, one broker is telling the other that each will keep the fee from his/her listing and not pool and split the fees. Obviously, if the commission I am liable for is $70,000 and the other side is liable for only $30,000, I'm far better off letting the other broker keep his while I keep mine.

The amount of commission in larger deals frequently depends on the value the broker places on himself at the time he lists the property. I have a high regard for my abilities, thus I feel I *earn* the substantial fees I ask for my services as a marketer of property. Other brokers, however, sometimes take high-priced listings at low percentages in the hope that a more qualified broker will sell the property for them. I run into these chaps from time to time and don't feel bad at all in using a YKYIKM deal.

From the Seller's Point of View

Dealing with a real-estate broker or salesman as the buyer of your property can be either a good way to go or a bad one. A lot depends on the nature of the broker or salesman and whether he/she was the original listor of the property.

First of all, there are several kinds of brokers and salesmen:

Type A: The salesman or broker who is in the business to sell real estate, but will from time to time buy what he is sold on himself after making a diligent effort to find another buyer.

Type B: The broker or salesman who is in the business of buying

65

real estate and utilizes his inside knowledge to make the best deals for himself.

Type C: Brokers or salesmen who didn't know there was a difference between Type A and Type B.

Naturally the three types described above are the clearest of all possibilities. In reality, there are various shades of the three.

From the seller's side of the deal, it makes little difference which category you deal with *as long as you know which one you are dealing with.*

I have many broker friends who are in fact investors. I deal with them in that fashion, realizing that they will participate in the deal. They are out to make the best deal they can for themselves and don't even have any clients to present the property to first. They are the clearest users of commission as a part of their purchase price.

From the Buyer/Broker's Point of View:

The buyer (broker or salesman) must be sure he has done everything he can to keep himself clear of any unethical dealings. The opportunity to take advantage of an unknowing seller is a constant reality.

Most buyer/brokers, however, view the taking of a commission rightfully earned in the sale or disposition of a property as both legal and ethical: Informing the seller of your intent and position, and giving him ample time to seek out other advice, is only logical; using your in-depth knowledge of your profession is prudent.

Pitfalls

For Sellers

Sellers should be careful of brokers or salesmen who list their property for sale and then, after some time, offer to buy the property themselves. Mind you, I said to be careful, not to avoid the situation. It's not unheard of for a broker to deliberately undervalue a property so that he can take advantage of a quick profit. One way to avoid this problem is to have more than one brokerage firm present you with a proposed marketing plan for your property. This program should include (1) a list of all comparable properties in the area that have sold within the last six months, (2) a list of all similar properties for sale at the moment, and (3) their suggested offering price for you to list the property.

It is a good idea for you to have some idea of the market yourself, and a good way to start is to take a look at several of the properties on the "for sale" list mentioned above.

Keep in mind, however, that as a property owner you will tend to overestimate the value of your own home.

For Buyer/Brokers

People who become real-estate salesmen for the purpose of investing in real estate must bend over backward to be open and aboveboard, lest their ethics be called into question. Buyer/brokers also face some interesting pitfalls when they attempt to get a full return of their commission in the deal. The usual problem in this kind of deal is the broker or salesman who forgets the real advantage of using a broker in the first place, and thus finds himself isolated in the deal.

I rarely negotiate my own deal. I don't want to meet the seller, except on the most social of occasions or for introductions. I never want to be in the same room with him when my offer is presented, and I don't want to do any face-to-face negotiating when I am the buyer.

Why? Simply because no buyer can make the best deal, in my opinion; he needs a strong and competent broker to negotiate the deal for him. The ability of the broker to take the heat of the transaction is important. A good broker will absorb the anger and the frustrations of the buyer and seller, rather than let them direct those feelings at each other.

I maintain this position when I make deals for others. I want the buyer and seller to blow up at me and not at the other party. I also want the buyer and seller to have time to think over their answers, not to have to come up with a fast answer while the other party is sitting across the table.

A good broker can negotiate a deal far better than the buyer's or seller's lawyer, by the way, because lawyers are clearly working only for their clients. The broker, on the other hand, is only superficially working for the seller. The seller is his client, and the broker has a fiduciary relationship to that person, but, without violating that fiduciary relationship, he becomes closely tied to the buyer and can soften the blows and make the deal.

Because this is real life, when I am a buyer I look for a good salesman to stand between me and the seller. That salesman (found at Cummings Realty) *earns* his percentage of the deal, and all parties end up happy.

12

Cash Out the Land

THE CONCEPT of selling the land under a building and then leasing it back isn't new. In fact, in some societies the fee-simple ownership of land by its users is rather rare. The real-estate investor looking to better his cash position and reduce his capital outlay in buying can use the land-lease technique in many ways. The following is one example that can work nicely in some instances.

Due to the lack of tax shelter inherent in land, there is no economic benefit of ownership of the land itself as long as the cost to lease it is less than the cost to own it. In essence, if you can lease land for $10,000 per year and in doing so free up $100,000 of cash that would have gone to buy the land (or can be generated by the sale of the land), then the economic questions to ask are: "Can I make more from the $100,000 than the annual cost of $10,000?" "Will I have to forgo the purchase of the property because I can't come up with the extra $100,000 cash down?" "Can I lease the property on terms that will enable me to get full use of the improvements and to benefit from appreciation at the same time?"

All real-estate investors must be cautioned that leasing land does have some disadvantages to both the buyer and seller. This chapter will cover those disadvantages, and advantages, from each of these points of view.

As a buying technique, selling land and then leasing it back is a very refreshing way to structure your transaction. It can enable you to break down some real barriers with stubborn sellers who have some specific problems. In short, this technique can frequently get you a property that has eluded more "astute" buyers.

Suppose you are interested in buying a motel, but you don't have the $500,000 cash required by the seller. The simplest use of the land-lease technique would be to tie up the property for sufficient time to enable you to find a buyer for the land under the motel. This buyer will agree to pay you in cash for the land, which you in turn lease back.

EXAMPLE: Charles was negotiating on a 100-unit hotel in Myrtle Beach, South Carolina. The deal was all set, but Charles knew that he was going to be short $400,000 in cash on making the deal. He had time, however, to set up the deal and go out to find a buyer who was interested in a management-free income, who would buy the land and allow Charlie to lease it back. The closings took place at the same time: Charles got the motel; the owner of the motel made his deal; and everyone was happy. (Charles, by the way, had an option to buy the land back a few years later. The intention was to eventually refinance the property and pick up the land at the same time.)

In another transaction, Brad was trying to get a seller to hold a large second mortgage on a small strip store he was trying to buy. The owner of the strip store was reluctant to hold a second mortgage, so Brad shifted techniques: He suggested the owner keep the land, sell Brad the improvements only, and Brad would lease the land.

The economics of the land lease, which was much like an interest-only mortgage, were in fact more favorable to Brad as long as he was able to buy the land in the future. The owner of the strip store took the land-lease deal because there was always the chance that Brad wouldn't be able to pick up the option, and then ownership of the land subject to the lease would be better than the mortgage.

This, then, is a part of the quid pro quo in using this technique. The finesse of the deal depends on these five elements:

1. *The terms of the leaseback.* If the payments on the lease are much the same or less than mortgage payments would be, then the first part of

the comparison of ownership versus leasehold is solved. On the other hand, if the lease would be more costly than a mortgage, there is no economic benefit in the lease. There can be other benefits, however: For one thing, it might be the only way to make the deal, due to the seller's demands.

2. *The conditions of the lease.* The lease must be realistic for the technique to work well. A three-year lease with an option to buy at the end of that time would be ridiculous, and would obviously force the buyer to pick up the option. Also, the IRS will look at the terms of the lease as well as the conditions to the deal if there were any question as to the establishment of a lease or a mortgage. This difference could have tax consequences for the seller who didn't want to have a sale (even an installment sale) in that year. A mortgage denotes a sale, while a lease means he still owns the land.

The buyer of the land wants to set up the best terms for himself, of course, but the investor using the technique does control the deal to the extent that he can insist on certain requirements to make the whole deal work.

3. *The terms of the buyback.* In this technique, the investor will want to have an option to buy back the land he is leasing. This, in my opinion, is very important, because even if the economics of leasing are favorable throughout the life of the investor, another investor looking to buy the property might think differently. Transactions with land leases with no options to buy them out are not as attractive as a similar deal with a buyout option. If you are the investor putting this technique to work, make sure this option is not too restrictive, or you may get caught in a tough money market and lose the opportunity to buy out your land lease. I've seen 99-year land leases with options that read: ". . . can be exercised in the month of November, 2068, and at no other time."

Make sure you have a reasonable length of time in which to exercise your option. The optimum for the would-be buyer is "can be exercised at any time."

4. *The escalators.* If you can obtain agreement on a fixed price to buy out the land and have a lease price that never goes up, then you don't have any escalators in the deal. But usually there are some, somewhere. Buyers of the land want a cost-of-living clause to enable the rent to keep pace with the rise of inflation. They also want to get a higher price for the land if and when the option is exercised.

Investors must take these escalators into consideration. If you anticipate exercising the option on or before the tenth year, however, you don't give up anything if your escalators begin at the tenth year. Unless, of course, your timing puts you right in the middle of a "Sorry, but we don't have any money to refinance your deal" epic.

5. *Getting a lock on the deal in the first place.* You sure as hell don't want to go out and knock down the forest finding a buyer for the land in your up-and-coming deal, only to find that, by the time you get back, the owner of the property has sold it to someone else. Always make sure you have the deal tied up. If you are the buyer of the land, make sure the entrepreneur has a firm lock on the deal.

Viewpoints

From the Seller's Side

If you are the seller and the investor is taking you out of the deal 100%, then the methods he uses to finance the deal are none of your business. However, if you are holding some paper on the deal, say a third mortgage, and you find that 100% of the cash the investor uses to close comes from a buyer of the land, then there may be a reason to worry. It's true that the ownership of the land would be subordinate to your mortgage (unless your closing agent slipped up or you had agreed otherwise) and its rights behind yours in foreclosure. However, whenever a buyer gets in without any equity or risked capital, it is possible that if the going gets tough the investor will step aside and let it go. In a scramble to protect your own rights in the foreclosure, you might find yourself spending more time and money than you want to (or have).

From the Investor's Side

As an investor, you will find that the land-lease technique works nicely to help leverage your deal. If there is existing financing at low rates, then instead of asking a seller to hold a second mortgage, give him the land-lease approach. Remember, your terms on the lease and the ultimate buyback will determine whether you have made a good deal.

Pitfalls

The biggest pitfall in this technique is the overextension of debt. This affects both parties because it increases risk for the seller who is holding some paper, and it adds excessive burden to the carrier of the property.

The majority of pitfalls, however, can be overcome or reduced through the use of sound economics in the deal. Does the buyer have the financial ability to support the added payments? Can the property support itself?

The use of a good real-estate lawyer in the drafting of the lease is essential. There are all kinds of leases, and unfortunately some lawyers use boiler-plate leases that don't fit anything but boilers. Each deal is different in this kind of transaction, and each lease would be tailored to fit the exact needs and intentions of the parties. The lease has to have certain provisions to protect the investor's option to buy out, or the technique will be far too risky for him to proceed.

13

Own the Land
by Selling the Building

IN THE previous technique, you sold the land to generate the cash to end up with the improvements. In this creative technique, the objective is to establish an income-producing land lease owned by you.

Owning land under some improvement and having a long-term lease on that land is not usually the optimum investment. The reasons for this are simple economics. If someone else has the use of your land for a long term (say beyond your fruitful life), he, not you, is the one to benefit from appreciation of the land. Even if you have rent escalators tied to the cost of living, the appreciation of the combined land and improvements will usually exceed inflation, hence the benefits to the landowner, who continues to have essentially the same income, are minimal.

This fixed, or quasi-fixed, income then isn't suitable for every investor unless—and I repeat, unless—you have used this technique as a *wealth builder*.

Let's look at the situation involving a 12% land lease. This term reflects the rent paid by the lessee in relation to land value. If the value of the land (as part of the total) is $100,000, then a 12% lease would have an annual rental of $12,000. Tie a cost-of-living increase to this on an annual-adjustment basis and you would have the rent going up by the same percentage as the cost of living. If the cost of living increased 15% over the first year, the rent would go from $12,000 to $13,000 (1.15 × $12,000). Value, however, often goes up faster than the cost of living.

Real-estate investors looking to build wealth in a hurry often scoff at this kind of investment as a slow way to build a fortune. But if the total investment you made to get this $12,000-per-year rental income was only $1,000, then you have hit on a potential gold mine.

The idea, then, is to use this "little old lady" technique to build your bank account.

Set Up the Deal, Sell the Building, and Keep the Land

Charles found a nice but vacant industrial building of 30,000 square feet. Its price was $900,000. The property had an existing mortgage of $300,000 at 9½% interest with 15 years to go. The seller indicated he would take back some secondary financing but needed at least $200,000 down. The rest of the price to the seller would be at 12% interest-only, with a balloon payment in 15 years.

Charles tied up the property with a contract subject to his finding a tenant for the building within 60 days. If he didn't find one to his satisfaction, the deal was off and the $1,000 deposit he had put up on good faith would be returned. (Yes, $1,000 is often all you need to put up on even a million-dollar deal.)

Charles turned around and restructured the deal, offering the building for sale. His ad looked like this:

OWN YOUR OWN
30,000 sq. foot industrial building. Can be yours for less than you'd pay for rent. $200,000 down. Annual payment to own $3.25 per sq. foot per year. Great tax shelter to boot. Call . . .

This deal would appeal to a user who either had some cash or could use another of our creative techniques to get the cash from some other guy. From Charles's point of view, here is what happened.

1. Charles tied up the property, as we have already seen.
2. There was an existing mortgage of $300,000 that had an annual payment of $37,590 in principal and interest. This mortgage would be paid off in 15 years.
3. The seller was going to hold a $400,000 mortgage at 12% interest-only with a payment of $48,000 per year.
4. $200,000 cash had to be generated by Charlie to close.
5. Charles formulated a land lease (subordinate to the existing and new financing). This land lease had an annual payment of $12,000 per year. The other terms were up to negotiation with the user.
6. The buyer of the leasehold had to pay all those amounts shown above. He got the property and the ultimate appreciation. He even was able to extract an option to buy the land from Charlie in the future.

Charles ended up with the land lease and the income.

You will note that the user might have circumvented Charles and dealt directly with the original seller. This could have happened, of course, and might happen to you if you don't make absolutely sure you have the property well tied up. Charles used the option technique to accomplish this. You should never tell the buyer of your deal that you are dealing with a contract until they are committed to buy. Keep that secret to yourself until the closing.

Learning the Power of the A & B Transaction

Anytime you split a property deal into its two elements—the land and the improvements—you are dealing with the A & B transaction. Buying this way can have great impact on your future, and save you taxes when you sell.

In the case of keeping the land in the kind of deal Charlie just completed, there were several interesting benefits that accrued. The most interesting and profitable was the ability to turn over a property with little involvement and low monetary risk. Charles had to spend some time finding the ultimate buyer, of course; but aside from his time, his total investment was the $1,000 deposit on the contract and a few dollars in sales ads.

Had Charles turned over the entire property for an instant profit, he would now be dealing with earned income—and higher taxes.

There are a lot of get-rich-fast schemes that will work for some of you in good times, and some of these schemes tell you to buy low and turn over fast at any profit. It is a great idea, except that it creates something called non-capital-gain-taxed income—as well as potentially classifying the investor as a real-estate dealer. When you are a dealer in real estate, you are no longer able to freely take capital-gains tax treatment. You want to avoid the "dealer" classification.

In the A & B transaction shown above, Charles didn't *sell* the property; in reality, he leased the property with an option to buy. He did this by "selling" a leasehold interest to the user of the improvements, subject to the land lease. As the title to the land is still in Charles's hands, there has been no actual sale of the real estate. A holding period of one year will then permit the taking of a capital gain and the saving of considerable taxes.

Tax considerations are important both now and in the future.

Since the land generally appreciates faster than the improvements, and since the IRS permits the improvements to be depreciated but not the land, the retention of both (A and B) in separate ownership each controlled by the same investor can have favorable results in future sales. The potential benefits will depend on your tax bracket and circumstances as well as the kind of property with which you deal. However, generally any property that is underimproved in relation to the zoning, or is outdated according to current growth trends, will reach a point where the value of the land surpasses the value of the improvements, and the value of the land is now the value of the total property. Any such property can be ideal for an A & B deal.

If the investor anticipates a fast turnover, the A & B deal can prevent his being classified as a dealer (or help, at least) and can be a good financing tool for the transaction.

Advantages and Disadvantages of Keeping the Land and Selling the Improvements

Let's look at the advantages to Charlie.

This technique can maintain Charlie's capital-gains position, since he did not "sell" the land, he only leased it, with an option to buy in the future. If the rest of the deal were a washout—that is, if the buyer of the lease paid the same for those improvements as Charlie did in the beginning—there would be no tax.

NOTE: As the purchase made by Charlie would show an allocation between land and buildings, some of the cash paid to Charlie should be allocated as *option money against the purchase of the land.* If the ultimate purchase of the land from Charlie was a part of the transaction in the form of an option (lease with option), then part of the down payment for the leasehold should apply as option moneys, which would be credited to an ultimate purchase of the land.

Why Do This?

Look at Charlie's purchase and allocate $50,000 of the deal to land value.

Purchased the Total Package:	$900,000
Value of the "A" Side (Land)	50,000
Value of the "B" Side (Improvements)	$850,000

Any price over $850,000 for the leasehold ("B") will create a profit. So Charlie does the deal described in this chapter as follows:

1. Charles sells the leasehold.
a)	Buyer assumes the existing mortgage	$300,000
b)	then assumes the second mortgage	400,000
c)	pays cash for the balance	150,000
		$850,000
2. Charles leases the land at an annual rent of $12,000 plus escalators on a cost-of-living basis.
3. The purchase of an *option to buy the land* sometime in the future. This money must be creditable to that ultimate price. The buyer pays $50,000 cash up front.

Because the $50,000 needed by Charlie to close the deal was paid to him as option money, he will not declare it as income until the year the option is exercised. As the money isn't known to be interest or part of a capital-gain transaction, it will not be taxed (according to current law) until the actual date on which the option is exercised.

The *disadvantages* to Charlie and most any investor are:

1. *Reluctance of many "buyers" to lock themselves into a land-lease situation.* This is due to a lack of understanding in most cases, and investors using the A & B transaction will have to spend time seeing to it that the ultimate user understands the advantages to him.

2. *Risk to the investment, which is subordinated to the existing financing.* As the land has usually been subordinated to the existing financing, a forfeiture on the mortgages by the owner of the improvements will cause the landowner to step in and protect his interest or lose the land. This can be very dangerous if the investor is not careful. Charlie was careful to make sure he checked the credit of the user. Of course, his risk was only $1,000. Yours might be much more.

The other side of the transaction—the ultimate user of the improvements—has no real problems other than the normal business decision of selecting this property over others that might be available. There should be no reluctance to make this deal, because the land is not being purchased. And if the values represented by Charlie are sound, then the user benefits by having a land lease at 12%, which may be below the current interest rate for mortgages. The overall benefits to the user are excellent and make the format acceptable in a wide range of transactions.

Finesse in Putting the Deal Together

As in any turnover, the key is control of the package. Charlie would have a very difficult time making this deal work if there were a wide selection of other properties below his total price, no matter what control he had over the seller. So he must control the deal in other ways—by being within the right price range and by using the land lease as a cheap form of "third mortgage" to make the package more attractive.

Never attempt to put this kind of deal into its "user" stage until you have a bona fide and signed contract from the owner; a handshake or verbal deal here, or anywhere, is a mistake.

14

The One-Lender, 100%-Financed Deal

DESPITE the ups and downs of the money market, it is possible in nearly any market to get *all the cash needed* from one lender. It is simply a matter of proper planning to ensure that one lender is all that is needed.

There are two basic areas in which this technique is used. The first is *new construction 100% financed*. The second—more commonly the case—is *existing property 100% financed*.

The New-Construction 100%-Financed Deal

Lenders, such as savings-and-loan associations, commercial banks, insurance companies, and pension funds, like to become involved with sound new-construction loans. Although these moneys are usually loaned at relatively high interest rates, the builder or contractor who uses these lenders to finance his construction frequently finds himself able to borrow 100% of the money he needs not only to build the improvements, but also to pay for the land.

Lenders make such loans on the basis of two facts:

1. Builders have overhead and profit that contribute to the total value of the end product.
2. Land value will most likely appreciate, and the builder's equity will be enhanced through the improved value of the land.

These two elements give the lender a buffer between the amount lent and the actual value, permitting what from the *builder's* viewpoint is a 100% loan.

Existing Property 100% Financed

Borrowing 100% of the funds needed to purchase existing property is more difficult than for construction. Still, with the concepts presented in this chapter and throughout this book, you will find that 100% financing is not only possible but in some situations downright easy.

Many partial-financing methods offered in this book enable you to borrow from a bank or savings-and-loan the balance of money needed. Certainly if the seller can be enticed to hold a $30,000 second mortgage on another property (the pyramid deal), you will find it relatively easy to obtain a $70,000 loan to complete the $100,000 purchase price of the property you wish to buy. Yet this is not truly a 100%-financed deal with only one lender, as the pyramid technique does create obligations to other sources of funds.

One-hundred-percent financing from one source is usually limited to the institutional lender, and the total amount of the funds almost always goes to the seller. There are exceptions to this, however, and later on I will show you several ways to use some of the cash in fixing up the property.

The Key to the 100%-Financed, Single-Lender Deal

Appreciation is the crucial factor in obtaining 100% financing from one lender. During the period between your obtaining control over the property and the moment you must close on it, there must be appreciation in the value. If you are able to tie up an office building with a five-month option to buy at $150,000, and during the five months you can increase its value to $200,000, the lender appraising the new value will find a $150,000 loan to be well within the parameters of "good business."

This appreciation can occur overnight, by the way, as illustrated by a situation involving one of my clients.

Harrison negotiated a fine purchase price with the owners of a vacant industrial building in Fort Lauderdale. The price was $200,000. I examined the building and the property and instantly knew he had a good deal. He had been on the inside of the deal at the right time and had acted quickly. He had a month or so to close, and now he needed to obtain the funds.

Harrison had a tenant for the building—one of his own companies—and an arm's-length agreement to rent the building was established. The terms were actually overly generous on behalf of the tenant, but the rent—along with an up-date appraisal—was sufficient to show a current value of $198,000. Harrison borrowed in excess of the needed $120,000 to cover all purchase costs and finance charges. His 100%-financing deal was obtained after we personally called on three of the local savings-and-loans.

Time Is a Major Factor

In seeking out transactions with the hope of getting 100% of the needed capital to buy through the lending market, you will be dealing with options or conditional contracts. These two forms of purchasing will give you *time* to let values go up naturally. If in that time you can also convert a building into offices, or a storefront to a specialty use, you will be aiding its appreciation. Time is on your side of a real-estate transaction when you can lock up the price for the duration of that time. Inflation will not work against you in this event, but work for you. If you can tie up the price of your desired investment and then let inflation up the value (not the price), this appreciation will be included in your equity when you get a loan.

Disadvantages of 100% Financing from a Single Lender

1.   Overleverage potential is a big negative, and it occurs no matter how many lenders you have. It's possible to overburden yourself with some properties. If the income you can quickly generate will not cover the debt and you are not getting other benefits out of the property to compensate for the negative cash flow—such as living in part of the facility or having your office there free—then you will have to carry the property out of savings or other earnings. This alligator will eat you out of house and home faster than you realize. The ability to obtain 100% financing can tempt you to go into a deal full speed and damn the risk. Prudent investors, however, will examine the total obligation and will avoid the potential alligator.

2.   Another negative: The sole lender can present problems that multilenders do not. First of all, if there is just one loan, then that lender has a clear decision ahead of himself as to whether or not to foreclose when you are in default. One lender also means one mortgage payment to cover the total debt. This can be a benefit, but it also has a drawback: Multilenders mean several loans and several *loan payments.* With several loans in a tough market, it is possible to keep current with one or more while letting others slide behind the payment schedule if you get caught behind the economic eight ball and don't have enough ready cash. You can pick on one or two weak mortgages and let them wait for a while, then later bring them up to date while letting others wait their turn.

Advantages

The simplicity of obtaining the one-lender loan is its big advantage. In the right circumstance—such as the development of a property or the sudden appreciation of a property tied up with a long-term option—the increased equity above the loan makes it a sound business deal for the lender. When the overleverage problem doesn't exist, then the second problem—the need to worry about manipulating the lenders for extra grace periods—disappears. In the sound deal, where the rent will cover the debt and still show a cash flow, this type of transaction is suitable for even the most cautious buyer.

Finesse in Putting the Deal Together

In seeking a lender, try not to spell out your purchase price. The less the lender knows about what the property is costing you, the better. If you are buying the property, most lenders will want to see your purchase agreement. In anticipation of this, have your lawyer draft an agreement that does not specify the total amount to be paid but shows a sum of money and other considerations. Better yet, use an exchange form on the contract, which, by the nature of exchanges, doesn't show any value at all.

There will be those times, however, when you will have a contract that shows the actual price to be paid. When this happens, you will have to overcome the natural reluctance on the part of the lender to lend close to or above this amount. Your ability to demonstrate an appreciated value will depend on the thoroughness of your homework.

Six Things You Can Do to Show Appreciated Value

1. List improvements made to the property. Don't show amounts paid, only the improvements that you have caused to be made after your contract and prior to the closing, such as:
    a) Revamping front yard landscaping
    b) Cleaning entryway
    c) Resurfacing driveway
2. Point out the time between your negotiations to buy and the present time *only if that time is sufficient to allow some natural appreciation.* If your contract was made yesterday and you are showing a 20% appreciation, you will have some difficulty explaining that appreciation.
3. Show recent sales prices of properties in the same price range

as the property you are attempting to acquire. Have your local realtor friends help you with this and other tasks by finding as many properties that have sold in the last few weeks. Cull these properties until you have as many as possible that are similar to the property you want to buy. It doesn't matter where these selected properties are; if you have fairly placed a value on the property, then the market conditions will automatically match similar areas. (NOTE: This is a shortcut method; the usual way of finding comparables is to scour the area for similar properties and then find those that have sold recently.)

4. Have a well-documented list of similar properties available for purchase. If your list demonstrates that your selected property is above the average offering, or that there is a very small selection, this is to your advantage.

5. Have a plan to effect even greater appreciation. If you have some good ideas on how you can create even greater appreciation by making improvements or by some change of use or whatever, *make sure this is known*. Lenders will sleep easier if they feel you have a good plan and they can clearly see the future increase in value.

6. *Don't do any of the above five if the end result would not clearly demonstrate appreciated value.* If you are unable to get the desired financing from one sole lender, don't worry—there are still avenues for you to explore. In fact, a prudent investor doesn't wait for all negative votes to come in before he begins to develop alternative sources. You should have some other iron(s) in the fire just in case the sole lender is not available at terms satisfactory to your needs.

15

The Second-Property Loan:

Borrowing Against One

Property to Buy Another

BORROWING MONEY on real estate is like supermarket advertising. Look in your Wednesday paper and you will see what I mean. The advertised specials are designed to attract the buyers: "Special this week on five pounds of ham"—that sort of thing. Meanwhile, the prime "buying items" are not marked down and the unaware buyers end up paying top prices for the majority of their supplies.

The parallel here is that you should borrow against that supermarket item. If you own a property that is a better buy in the "borrowing market" than one you are proposing to buy, then don't be reluctant to use it as security when you borrow the funds to buy the other property.

EXAMPLE: Charles wants to buy a four-unit apartment building and can do so with a $15,000 down payment and assumption of the existing financing. However, he can't get the 15 grand by borrowing on the apartment building without going into a hard and high-cost secondary-mortgage market. This would overburden the apartment and cancel out the good deal Charles has negotiated. However, Charles owns a home that has a low-percentage loan-to-value first mortgage; and when he talks to the savings-and-loan holding that mortgage, he finds that he can extend that mortgage by $15,000. His total overall cost will be less than going into that secondary market for the funds. Charles gets his $15,000 at a reasonable cost and saves his deal.

ANOTHER EXAMPLE: Jake needs $50,000 to make the purchase he has been working for, and finds that refinancing the property he wants to buy will be very difficult and costly. He owns some free-and-clear vacant land, however, and decides to mortgage that property. A few conversations with the local commercial banks produce a lender willing to provide a first mortgage on the vacant land at a cost far below the costs of either refinancing the property to be purchased or obtaining a second mortgage on that same property.

Pick the Most Lendable Property and Work from That

Lenders like certain kinds of properties as security on their loans. A free-and-clear single-family home in which the borrower lives would probably be the first choice, but it most certainly is not limited to that.

Make a list of what you own and your existing financing. This is the supermarket of items on which you can borrow. If you have established some rapport with a mortgage broker (and you should now if you haven't already), discuss the situation with him. Go down to your local savings-and-loans and commercial banks. Meet the lending officers there and discuss your problem. Your problem, by the way, is obtaining the maximum money to meet your needs at the lowest overall debt service.

Avoid undermortgaging your property for the sake of a limited amount of cash you might need to swing into one deal. If, for example, you own a free-and-clear home worth $100,000 and you need $40,000 to make a transaction work, there is no question that you can borrow those funds. The problem is, a $40,000 loan against the property is less than the maximum that can be borrowed. You might find that pushing the loan up to $70,000 would be more practical even if you didn't need the extra cash at the moment. Once you place a first mortgage, there may be no future opportunity to expand it to a greater amount. You can look to a refinancing of the loan or going into the secondary market to obtain additional funds you may need in the future.

The ideal situation, then, would be to have a property that will support the amount of money you need in a maximized lending situation. If you need $40,000 and have a property valued at $50,000 and can borrow the required amount against it, then that is as close to perfect as possible (unless you can borrow $40,000 against a property worth $40,000 or less).

It is possible that refinancing might be the way to go to achieve two benefits at the same time. Let's say you need $30,000 in cash to make a transaction work. You make a list of the property you own and it looks like this:

You Own	Estimated Value	Existing Financing	Your Equity
Home	$100,000	0	$100,000
Duplex	90,000	$42,000	48,000
Lot	50,000	0	50,000

It might appear that the best property to use would be the lot valued at $50,000. However, when you examine the debt service on the duplex, you find that the $42,000 balance is to be paid over seven remaining years at 14% interest. In monthly installments, this will give you existing payments of $787.08 per month. If you refinance to 15% on a 30-year term to a maximum mortgage amount of $72,000, your monthly payments would be $910.38, or an increase of $123.30 per month on the increased debt service of $30,000. This increased cost of the debt service is less than you could obtain in any reasonable market, and you are unlikely to find a reasonable market today. In essence, for only $123.30 per month over your current debt cost, you can generate an additional $30,000 in cash.

The fact is, of course, that you have to extend your payments over 30 or more years to accomplish this. But while this does increase the total payments over the life of the new mortgage, it does not reduce the value of the property. From a financing point of view, this method produces immediate cash at the lowest possible cost.

Being creative in finding the right property to refinance or use as security in a loan, then, is an important part of this technique. Using the blanket type of loan, wherein you would present the lender with several properties as security instead of one property, might do the trick when all else fails. Remember, the greater the security on the loan, the less the lender is risking. Anytime you can present a reduced-risk loan to a lender, you will gain his attention.

The Advantages of Borrowing Against One Property to Buy Another

The main advantage in using this technique is in obtaining money at a lower cost. Some investors have the idea that they must let each property stand on its own; they never look to one property for financing another. In my opinion, this is a shortsighted approach that often prevents their getting the edge in the financing arena.

The total payment to your lenders each month is what you should consider. Anytime you can borrow against one or more combined properties more cheaply than you can against the property you want to buy, you should consider doing so.

The Disadvantages

As mentioned earlier, in techniques involving high leverage and potential overextension of debt it is possible to get in over your head. What you want to avoid whenever possible is the borrowing of money simply for the expediency of having the cash. If the new property won't support the total added debt plus the existing debt on that property, then you are flirting with disaster.

Mike, for example, needed $25,000 to put down on a small four-unit apartment building he had tied up on a 90-day option. He scraped up the money by obtaining a second mortgage on a property he already owned. The problem was that, after the smoke had cleared, Mike found himself the owner of a property with a heavy four-year payment on the second mortgage. The income from the apartment building didn't cover his total expenses, and the first property—a nice three-bedroom home where he and his family lived—was not an income producer, so there was no support there. He had placed his holdings in jeopardy by overextending his debt to a point where the income from the apartment building wasn't sufficient to ward off foreclosure.

There is no hard-and-fast rule about overextension. Sometimes it is warranted, if you are ready to carry the load until you can increase the income of the property to cover the total cost and, of course, put some money in your pocket.

To be on the safe side, however, in a tight situation you should have a margin of at least 5% vacancy in the *current existing income* from any income property you hope will cover your debt service. It is nice to be able to increase rents, and sometimes the market will go along with that desire. But then sometimes it won't.

Be cautious in any lending situation. The total impact of the debt service is the key. Look at it, then see if alternative mortgage situations are available to reduce it.

Never view any single method as either the best or the most readily available until you have used creative thinking to locate or manufacture another.

16

The Private Punt:

Private Mortgages with Kickers

WHEN IT COMES to borrowing in a tight money market, there are times when you can offer *private* lenders some benefits that will get you the loan. These benefits may or may not be cash, and often take other forms of return. "Kickers" you offer to lenders—or which are demanded by lenders—will vary greatly. This chapter can only hint at the creativity of some lenders in their quest to better their investments.

Some Examples of Private Mortgages with Kickers

· Ron needed $75,000 cash to close on the apartment building he wanted to buy. He ran some ads in the local papers offering private lenders a blanket mortgage on several properties, including second position in the apartment house. His "kicker" to the lender was the additional security of having several properties to look to and, because of that, a lower loan-to-value ratio or risk.

91

- Lamont needed only $30,000 cash to close on the North Carolina home he wanted for vacations. He offered private lenders, as a kicker, three weeks' use of the home each year for the term of the loan.
- Phil needed $100,000 to buy an office building. He offered private lenders 20% of all net income in excess of the previous year's rental figure for the duration of the loan.

In each of these three examples, the borrowers were competing with the normal terms of the market. The kickers were offered not only in hopes of softening those terms but to *entice the money to come to them, instead of to another borrower.* Some lenders will take the kickers you offer and not report them as value received, hoping in this way to avoid payment of income tax on the value of the kicker. After all, who would ever know about the three weeks in North Carolina?

My suggestion to you in offering kickers is not to get involved with the motives of the lender. If they don't plan to report the kickers as value received, the trouble they will find with the IRS is the pitfall lying in wait for them. Don't be an accomplice. Be sure *you* report the value of those kickers as *interest paid* when you file your income tax.

What Kickers Should You Offer?

When dealing with private lenders, the kickers needed to make the deal work depend on the lender and the deal. Each lender will have something that can motivate him into a deal, and if you can provide that motivation, then you are on your way.

Some lenders will simply hold out for hard items like (1) percentage of income, (2) increases in interest, (3) cost-of-living adjustments to interest, (4) part of the depreciation, and/or (5) use of part of the property. These five items can hit you hard in the pocketbook, since they can reduce your net profit on the property. If at all possible, you should avoid this kind of kicker *unless* you are satisfied with your own return. Instead, try to use *soft kickers.*

Some Soft Kickers

1. *Noneconomic use of the property.* If there are times when the property isn't producing income, then offer that.

2. *Use of some other property during its noneconomic period.* If you own a mountain cabin, for example, offer time in that facility to the lender giving you cash to buy something else.
3. *Professional or craft services that you do personally on some limited basis.* If you are a dentist, doctor, plumber, carpenter, electrician, or whatever, you have a kicker to offer that need not take away from your normal economics.
4. *Kickers that you can buy at a discount.* You might find that the lender will make the loan if you give him a trip to Paris each year during the term of the loan. If you calculate the cost and then make a deal with a travel agency to give you a commission on the sale of the travel, you can reduce the overall cost to you.
5. *A percent of future profits when the property is sold.* This is a hard cost on one hand, but it is not paid until the ultimate sale of the property and can be limited.
6. *The opportunity to buy at a discount.* If you are building on or re-developing an existing property and plan to sell units or condos or subdivided lots, you could offer a lender the opportunity to buy at a discount. This cuts into your pocket on one hand, but generates some sales right away on the other.
7. *The right to buy into a future deal.* Some developers might offer to let their lenders come in as partners in future deals.

A Look at the Private Money Market in General

In any given society there will be private persons who have horded cash. It is a basic and a natural human syndrome. The tougher the times, the greater the amount of cash some people will accumulate. They will do this out of fear of the market or out of prudence. But whereas having cash at the turn of a sellers market into a buyers market will put them on the top of the pile, holding on to cash can be very frustrating. What do you do with it? Long-term, short-term? Stocks? Bonds? CD's? What?

As this cycle develops, and as the money market gets tighter, the institutional lenders begin to dry up. They eventually lend only to prime clients, and then only if they have the funds. The secondary market in institutional terms no longer exists.

Private lenders can be lured into providing the necessary funding for small, moderate, fixed investments by giving them the yields the institutional lenders demand, plus some of the kickers mentioned or which will be devised by creative lenders and borrowers.

A great advantage of dealing with private lenders is the often reduced cost of the loan. Big banks and savings-and-loans like to collect big points, which are additional interest in the form of up-front expenses. Private lenders rarely charge these points, and the actual cost of setting up the loan documentation need not be expensive.

A big drawback of dealing with private lenders can be the nervous nelly who has just made his first real-estate loan and will call you every time the wind blows or your grass hasn't been cut for over ten days. It's easy to say, "Stay clear of newcomers to the lending market," but that isn't sound: Some of the best lenders you can develop might make their first loan with you. A few, however, will be so nasty and scared that you will never want to see them again. Remember, when you are dealing with institutional money, the people you deal with are removed from the money—it isn't *their* money. On the other hand, that private lender has worked hard for his cash and will take a personal interest in having it paid back—on time.

Where to Find Private Lenders

Private lenders exist everywhere. They are wealthy people. People with newfound cash. People who like the yields and security obtained through real-estate lending.

However, they often hide behind rocks, trees, lawyers, and accountants. You can write letters to the last two mentioning that, as a real-estate investor, you are interested in knowing if any of their clients are potential lenders to good, sound, excellent-yielding real-estate loans. In doing this, you will also draw out any lawyers and accountants who might have available cash. But don't rely solely on your letters; arrange personal visits with real-estate lawyers and accountants in classy areas in town so you can see each other face-to-face. (On the other hand, if you are one of those shifty-eyed types who look like they've never done an honest day's work, stick to letters and phone calls.)

Newspapers are a good advertising source you can use. Most classified sections have a column headed "Money Wanted" or "Investment Opportunities," so put your specific ad for the specific deal in the paper. "Charles the investor needs $50,000 for sound real-estate transaction and will give the lender great terms with fantastic kickers. Call . . ."

Some private lenders will place ads themselves, searching out good loans. Look for such ads, sometimes found in "Capital Available" or "Money to Lend" columns.

An active borrower, however, will look beyond newspapers for his lenders. There are three sources of private money in your neighborhood.

Investment Brokers

These are stockbrokers and other investment counselors, and they are easy to find. If you have one or two yourself, then those are the ones to start with. Make absolutely sure that you are very clear in dealing with these people, however, and make it particularly clear that you expect to pay them a *fee* for finding you a lender. The usual fee would be 1% of the amount of the loan. If they demand more, you must weigh the total cost against your need for the funds. In any event, be sure to weigh carefully the total cost of any money you borrow.

Accountants

These professionals know their own clients' specific needs and financial capabilities. If you are offering secure mortgages and borrowing is usual in your business, they will sometimes be of help to you. If these chaps (or any lender) think you need the loan *to save your butt*, then the chances are you won't get it—or it will be offered at terms that won't save you anything.

Accountants should not be offered a fee, but you should be willing to pay if *they* bring it up.

Lawyers

I mention lawyers, but I put them at the bottom of the list. Your own lawyer might be okay, and you should let him or her know that you are looking for private lenders. Other lawyers will usually see your need for money as a weakness, which they can take advantage of. This is not a condemnation of lawyers, just an insight on how some of them tick.

Some Tips

Private money can be very good if you play your cards well. When you repay the loan, chances are the lender will ask you if you need more money. If you develop a good rapport with the private lender, he or she can be a lifelong partner in your ventures.

You should therefore take care to always be prompt with the loan payments—even more so with private lenders than with institutions. The institution has taken into account the potential wait for its funds, and none of its employees have loaned their own money, so there is no one to upset. The private lender, on the other hand, will sit at home waiting for the mail on the first of each month to make sure he has gotten his payment on time.

Keep in mind, too, that the wrath of a private lender can, and usually will, be far more swift than that of the biggest and toughest savings-and-loan or commercial bank.

17

The Public Punt:
Institutional Mortgages
with Kickers

MUCH LIKE the private loan, the institutional loan can and does function well when there are kickers added. As money becomes tighter, the big lenders find that kickers are not only needed to entice them into the deal, but that without the kickers their ability to survive the market will be slim.

To understand the risk of surviving in the financial marketplace, it is helpful to examine the differences between the private lender and the institutional lender. There are several very important differences between them. Now that I have introduced you to the private lender in the previous chapter, it's time that you had a better understanding of the institutional lender.

Who Are the Institutional Lenders?

The financial community of lenders centers around the big banks, of course. Chase Bank of New York, Barclays Bank of Tokyo, Bank of London, Royal Bank of Canada, and so on. Each bank is a major factor within its own circle in the ultimate cost of money.

Combined, these and other banks set what is called a "prime rate," which is the supposed interest rate that the preferred clients of these banks must pay when funds are loaned to them. All other clients—those of lower quality in terms of risk—will pay *over prime*.

The savings-and-loan associations and other savings institutions make up another part of the institutional market. These "banks" function much as limited competition to the commercial banks within the usual markets, and have been in the past primary lenders in the residential and small commercial real-estate market. These lenders are governed tightly by the laws that grant them existence, and are heavily hurt by declines in the real-estate industry, which is their lifeblood of lending.

Nearly all of the money loaned by these two "banking sources" is money given them in the form of *deposits*. These deposits are given to the institution for safekeeping and for the interest the institution pays to the depositor for the use of the money. The bank or savings institution then loans the money to others in the form of real-estate or other kinds of mortgages and loans.

The importance is this: The deposit comes in and, within a short time, the money is given out. The mortgage loan with the borrower might be over 15 to 40 years at an interest rate that in the past has been fixed for the life of the loan at not more than 3% to 5% over the rate the bank is paying the depositor.

For years this system worked pretty well: You put money in your savings-and-loan account at 5¼%, and they lent it out at 8¼% or 9%. As long as the level of deposits continued to grow, the institution could grow. Based on the level of existing deposits, they could borrow additional sums of money from other lenders, namely the Federal Reserve, at relatively low rates and lend out that money, making a nice profit all the while.

The institutional lenders weren't lending *their* money, they were lending the *depositors'* money or the Federal Reserve's funds. The yellow brick road looked like it could go on forever, but it didn't.

The Long-Term Contract: Boom and Bust

The long term of the mortgage loan is what has made real-estate financing within the United States much easier than almost anywhere else in the world. An 18-to-40-year loan is not unusual in the U.S., whereas 5 to 10 years in some countries is considered a very long term.

As the institutional lenders began to lay out the funds on these long-term loans, they discovered that the average loan was paid off somewhere between the seventh and the ninth year. The original term of the loan apparently didn't matter much, since borrowers found it economically prudent (in times of relatively cheap financing) to refinance after seven to nine years. This average life caused lenders to make their contracts even longer in some cases, as an enticement to seek out their funds: After all, borrowers like long payouts, even though they might choose later to cut them short.

The big problem came when interest rates, formerly held down by usury laws, went up and up as those laws were removed. Economic measures that will be argued about for centuries were taken by the federal government in hopes of "fixing" the national economy. Interest rates were permitted to rise, and in fact encouraged to do so by a tightening of the Federal Reserve rate to the institutions who had to have those funds from time to time to survive the ups and downs of their cash-flow problems.

As the rates went up, the institutions found that they had to pay more and more to their depositors to keep a flow of cash in their vaults and to stem the tide of withdrawals moving into higher-yielding money funds. By mid-1981, the depositor could get a safe return of more than 18% on his certificate of deposit, which was a far cry from the 5½% or so his savings were earning just a few years earlier.

For the lenders, the situation grew critical. The money taken in a few years earlier in the form of deposits had been lent out already. A 1976 deposit of $100,000, on which the institution had to pay 6%

interest, was sitting in a loan of $100,000 (the principal that had been repaid was quickly lent out, of course) at an average rate of return to the lender of 11%. The deposit itself, however, had been withdrawn from the institution and placed somewhere else, where it could earn 18% instead of only 6%.

The institution couldn't pick up the phone and call the people they had lent the money to back in 1976 and say, "Kindly send up the hundred thousand we lent you as the depositors want their funds back." So they had to go into the current market and borrow money (through Fed, or other depositors) at the current rate.

Now, instead of having a deposit for which they paid 6% and on which they earned 11% by lending it out, for a whopping 5% profit on the total funds (none of which was theirs), they had to borrow money at 18% to make 11%—a loss of 7% and all of those funds were theirs.

At this point the institutional lenders realized that this kind of punishment would drive them to close their doors and declare bankruptcy very shortly. So they began to seek out *kickers* to make their loans palatable to the market. They also began to tighten the reins on their existing loans, because of another event that began to occur at the same time.

As money became tighter and tighter from 1979 through the early 1980s, a great slowdown within the real-estate industry began to develop. People began to talk about the high cost of borrowing money for buying their home or apartment, and lenders running out of cash to lend began cutting back (out of necessity) the amount of loans they made. This combination of events meant property owners were not going to refinance those low-interest loans they had taken out seven to nine years ago. With a mortgage below 10% and in some cases below 8%, why saddle oneself with a 30-year, 18% python of a loan? Better to keep the old homestead and pay off the loan over its remaining 20 years.

Thus, lenders who planned on those rollovers within seven to nine years are now faced with the prospect of holding on to a below-10% loan for its full life, and at an annual loss that drives savings-and-loan presidents to contemplate suicide.

Okay, now you see the urgency of the savings-and-loans to do something about their dismal future. They have to unload their old loan portfolio and start out from scratch. It isn't the tight money that's killing them—it's the easy money they lent in the past. One idea I would suggest is that they sell their old loans to Social Security to save both institutions.

The problem in a nutshell: Institutional lenders give as loans the money they get from others, lending it at a higher interest than they pay, and pray at night that they won't have to give back the money they received or borrow it at a higher rate.

Private lenders differ greatly from institutional lenders in that the money they lend comes from themselves—they are their own depositors. They take their own cash and give it to you in the form of a mortgage. You pay them back in the form of loan payments, and that is how *they* get their cash back. The private lender will never have a run on his deposits unless he has acted like an institutional lender by borrowing the money he lends. (Nasty habit.)

In the vast majority of "small" loans (small in relation to the size of the lender), the private lender is using his own cash. This makes for a more stable lender in normal times, but one who frightens easily and wants to foreclose quickly in tough times.

Taking the institutional lender to task is far easier than with the private lender. In the first place, when money gets tight, the logical conclusion in that the institutional lender will become tough just like the private lender. After all, it will be the institutional lender who will be losing by having to borrow at rates in excess of those earned on the old mortgage. However, institutional lenders have restrictions that require them to *reserve funds* for potential foreclosure losses every time they foreclose on a property. In short, even though they will threaten it, most institutional lenders will avoid foreclosure, even to the extent of absorbing considerable loss. (They will, of course, eventually foreclose in the end.)

Living with these facts isn't easy for the institutional lender. But they have some tools to fight back, and they are getting smarter about getting the edge in lending. You see, to simply be a lender will in the long run kill you. You have to get some of the other benefits that go along with the real estate, not just the interest on the loan.

With this in mind let's look at some of the kickers that the institutional lender can and will request. If you find one that is more palatable to you than the one the lender is requesting, suggest a trade-off—don't wait for the lender to bring that possibility to your attention. Lenders are not as creative as they could be (look at the mess they are in).

Three Kickers Institutional Lenders Use

The Land-Lease Ploy

This can be a good kind of kicker for both the lender and the investor. Here the lender takes a look at the total amount of funds to be lent, then allocates part of the money to a *purchase of the land,* which the lender then leases back to the borrower at the same or a slightly higher rate than would have been paid on a mortgage.

EXAMPLE: Charles needs $1 million to finance the construction of an office building on his lot. The full $1 million is paid over to Charles, but he has a mortgage of $700,000 and gets $300,000 for the land. He has to put the $300,000 into the building, of course, and he uses the land under the terms of the land lease.

Charles's total debt service is much the same as paying on the $1-million alternative loan. But he isn't given the alternative option: It's "Take the deal this way or not at all." Charles looks at the total picture and realizes that he will be faced with increases in the land-lease rent sometime in the future. But it is all a matter of economics. The land isn't a tax-shelter item, and it might be good for Charles to take the deal. After all, he needs the building and hasn't any other way to go.

*100% of the Financing Up Front for a
50% Preferred Percent of the Profit*

More and more lenders are coming into deals as partners instead of lenders. They do put up all the cash at times, however, anticipating their judgment of the reputation, character, and credit-worthiness of the investor to be prudent and the profit potential sound.

A preference position is kind of neat, too. In this way the lender (private lenders or investors can use this technique also) puts up the money but gets a yield, such as interest, off the top. The borrower doesn't get any return until the lender is paid his yield, and then the borrower receives the next yield, until they are equal, after which all is split on a fifty-fifty basis.

This technique, of which there are many variations, is used for income-producing investments such as apartment buildings, office buildings, shopping centers, and the like. Income on such properties has a tendency to grow over the years, and to be a partner in such a venture can be a great advantage to the lender. As he is advancing all the cash needed, he is in essence buying the investor's expertise and of course the investor's package deal.

Percentage of Income over a Set Gross

This kicker is more common than the one just mentioned with insurance companies who don't want to become partners with builders and investors. In this transaction, the lender advances the agreed-upon sum of money on the mortgage and collects the monthly mortgage payments as in any other loan. At the end of the year—or during the year, as might be agreed on—the borrower will calculate the *gross income* of the property (the rents that have been collected) and will pay to the lender a percentage of any income in excess of the ceiling established by the loan agreement.

EXAMPLE: You want to borrow $500,000 for a 20,000-square foot strip store. The lender (if they want to impose this kicker) calculates the comfortable gross income needed to support the expenses of the strip store. Let's say that the current rent is $140,000 per year and operating expenses are $40,000 each year. This would leave $100,000 for debt service and return to the investor. The debt service on $500,000 at the term and interest rate demanded by the lender might be in this case $85,000 per year. Assume the lender allows you, the investor, another $15,000 on top of that for your return. This has then used up the entire $140,000 of income.

However, as income is going to go up as rents increase, the lender tells you that to get the $500,000 you must give them 50% (or whatever percent you can get them down to) of all gross income above the $140,000 gross during the life of the loan.

These three kickers are the usual ones requested by institutional lenders. They will come at you with various twists, but these are the basics.

Four Key Points in Dealing with Institutional Lenders

1. The farther the institution is from the actual property, the more information you must give them. This is sometimes not examined too carefully—until you leave out something important.

2. The people you deal with are not lending you their own money. They will therefore have an impersonal approach to the entire situation. Because they do control the situation to some degree, they do at times like to make borrowers squirm.

3. Loan officers don't like to make bad loans—because each time they do, they earn red marks on the president's checklist of Loan Officers to Fire Next. Therefore, they will try to cover their tracks to be sure it isn't their ass that gets burned if your loan goes under.

4. Deal with the president if at all possible. Since he cannot cover his own ass so well, he will make damn sure that foreclosure on your loan is the last possible recourse.

18

The Family Loan

THE FAMILY LOAN—a very simple event: "Dad, how about loaning me fifty thousand so I can buy that run-down gas station and turn it into a fast-food restaurant?"

But obtaining a loan from that single most private source—your own family—can be one of the hardest ways to finance a deal. I say this for several reasons. First of all, asking for the loan might be next to impossible for some people.

Second of all, there is frequently a good deal of reluctance on the side of the potential lender. "A loan? No one gave me a loan when I was just starting out."

One objective of this chapter is to help you to decide whether you should ask, and, if you do, how you should set up the family loan. Another objective of this chapter is to help family members ascertain whether the loan request is a prudent one, and, assuming the funds are available, whether the loan should be granted. The natural reluctance to lend because "the kid hasn't any idea of what money is" should not enter the picture. If the deal is well secured, you should approach the loan with as open a mind and as businesslike an attitude as you can muster.

Begin with the Problem

Brad comes from a nice family in California. Not a wealthy family, but a nice one. He has finished college and is working for an electronics company in Utah. He has the opportunity to tie up a small duplex in the Salt Lake City area on an option. Brad figures he can put some money together by the time he has to close on the deal in four months. If he can't he will lose the $2,000 he put down on the option.

Brad strikes out at the local savings-and-loans and everywhere else he goes for the loan. It isn't a question of the value of the duplex— that is sound, and Brad's deal is an excellent one as far as the purchase goes. However, the lenders in Salt Lake just aren't lending to anyone except their long-standing customers. Brad is out in the cold. He figures that he will need $10,000 to close the gap between the money he can scrape up and what he needs. Where should he turn?

"Dad," he says, "I have a proposition for you." He knows something about his father's finances. He knows that good old dad has some cash tied up in CD's and some more in stock. The stock isn't doing so hot at the moment, and Brad is willing to pay an interest rate equal to or better than the rate dad is earning at the bank. In fact, if he must, he will offer dad a kicker or two to entice him into the deal.

Dad looks at the deal and decides he will make Brad a second mortgage provided Brad moves into part of the duplex himself. Dad figures that this will cut down on Brad's living expenses, as the apartment closer to town where Brad is now living costs about $100 more per month than the small side of the duplex would rent for. In addition, Brad will be on the site to fix up the property, which needs some tender loving care.

Each party has approached the loan as a business venture. Sure, there was personal interest that went beyond the hard economics of the transaction, but in the end it was a sound business deal that offered real economic benefits to each party.

A lawyer was hired to draw up the necessary papers at a nominal cost, paid by Brad, and the deal was made.

This example is not typical. Most family loans breach all business sense and end up proving the adage "Lend to the family and you will break up a family." (That statement was made by an orphan, I do believe.)

It doesn't have to be like that, of course, as Brad and his dad have illustrated. If both parties follow the checklists in this chapter, they will have a clearer understanding of their positions.

When Should You Ask the Family for a Loan?

There are two simple answers to this question, and they are in the form of questions themselves:

1. Isn't it better to keep the interest in the family?
2. If all *other* sources fail, shouldn't you give up without trying this last possibility?

In reviewing these questions, there are factors for each party to consider. In the first question, the theory is simple enough: If you are going to borrow money and pay a profit to a lender, why not pay that profit to a member of the family? The theory breaks down, however, in the application of the business sense. If a member of the family turns you down for the loan for any reason at all, the matter should not be taken personally *if* you are being businesslike about the request. After all, you aren't going to take umbrage if the local savings-and-loan turns you down, are you? Any lender must occasionally turn down what appears to be a good loan. They do so because of other commitments, or simply because they don't want the risk at that moment. Respect this concept of lending.

The fact that you have sought the funds elsewhere and have failed doesn't mean that the loan is not sound. It could mean that the local lenders you have approached are out of funds. Or perhaps you actually got offers of money, but at terms that strangled the deal. It is one thing to pay top interest and closing costs, but to have to pay through the nose, too, might mean a reassessment of the project. No project or investment can support *any* debt service. There is a limit. I point this out because any good deal can find funds if you are willing to pay any price for the money. Loan sharks and that sort of money lender must be avoided as they are not a good business source of funds.

If you have approached the investment properly, you will have examined several alternative forms of financing to solve your cash needs. This book offers many such alternative forms of purchasing real estate without cash, and some of these techniques used together or by themselves might be your answer. If none of the others produce the funds at a cost that makes the investment a potentially successful one, you then follow up with this technique. On the other hand, if you have had some past history of borrowing from the family, and you have always been a good risk, then the family might be the very first source of funds to reach out for.

No matter when you go to the family, first or last, the time to do so is only when you can present a prudent risk to the lender. You must be ready to meet the market as to interest and terms. You must also be ready to pay the penalty of *kickers* if that is what the market demands, and accept the punishment of foreclosure if you are behind in your payments.

What Makes a Prudent Risk?

No lender should approach a potential loan without wanting to know the present and potential value of the property and the background of the investor. In approaching your family for a loan, you should be ready to answer these questions in depth and with backup documentation to support your evaluations. Unlike an institutional lender, the family won't have the advantage of an appraisal department to check out those values. If you can obtain an independent appraisal to support your own evaluations, then this will be a good idea. *Never use family relations as an excuse for a lack of professionalism in obtaining the money.* "Gee, dad, don't you believe me?" after you have told them the property you are buying for $50,000 is really worth $120,000. It might be, but document it. A bank would want to know, so why not Uncle Charlie, or mom and dad?

A prudent risk for a lender, then, is the chance one takes in lending money where the present value of the property will be reasonable security for the amount of money lent if the lender has to take the property back through foreclosure.

If I give you $50,000 in cash, I want to know that, if I have to take the property, a foreclosure sale will return me my unpaid money, *plus* unpaid interest, *plus* costs, *plus* aggravation. Sometimes this all adds up to quite a lot of money. For this reason, lenders are careful and borrowers have to pay high interest to get money.

Naturally the lender looks to the borrower and not just the property. Two people wanting to borrow the same amount of money on the same property will be viewed in different perspectives if one is a wealthy well-known owner of real estate in the area and the other is just out of school and doesn't have a job.

Since the majority of family loans will be within the secondary-loan category, some of the problems of ascertaining the risk are alleviated. A secondary loan, by the way, is the placing of any mortgage on a property that has an existing mortgage already recorded against the property. Most investors reaching out to the family for a loan will be attempting to get part of the down payment, leaving intact the existing first mortgage.

Secondary mortgages are riskier than first mortgages because, in the case of a default, the first mortgage is covered in the foreclosure sale ahead of any other mortgage. Sometimes there aren't enough proceeds from the sale at the courthouse steps to cover the first mortgage, costs, interest, etc., and the second mortgage is wiped out. This leaves the secondary lender in the terrible position of having to take the loss or go after the borrower by obtaining a deficiency judgment. This kind of judgment is very tough to get in most states and in most circumstances. And even when you can get the judgment, it is tough to collect. So as the risk goes up, the cost of money also goes up.

How to Reduce the Risk or Eliminate It Altogether

Back in the picture once again come the kickers. You can do a lot of things with kickers in the family that you wouldn't do with other loan sources. For example, Rick needed $10,000 to put down on an FHA-financed home. He had scraped up $5,000 of his own money but was short the other $5,000. He asked his dad for a loan, and the kicker that enticed his dad into the deal turned the transaction into something quite different, not a loan at all though the end result was the same for Rick. The home was put in dad's name, and Rick's

$5,000 was given to dad as an option allowing Rick to buy the home in the future. Rick rented the home for a few years from his dad; and when he had saved up $5,000, he exercised the option to buy the home from dad and closed on the deal. In the few years between deals, dad had an arm's-length transaction where he had bought a home and rented it out. This gave dad a nice tax shelter on the home (depreciation), which Rick wouldn't have been able to use anyway as it was to be his own residence. The risk of a loan was reduced greatly in this kind of a deal and worked to solve Rick's need for a house.

It is likely that any investor seeking funds from his family will have something else of value that can be "blanketed" into the loan. Pledged as additional security to the loan, this other property (car, lot, another real-estate property, etc.) will help eliminate risk.

How to Ascertain if the Loan Should Be Made

The following checklist should help families faced with this critical decision. There are many aspects which should be examined that might mitigate some of the potential negative answers you can get as you go through the checklist, and I will elaborate on them at the end of this chapter.

The Family Preloan Checklist

1. Does the borrower have a history of loan payback? Simple question—tough answer. If the member of the family asking for the loan has never borrowed money before, then there is no plus or minus on this point. However, if he or she has and the results have been late payments or foreclosure threats, this is a definite negative.
2. Examine the investment-property data carefully. How well documented is it? If it's sloppy, send it back to be returned as a neat and well-presented package. If other "experts" are brought in, check their credentials and their willingness to put their spoken words into written words.
3. Ask this question: "Why are you buying this property?"—and expect a good answer. If it is a closed restaurant and the idea is to turn it into a steak house, then examine the qualifications of the investor to do that.
4. What are the other financing details. If the property has great existing

financing, this can make a moderate deal great. On the other hand, if the existing financing is 85% of the price and at 18½% interest per annum, there might be a problem of overburdening the deal with excessive financing.

5.   What investment alternatives does the investor have? What you want to know is whether he or she would be better off buying a nice office building than buying an apartment building. You also are seeking to learn how well the investor has scoured the market.

These five questions to consider will serve to bring to the forefront items the investor himself should have examined. If they were examined, then the answers will be fast in coming. If not, then perhaps you will do the investor a favor by *not lending the money* until the full background of this investment and the alternatives have been examined.

Factors That Mitigate Sound Business Reasoning

If you have a program of bit by bit transferring parts of your estate to your children, then you don't need sound business reasons to make a loan. It is possible, through lending at low rates of interest or at *no* interest at all, to enable your family members to benefit at a minimum of tax consequence to you. I won't expound on the many ways this can be accomplished, except to say that you should seek the advice of a good tax counselor to set up a program that best suits your goals.

Wrapping Up the Loan with the Family Member

Do it legally with a lawyer or a title company, and make it simple, clear, and concise. Then live it up. You should have nothing to worry about if your risk in making the loan is compensated for and you can better your yield over other investments you presently have.

In short, if it's done in a businesslike way, there is no reason not to lend to a member of the family.

19

The Presale Refinance

IN THE refinance-prior-to-closing technique, the seller arranges for new financing prior to the closing and transfer of title. The buyer then comes into the deal and takes the property subject to the new existing financing.

There are several instances when this technique is the ideal one to use—such as when the buyer cannot qualify for a new mortgage, or when it is in the seller's best interest to approach the sale this way. For example, look at Lou's and Bob's transactions below.

Lou had lost two deals in the past three months because he had been unable to qualify for the financing he needed. It wasn't that he was a bad credit risk, only that he was property-poor and had few liquid assets. This scared the lenders, but it didn't scare Lou. He was eager for more property and kept looking.

Soon he found a home he wanted to buy. It was priced at $65,000, in a good area of town, and its zoning would permit professional offices. He knew he would be able to convert the home into a beautiful doctor's office and quintuple the existing rent.

The seller owned the property free and clear, however, and did not want to hold any paper; he wanted to be taken out of the deal with 100% cash.

Lou studied the deal and decided that the seller could get the price he asked and over 80% of the cash he wanted if he would simply follow the plan Lou offered him. All the seller had to do was take out a new mortgage, let Lou take over that mortgage, and accept from Lou a second mortgage equal to the balance of the funds needed.

Lou calculated that if the seller placed a value of $70,000 on the home, he would be able to borrow $56,000 (80% of that value). There would be some closing costs on the mortgage, and Lou anticipated that would total $2,000. This then would net out $54,000 to the seller. Lou would assume the $56,000 loan and give the seller a second mortgage in the amount of $11,000 ($11,000 plus the $54,000 cash to the seller equals $65,000).

It looked good on paper. After all, the seller was walking out of the deal with a lot of cash, he would keep his price firm, and only had to give in a little on the paper part of the transaction. Lou, by the way, was willing to pay a good rate of return on the second mortgage, and that could have clinched the deal right there.

The seller, however, had read several of my books and knew that letting the buyer walk in with no cash and little risk wasn't prudent. To counter this, Lou offered to *blanket* the $11,000 second mortgage by adding additional security—a set of sterling silver tableware appraised at $9,000. Lou had been holding the silver for his younger daughter's dowry, and decided it might as well sit in a safe-deposit box as security on this paper.

It was just the kicker to make the deal work, and Lou bought the house. He kept the silver, of course, as he only "gave" it as security. As long as he paid the mortgage, the silver remained his.

Bob, on the other hand, was a *seller* who had a problem. He needed to unload a property he owned because he was short of cash, but would have tax trouble if he sold any more property that year.

He had a buyer ready in hand to buy the property—a small apartment building that was beginning to be more aggravation than it was worth. It needed fixing up, and Bob was on the move all the time and didn't have time to look after it.

As he pondered what to do, he remembered that *money borrowed is tax-free money*. This meant that if he simply took out a mortgage on the building, that would generate the cash he needed without the tax worries.

So what Bob did was this. He made a deal with the buyer on an option basis to take over the management of the apartment house with zero cash down. The buyer could purchase the property at the end of one year, provided the terms of the option had been lived up to—namely, fixing up the property as outlined in a detailed list of improvements needed.

Bob then borrowed the cash he needed, and during the year didn't have to worry about the operations of his improving apartment building. At the end of the year, the buyer exercised his option to buy (adding cash to the deal, which he obtained from a second mortgage on the now like new apartment building). Bob solved his problem and made it possible for another buyer to get a zero-cash deal.

These are just two examples of refinancing prior to a sale to solve separate problems. The use of new financing to help the transaction along can be a marketing technique as well. It is possible for some owners to have so much equity in their property that a sale is difficult. Buyers with heavy cash availability are generally the investors who hate to use it. The majority of investors around like to buy in with as little cash as possible. Therefore, investors who have a lot of equity may find that placing a mortgage on the property prior to closing not only is prudent, it can make the sale.

Keep in mind that the mortgage need not be placed on the property until you know you have a buyer in the wings, but it is a good idea to make sure you have a lender ready to make the desired loan.

Setting Up the Lender for the Deal

From the Seller's Point of View

Any seller approaching this technique should be candid with the lender—at least to a point. Tell the lender that your intention is to finance (or refinance, as the case might be) a property you own and ultimately plan to sell, and that you want the loan to contain provisions allowing it to be assumed by a future buyer. The lender may impose limitations on this—such as their approval of the buyer, adjustments of interest rate to a current level, and the like. But be honest with them on the ultimate intention to sell.

A commitment from such lenders as savings-and-loans or commercial banks can usually be obtained without cost, and when a lender has made the commitment, the balance of the deal can be put together.

From the Buyer's Point of View

Once the commitment has been obtained the buyer can proceed with the purchase. There is the matter of his assumption of the loan being approved by the lender, but such approval is frequently easier to obtain in purchases subject to newly placed financing than in the original loan application. Keep in mind that the fact the new buyer's willingness to substantiate the value of the property by a purchase contract will aid in his being approved. (The lender is relieved to know that a buyer agrees that their evaluation was correct—or low.)

Be Sure You Understand the Difference Between the Mortgages

One of the toughest things to fully appreciate is the cost of the debt service. This single element—*the total cost of the mortgage*—is vital in developing *beneficial* refinancing instead of simply getting new money at future detriment to the investment.

The mathematics of mortgages is such that a $100,000 loan at 15% interest per annum payable over 30 years will have an annual payment (combination of 12 monthly installments) of $15,730. This payment will continue, in the average amortized mortgage, at the rate of $1,310.84 per month for a full term of 30 years, over which time the principal of $100,000 is slowly reduced until it reaches zero. The reason it is "slowly reduced" is that the bulk of the payments are interest. In fact, to pay back the $100,000 borrowed will cost $471,900 over the 30-year life of the mortgage at 15% interest: $100,000 of principal and $371,900 of interest.

In the beginning the total cost, on an annual basis, of principal and interest is 15.173%. This percentage is often called the "constant rate." If you look at table A in the Appendix, you will find a series of interest rates and corresponding columns of years. A 15% loan for 30 years will have the 15.173% constant shown under the 30-year column at the 15% interest level.

The annual payment for this $100,000 mortgage, then, is the amount owed multiplied by the constant rate for the remaining term of years. $100,000 × .15173 will equal the annual payment over the term of 30 years of $15,173 per year. (Remember, when using a percentage in a math problem, move the decimal two places to the left: Thus 15.173% becomes .15173 in the problem.) Divide that annual payment by 12 and you will have the constant payment per month for the next 30 years, which will cover interest and principal.

Back to the cost for a moment. In the very beginning you have a cost then of 15.173% for both the principal and interest part of the mortgage. I say "in the beginning" because as the loan pays off principal, the percentage increases. For example, by the time the loan has five years' maturity, the balance owed is $98,718.28. That's right, five years of payments at $15,173 per year and all you've paid off is a little more than $1,200. The rest is interest. As the annual payment (total of 12 months) is constant, and remains at $15,173 per year, the cost relates back to a lower principal, therefore showing a greater annual percent. If you look at table A's 25-year column at 15% interest per annum, you will see the constant rate for a 25-year-remaining-term loan to be 15.370.

Continue down the years now and examine what happens at the midpoint of this original 30-year loan, when the loan has 15 years remaining. If you look at the 15-year column at 15% interest, you will see that the constant is 16.795%. To instantly find the remaining balance owed on the loan, divide the annual payment ($15,173) by this new constant rate (.16795). The answer is $90,342.36. In short, although the loan is half over, more than 90% of the amount borrowed is still outstanding.

When you reach the point where only 5 years remain of the original 30-year term, things will look even more dramatic. Look at the 5-year column at 15% in table A. The constant rate is now a whopping 28.548%. Using the same fast technique to find the amount owed, you divide the annual payment of $15,173 by this new constant, .28548, and come up with $53,149.08.

The loan payment cost started at just over the annual interest rate and had a constant cost of 15.173%. The constant rate started to move up as the principal was paid off. By the time the loan was about half paid off, 25 years had passed, and the constant for the remaining 5 years started at over 28% and went up.

The point here is that refinancing can bring down the overall cost of the money borrowed even if you have to borrow at a higher interest rate. Borrowing $65,000 at 16%, for example, at an original term of 30 years, will give you 16.137% constant. This is an annual cost of $10,489.05, or a monthly payment of principal and interest of $874.08. If you are buying a property whose original $100,000, 30-year mortgage is now 25 years old, the balance outstanding is the $53,149.08 shown above. Your annual cost on that amount is $15,173 per year. A refinance *even at higher rate*—let's say 16% on a $65,000 mortgage—will generate some cash and will lower your annual cost by $4,683.95. This reduced debt service will come to you as additional return on your investment.

The "take away" side of that story, of course, is that you have just refinanced yourself back to a 30-year mortgage program from a mortgage that had only 5 years to go. In doing that, you will have to go 25 years and more to bring that $64,000 down to its halfway mark, and your constant rate will grow just the same as the 15% one did.

However, if the interest market drops in a few years from the 16% level, then you will simply refinance again, taking out more cash (which, since it's borrowed money, is tax-free) and reducing your debt service at the same time.

It pays to learn about constants as a shortcut to understanding the mortgage market and just where you stand with overall cost. From time to time as the book develops, I'll give you more uses of the constant tables.

20

The Policy Loan

BORROWING against your life-insurance policy can be good business and may be the lowest-cost loan available to you.

Charles had just about given up trying to find $10,000 to nail down a deal he was putting together. The triplex he had tied up was a real gem and he knew he would be able to turn it over in a few months at a nice profit after fixing it up. But he was ten grand short.

He was able to find lenders, but the property already had a first and second mortgage, and he was reluctant to add a third. The lenders saw the potential, of course, and thought they had Charles over a barrel. They were hitting him for maximum interest and kickers that made the deal only fair to poor, a risk Charles didn't want to get involved with.

He then remembered that his life-insurance policy had a cash value, and that he could borrow against that cash value at a low interest rate.

He went home and, after a few hours' hunting around in his den, found the policy. It was an old one, taken out nearly 20 years before, and there was a provision enabling Charles to borrow up to the cash value at an annual interest rate of only 7%.

At first Charles was cautious about borrowing on his life insurance. After all, what if he died, or was crushed by the weight of his mortgage payments? Then he put it down on paper. Borrowing money from the insurance company didn't mean he wasn't still insured for the amount of the policy—only that he was getting some of that insurance early. Surely if he was still insured for his policy amount and could borrow the funds he needed now at 7%, that was much better than being held up by a loan shark third-mortgage lender at 18% plus three fingers and part of the profit.

There is no real trick to borrowing on your life-insurance policy, the only question is, *can* you borrow on it, and how much?

Not all insurance policies have a cash value, and not all that have a cash value will permit low-interest loans. You need to know just where you stand with your own life-insurance company.

Is There Any Reason Not to Borrow
Against the Insurance Policy?

Of course. It could be that you have overlooked a better source of money.

Prior to beginning this book, your repertoire of techniques to finance your real-estate purchases was most likely limited. Well, it's growing now, and by the time you finish this book it will be far richer than when you started. But that isn't all there is to the game: In addition to the 40 techniques offered here there are 40 more techniques (which will be covered in the future in another book). These techniques, with their blends and variations, will give you hundreds of alternative methods to make your deals work without your digging into your own pocket for the cash to buy.

Don't use your insurance cash value for your loan unless this loan technique provides the *maximum benefit*. You wouldn't borrow $15,000 against a free-and-clear $100,000 property if you could use a $17,000 property or $20,000 investment as that security.

You don't have an easy second chance in refinancing real estate, so you want to get the maximum benefit from the first loan. Of course, when you borrow from your life-insurance cash value, you do have a freer in-and-out privilege. Usually you can borrow and repay, borrow again, and so on at a high percentage of the cash value building up and at the low rate provided by most insurance contracts.

Ultimate Investment Goal Will Affect
Your Borrowing Program

If you are interested in buying a four-unit apartment building with the idea of fixing it up for a resale, the method you choose of financing the purchase may differ from the one you would have chosen if your intention was to move into one of the units and keep the property for long-range income. Now be careful you follow this next part. I said *"may* differ" because you alone don't call all the shots: The deal will be made between you and the seller. It is possible that there will be only one way you can make a deal—the seller's way. If that fits your economics, okay—though you will still find that many of the techniques in this book will help you in meeting the economic needs to make the purchase even on the seller's terms.

For the fast-turnover kind of purchase, I recommend you use techniques that load on the property in question rather than on other investments you have. The idea here is to keep the maximum financing *on the property you are buying,* rather than develop high equity in property already purchased.

EXAMPLE: The four-unit apartment building you're interested in is priced at $92,000. It has a first mortgage of $50,000, and the seller has already agreed to hold a $20,000 second. To generate the $22,000 cash to buy, you might find your insurance policy an ideal source. However, that puts you into the apartment building with $22,000 equity (cash you borrowed from the insurance policy). This might be the ideal thing to do—except that when you sell the property you must *get that cash back* to pay off the loan. Since you plan to fix up the property and sell it for around $125,000, you can see that you will have a $55,000 equity in that new price above the existing first and second mortgages.

An alternative might be to *temporarily* borrow the funds from the insurance policy, fix up the place, *then refinance* the now more valuable property with one new mortgage. This way you can pull out your cash equity, pay off the insurance loan, and have a property that will be easier to sell.

However, that might not work in a tough money market, because you simply may not be able to get your cash out with a new-mortgage rate that will *enable* you to sell the property.

It might be better in this situation, then, to see if you can change the seller's mind about the amount of paper he will hold. If you can entice him into holding more of a second mortgage, your equity will be reduced when you go to sell.

Should You or Should You Not Borrow Against Your Insurance Policy?

It really boils down to the proper matching of what you want to do with what you can do.

This matching of ideals with opportunities can rarely be done to perfection, but you *can* learn to avoid deals that require of you more than you are able to give. The trick here is to fully understand what you are able to give, and what you wanted to get out of the investment in the first place.

In my opinion, there are three questions you should ask yourself before deciding to borrow against your insurance policy. If your answer to one or more of these questions is "yes," then the likelihood is that this is a good way to go. Keep in mind, however, that you must be very honest with yourself in answering these questions.

Three Questions to Ask Yourself

1. Does the added debt service jeoparadize the investment, and have I attempted and failed to obtain the funds through the other techniques offered in this book at a *cost* lower than or equal to the total debt service for the insurance-policy loan? (If you have not examined the situation in this totality, do so before going on to the other questions.)
2. Is my long-range goal to hold on to the investment? (If so, the security for the loan should be the security that provides the *lowest loan cost.*)

3. Can the needed funds be fully attained through the insurance-policy loan? (You should not dip into this well for only a portion of the needed funds, unless you already have the balance tied up in the contract or from other sources. Your insurance policy is like cash in the bank and should be sought only if you are ready and willing to commit the deal.)

21

Collect Autographs: Cosigners Can Make Your Deal Work

WHEN you are at your last thread in putting a deal together, you might find that the source for the funds was right before your nose all the time. All you needed was some signature power behind you to clinch the loan. In short, a *cosigner*.

The cosigner may be a person, corporation, partnership, or any entity that will entice the lender into making a loan that would not be made to you otherwise.

Let's say you were using a substitution technique, such as a pyramid, where the seller was holding a second mortgage on another property and you were trying to refinance the purchased property with the local savings-and-loan association.

The savings-and-loan cuts you short, however, by lending less than you had planned. If that happens, this technique can pull your deal out of the fire. Let's look at this situation in more detail.

Charlie was trying to buy a small strip store. It was 10,000 square feet of local shops and generated a nice income as well as sufficient tax shelter to be attractive to Charlie. The price was $450,000 and the property had a low first mortgage of $150,000. Charlie felt that any local savings-and-loan association would lend 75% of the value, or $337,500, if he went to them. Figuring that there would be loan costs totaling about $7,500, he calculated that if he could get the seller to hold as part of the deal a $120,000 second mortgage secured by a farm Charlie owned, the seller would be well secured as the farm was worth well over $350,000 and the first mortgage was only $50,000. In this way the savings-and-loan would not have to consider a loan on a transaction that would have any secondary financing. Charlie would not have a second mortgage on the strip store—but on the farm instead. (See the discussion on "pyramiding" in chapter 23.)

All was going according to plan until Charlie got the results from the savings-and-loan association's loan committee. They said they liked the strip store and would loan $307,500, not a dime more.

That upset Charlie's plans, as you can see below:

What Charles Wanted to Do		Deal after Loan Committee	
Cash Down	0	Cash Down	$ 30,000
Net Loan	$330,000	Net Loan	300,000
Seller Takes		Seller Takes	
Second on Farm	120,000	Second on Farm	120,000
Price	$450,000	Price	$450,000

There was no logical reason for the savings-and-loan to refuse the amount of money Charlie needed except that the times made them reluctant to risk more loan on poor old Charlie. They needed to be enticed into the deal.

Charlie asked for a conference with the loan officer and gave him some new ammunition to take back to the committee—a cosigner to make Charlie less of a risk. This gave them a reason to increase the loan to its more realistic level, and the deal was saved.

Your transaction won't be exactly like this, of course, but it is possible that you will find that you can and will be able to use the cosigner technique effectively.

Sometimes It's the Seller Who Needs to Be Satisfied

If the seller—the most motivated of all lenders—is balking at giving you more paper, it may be because you are a higher risk than he wants to accept. In the case just discussed, if the savings-and-loan had ultimately turned Charlie down on the increase needed, or didn't come up to the required level, he could have gone back to the seller and said: "The savings-and-loan is about to blow your deal. It seems they are just about out of money, and I'm short thirty thousand to make the deal work. I'll give you a second mortgage on the strip store for thirty thousand, however, with a cosigner to add to your security. Don't forget, Mr. Seller, you will still get one hundred and fifty thousand in cash when we close." (Of the new loan, $150,000 would go to pay off the existing loan, and the balance would go to the seller.)

Where You Can Find a Cosigner

There are many places where you can find a cosigner. Here's where they hide:

1. Home (dad, mom, brothers, sisters, other relatives)
2. Office (partners, coworkers, boss, employees)
3. Social Circle (your bartender, hairdresser, friends)
4. Neighborhood (neighbors, shopkeepers)
5. Financial Circle (the broker, the seller)

For the most part, the cosigner is taking little or no risk if he uses any prudence at all. For this reason, the most useful cosigner is apt to be found at home. If your parents, for example, can improve your future by doing nothing more than placing their names on the loan with yours, then that might work out nicely. If the loan is a low one in relation to loan value one (unlike Charlie's deal—a 75% loan to value), there is substantial property value securing it. At the same time, the lender knows there is a moral obligation on the part of the cosigner to ensure that the loan is more secure, even if in fact there is little or no risk on the part of the cosigner.

Use Kickers If You Must

If you know you can lock up the deal by simply adding a signer to the loan, then look at the possibility of giving the cosigner something for his "risk." In the previous chapters on loans with kickers, I suggested several kinds of kickers you can offer someone who is lending you money. Cosigners shouldn't expect much—if anything—but be ready to offer something if you are in a tight market.

In my opinion, the best kicker to offer a cosigner, if you have to, is something that has to do with a future benefit. It might be a piece of the profit, or perhaps some future use of the property.

The benefit for some parents in aiding their offspring will be getting them out of the house while at the same time watching their children grow and develop their own wealth—kickers of this nature can be cultivated. But remember, a start in the financial world doesn't just center around the use of another name; that name has to have something behind it to make it worthwhile from the lender's point of view.

What Is the Combined Net Worth
of You and Your Cosigner?

This is a question lenders will ask. Remember what I've said about dealing with institutional lenders: You're dealing with people who lend someone else's money, not their own; and these middle men want to make damn sure that if anything goes wrong and (heaven forbid) the institution has to foreclose on you, no one will look back at them and say, "Stupid, how could you have recommended a loan to this jerk?"

To get his ass out of the fire, the loan officer will say: "I can't understand what happened! We made him get a cosigner, and look at this net worth—it's better than our normal loan!"

To be sure he can say that, the loan officer will insist that your cosigner look as good in the credit reports as he does on paper. It's no good getting mom or dad to cosign if they are about to file for bankruptcy. And your wealthy partner won't do you one drop of good if he is on his way to the penitentiary for grand larceny. Pick a cosigner who can show a better net worth than you. (Your net worth, by the way, is your total assets less your total financial obligations.)

In determining an individual's net worth, there are two kinds of assets that a lender will examine carefully: liquid assets—cash, or those items that are just as good as cash (money, gold, stocks, etc.—things that can be turned into cash with a phone call); and nonliquid assets. (Real estate is one of the top nonliquid assets around: It can't be quickly turned into cash.)

Obviously, lenders prefer strong liquid assets to nonliquid ones. On the other hand, most real-estate investors have a far stronger nonliquid-asset list than cash equivalency. Since this will become your problem as you develop a real-estate portfolio, you will need to make your nonliquid real estate look as important to the lender as it is to you.

All lenders want you to fill out a financial report. *Use their form* even if you have a dozen of your own. However, never fill out a lender's financial statement without giving a backup package on all the real estate you may own. If real estate is the bulk of your assets, you should show the income or profit potential of that real estate in hopes of softening its nonliquidity. Thus, if you own income property, spell out clearly the cash flow you earn and its potential for increases. If you have vacant property, then hint at your intended use or how and why it is going up in value.

The enhancement of your assets may not eliminate the ultimate need for a cosigner, but it will aid both of you in presenting the strongest lending package possible. In this way you will have the greatest opportunity to get the maximum loan at the most favorable terms.

22

The Double Scoop

IN THIS TECHNIQUE, you get the seller to hold some paper while you finance the rest somewhere else—and *you get cash.*

The fact is, there will be times when you can buy a property and walk out of the deal with cash at the same time. When you use the "double scoop" technique, you may not always put cash in your pocket, but, if used properly, you will always finance your deals 100%.

There are many ways to double-scoop your purchases; in fact, most of the techniques in this book can be used with this method of building your wealth in a hurry. The main ingredient in the double scoop is a *motivated seller* who needs to unload the property *and also needs some cash.* A motivated seller is important in any real-estate transaction where you hope to get the upper edge, but not all *sellers* are that strongly motivated. Your job, then, is to either *find* a motivated seller or come up with a plan of purchase that will motivate *the seller.* Obviously, however, if you go around looking for the seller who has a sign around his neck that says "I'm a Motivated Seller—come and steal my property," you will be looking for a long time.

Finding a Motivated Seller

There is only one real way to find sellers who are motivated to do business with a hard nut of an investor like you. MAKE OFFERS, MAKE OFFERS, MAKE OFFERS, and then MAKE SOME MORE OFFERS. By constantly being a ready and willing buyer (on your terms, of course), you will be ready when the seller who wasn't motivated yesterday all of a sudden becomes motivated today.

The basic law of successful real-estate investors centers around this simple fact: You have to ask someone to do what you want them to do before they will do it. This works most emphatically for the double scoop, as well as other methods of buying without any of your own cash.

(Oh, yes, while I'm on this subject. The guy who has overpriced his property may not appear to be a strongly motivated seller, but I love to see him because, if his property is overpriced, it isn't going to sell; the average buyer will pass it up in favor of a more reasonably priced investment. However, if I like the property, I'll hang in there and make one offer after another, change from one buying technique to another, not in the hope of breaking the seller down to a lower price but to let him know I'm a taker of his property when he becomes motivated.)

The double-scoop method works on the motivation of need. The seller must *need* some cash. Here's an example of a double scoop.

Charles found a beautiful office building that could be purchased for only $150,000. The building had some major drawbacks, the most important being the fact that it was currently 100% vacant. The property had been on the market for over a year, during which time Charles had watched one tenant after the other leave the building. The price dropped a little each time, until Charles was ready and willing to step in and make the deal he wanted.

Charles offered the seller $100,000 in cash, out of which the seller would have to pay off the small $30,000 first mortgage. On top of the $100,000, Charles would give the seller a note for $50,000. The note was not secured by the building, but Charles agreed to pay off the note within five years or at that time secure the note with a mortgage on property worth a minimum of twice the remaining amount of the note (as a kicker) and to then pay off the balance within four more years.

Charles knew he was making a good deal as he already had a tenant lined up for the building—an insurance company that needed just that sort of building. Based on the lease Charles knew he could work out, he went to a savings-and-loan and showed the now improved value (improved because the building would no longer be vacant, but, instead, rented at top dollar). That new value was estimated by Charles to be $225,000.

The lenders agreed that the rent justified this higher value, and Charles was able to borrow $140,000 on the basis of this new value and still offer the lenders a strong loan-to-value ratio. This gave him a good loan at the best rate of interest. The seller would get $100,000; another $10,000 for closing costs left Charlie sitting pretty.

Charles double-scooped on this deal because he had over $30,000 cash in his pocket after paying the closing costs on the mortgage and taking title to the property. That $30,000 cash, by the way, was tax-free to Charles and was promptly put to work as a down payment on another property.

Finessing Your Double Scoop

Look *strong*, look *successful*, act *confident.* These three important images are even more effective if they are more than skin-deep, but in the beginning you must at least *appear* certain that what you are doing is going to succeed.

Other key factors that will aid you in making your double-scoop transaction:

1. *Buy free-and-clear property.* When you are dealing with sellers who own their property free and clear of any mortgages, then you have a greater potential for generating cash for the seller as well as yourself. If the seller has a high percentage of financing already on the property, you need to seek some other method to make the deal work, as there would be little room to refinance.

2. *Find sellers who can't exercise control over their property.* If the seller is moving out of town, or can't deal with the

public, or has a full-time job that doesn't allow him time to look after his own interests, then you have a seller who has lost or is about to lose control over his property and will more freely accept any deal that will solve his imminent problem.

3. *Deal with sellers who need some cash.* You have to examine the times to know who they might be. In tight money markets, they might be builders or developers looking to unload their don't-needs to protect their projects. A seller who has had some economic tragedy befall him should not be overlooked. You aren't out to take him—only to aid him in his search for cash. The important factor here is the need for *some* cash, not a *lot* of cash.

4. *Buy property that lenders like.* You find out what kind of property lenders like by asking them. Visit mortgage brokers and loan officers, and ask that big question: "What is the most borrowable property in town?" Work from that. Smart investors don't buy what they are in love with, they buy what the lenders are in love with. Wise up on this score. Once you are wealthy and can blow your cash, you can spend money on property you've fallen in love with.

5. *Think big and act big.* If you've just obtained an option to buy a property for $130,000, don't be afraid to up the value on that property to $250,000 when you approach a lender. Make sure you can back up the new value of $250,000, but *never, never* point out the increase. Simply say: "Sir, the value of this property is two hundred and fifty thousand dollars because I have a letter of intent to lease this building from IBM for fourteen dollars per square foot on a triple net lease with cost-of-living adjustments every year over the next twenty years." If that doesn't do it, nothing will. If you point out that this figure represents an increase of value, you tie it back to the old value. The past in real estate is gone forever. Don't raise values, however, on a whim. Have a sound basis for doing it, and stick to it.

6. *Shop around for mortgages.* You have to look for financing; it doesn't seek you out. Only really big investors have money barking at their door—and remember, what barks also bites. When you seek a loan, visit with a minimum of four savings-and-loans and one or two commercial banks as a good start.

7. *Do not take the first or second no.* When a loan committee turns you down, try to find out why. Then try to counter the objec-

tion with a new loan submission. Try a kicker, or a cosigner, anything, but keep at it until you obtain the financing at terms you can live with.

There will be a point, of course, when you must finally take a no gracefully if it keeps on coming back to you. After all, you don't want to burn your bridges with something dumb like "I'll never come in here for a loan again."

The Disadvantages of the Double Scoop

On the Buyer's Side

Again we see the potential overextension of loan to value. You will have a mortgage with the lender and another with the seller. If you aren't careful, that will burn a big hole in your pocket in a hurry.

On the Seller's Side

The seller is taking a risk, of course, by taking a note back on a deal not secured by any mortgage. But some sellers, anxious to get the cash and trusting the buyer, will do just that. In fact, if you were a seller you might *seek out* a prime candidate you trusted and sell him your property just that way.

Risk, after all, is a two-way street. If the seller can get a good price and a lot of cash by taking a risk on a person he already believes in, that isn't such a bad risk after all.

The Advantages of the Double Scoop

This is so obvious. You finance 100% nearly all the time, and much of the time you can walk out of the deal with cash. There are, however, some times when you are unable to do the double scoop as I've outlined it in this chapter. In fact, there are times when the seller will go along with everything except the unsecured note.

When this happens, and it will happen, you can fall back on the "pyramid" and its several variations. In the next two chapters, we'll discuss two pyramid techniques that offer fantastic opportunities to launch yourself into sudden equity and greater wealth.

Ready? Go!

23

The Grand Pyramid

ALL PYRAMID TECHNIQUES rely on the human tendency to view the grass as greener on the other side of the fence. In all pyramid techniques, the seller holds some paper as a part of the transaction; what differentiates the pyramid deal from the usual situation—where the seller will take back a second mortgage when he sells—is that, in a pyramid, the seller holds the paper on *some other property.*

EXAMPLE: Charles has found a great vacant lot on which he will build a rental apartment building. That is, he will build it if he can put his transaction together so he can finance out on the building.

The lot is priced at $30,000. Charlie will put seven apartments on the site at a total construction cost of $140,000. He calculates that other costs—such as plans, interest on financing, and miscellaneous items—will bring his total costs for land and building to $190,000. He is sure, however, that by the time the building is rented (and the current low vacancy rate in the area indicates that will happen before the building is completed), the value will be at least $225,000. As he has found a lender who will lend 80% of the *pro forma* (future) value ($225,000 based on realistic income and expenses), Charlie can see a potential loan of $180,000. This leaves him

$10,000 short—and with no real cover for contingencies. So he goes to buy the lot and offers the seller the following:

1. $15,000 cash, to be paid out of the first construction draw when Charlie breaks ground.
2. A note and mortgage in the amount of $15,000 at closing. The mortgage will be on a beautiful three-bedroom home Charlie owns in Vero Beach. True, it will be a second mortgage, but it is a beautiful home and the first mortgage is quite low.

The seller really wants to sell the lot, and this deal is a secure and safe one: He gets some cash, and he holds a strong mortgage, even if it is a second-position mortgage.

As Charlie has no secondary financing on the lot he is buying, the lender assumes Charlie has $15,000 equity in the deal. He lends the $180,000 as anticipated by Charlie, and Charlie advances the first $15,000 to the seller as that purchase agreement calls for.

Here is how the deal has shaped up:

At the outset, Charlie owes $15,000 in cash on the lot. The construction will cost another $140,000 as anticipated. On top of that, there is the extra $20,000 in other costs (plans, interest, etc.), giving him a total cash outlay of $175,000. Since he has borrowed $180,000, he now has an extra $5,000 to use as a buffer. (The cost of the financing, by the way, was part of that extra $20,000 already calculated in, so Charlie didn't have some hidden charge waiting in the dark.)

The use of the pyramid to generate 100% financing is a sound way to approach any building program. In Charlie's case, if he had some extra cash left at the end of the project, he could pay down the other mortgage (the pyramid) that he gave to the seller.

ANOTHER EXAMPLE: Mike wanted to buy a 35-unit motel on route A1A in Fort Lauderdale. It was a nice property and was priced at $1,225,000. The present owners had owned the property for over 15 years and had paid the financing down to only $210,000. Mike saw this as a real opportunity to use the pyramid, so he approached the sellers with this deal:

1. He would give them $700,000 cash.
2. He would take over the obligation of the existing mortgage.

3. He would give them a first mortgage of $315,000 on a large vacant tract he owned near Naples, Florida. The terms of this mortgage were such that Mike knew the sellers would not object.

The sellers looked at Mike's offer and realized they would get more cash out of the deal than they had hoped for. They had anticipated that a buyer would not come in with more than 30% to 40% down, so getting $700,000 cash out of the deal was very attractive. On top of this, they didn't even have to hold mortgages on their motel.

What Mike did next should have been in the back of your mind by now. He went to a lender (who he knew liked motels) and cut a deal to borrow 75% of the purchase price. That gave him $918,750 in cash. Out of that, he made a deal to pay off the existing first mortgage, which was at a very low rate of interest. The holder of that paper was so glad to get cash that the mortgage was discounted down to a round $200,000. Mike then gave the seller his $700,000, paid $15,000 for the mortgage closing, and was left with $3,750 in his pocket.

Now watch what goes on when you pyramid. In the first place, there are more motivations at play than just the "grass is greener" one. In most cases the sellers are actually *glad* they aren't being asked to hold a mortgage against their own property. The reason for this is rather simple.

When the seller bought the property, he probably paid much less than he is now asking. In the seller's mind there are mixed emotions. Suddenly he loves the property to death: It is a pot of gold, his diamond, his life and blood, he can't part with it, he'll never find another parcel like it, he'll kick himself forever in the head for selling it . . . you know, you've either had these emotions or you will. On the other hand, he wants to sell, must sell, can hardly wait until he is rid of the dump, can't stand being there any longer, the world is about to end if he doesn't sell. And yet everyone has told him that if he sells he should never hold a second mortgage on the property he just sold unless he gets a million percent per week—18% to 25% is minimum.

But an ultrahigh second-mortgage interest rate won't sell the property, and one deal after another is blown because the seller doesn't want to hold paper on his property without such compensation and buyers can't make the deal work with such high debt service. On top of that, sellers frequently object to holding paper for another reason. Remember, they paid less for the property when they bought it—so much less, in fact, that they may now have a hard time accepting the fact that the property is really worth as much as it is. I've had sellers who a few weeks before had ranted and raved about how their home, which I was trying to sell, was worth over $300,000 and now that I had an offer that called for them to hold a small second mortgage looked me in the face and said, "Hold a second mortgage on this place? That's too much risk."

Setting Up the Pyramid Takes Finesse

You don't just blunder into a situation and try to spring a pyramid on the seller. You need to feel out the seller to some degree to get a pulse on his motivations. Just how low will he go in price? Can you break him down on cash needed to make the deal? Your first, exploratory offers should be rather low, just on the chance that you have found a seller so motivated that one of your low offers hits the right nerve at the right time and he grabs the offer then and there. But even if this doesn't happen, a low offer—say, $95,000 on a $150,000 home—lets you out if that is what you want, and is a shocker of an offer.

If you are making this offer through a broker, you must sit down with this broker and tell him you think this property is overpriced but you know you would like to own it; you are ready to make this $95,000 offer and would like the broker to present it.

The broker will react to this if he is worth his salt and attempt to dissuade you from making this ridiculous offer. "You don't want to insult the seller, do you?" he will say. At this point you must *stand firm. Never give the broker or salesman any indication that you will come up.* Never say, "Well, let's see what he says." Simply say, "I would like to buy this property and I wish you would present this offer."

Do not worry if the broker tells you that the sellers have turned down more; if they have, it is possible they now wish they hadn't. Simply stick to your guns and insist that you want the offer presented. Don't be nasty about it, don't threaten to turn the broker in (to the police?). In fact, if you want to make your point even stronger, write out a check to the broker's escrow account for a modest deposit and hand it to him while at the same time, in a much lower voice than before, you nearly whisper, "We love this property and want very much to own it."

If you have played your role well enough and the broker or salesman isn't a real nincompoop, he will get the picture: You *really want to own the property.* But you haven't given him any indication that you will come up in price.

The moment the salesman thinks you *might* come up in price, he will assume you *will.* That feeling will be imparted to the seller and will come back to you in the form of a counteroffer higher than it might otherwise have been. On the other hand, if the salesman gets the feeling you *will* buy, he will work harder to bring both of you together—even if he has to take up some of the slack by reducing his commission.

As a salesman I hate to give away any secrets, but brokers do from time to time cut their commissions. The deals they are most likely to do that on will be the deals they have worked the hardest to make, and in which there is at least one party who appears to be appreciative of their efforts. Keep this in mind no matter which side of the fence you are on, because the opposite is also true: Brokers will stand so firm that their commission blows a deal when both buyer and seller take the posture that the broker is the only thorn in the garden. Alas, how easy it is to forget who watered the flowers.

Okay, so you are being nice to the salesman and he is out busting his buns to make your deal work. If you have done your job right, you are offering *less* than the seller may take and there is going to be some kind of a counter. That is almost a 90% sure thing.

Dealing with the Counter Is a Move to the Pyramid

When you move into the real nitty-gritty of the purchase negotiations, you should be ready to get serious. Your original offer, if countered at all, will be countered with an offer much higher than you would like. *Now* you can let the salesman bring you up, while at the same time you learn more about the seller. Before making your second offer (counter to the counter)—which could be your final offer—you should be sure you have the answers to the following questions:

1. *What are the existing mortgages and other financial obligations against the property?*   You may have thought you knew what they were—in fact, the salesman may have thought *he* knew—but sometimes the first offer brings out some hidden mortgages or tax assessments. You must know exactly where you stand with the actual financing and hidden obligations. You need to know more than just amounts. Who holds the mortgages? What is the payoff penalty, if any? What is the interest rate, etc.? You won't be able to pyramid—or, for that matter, use many of the no-cash-down techniques—if there is a whopping mortgage that everyone thought could be paid off only to find that it cannot be paid off without killer penalties. Tax assessments are essential, too, as they may require sudden cash payments.

2. *What is the owner's real reason for selling?*   The owner of a hotel told me he wanted to sell because he wanted a larger property. I made a thorough inspection of the hotel he wanted to sell and found it to be in horrendous condition. "Thor," I said, "did you know about the condition of the property?" "Now you know why I want to sell," he replied.

You may never find out the full extent of the reasons for sale. Some sellers will be impossible to understand, as not everyone operates logically. But some idea of the reason for the sale might open up alternative techniques of buying that neither you nor the broker would have guessed. If it turns out that a seller wants to get out of his large, electricity-eating house and into a more economical property, a buyer can seek out some possible solution to that need. If another seller discloses a desire to travel around the world, the buyer might make that dream come true—not by paying cash but by making travel a part of the deal. Only by knowing where the seller wants to end up can the buyer fit his buying techniques to the benefit of each party.

3. *What are the seller's feelings about holding paper?*   This one is hard to get at because sometimes the question is asked negatively by the broker: "You wouldn't want to hold a forty-thousand-dollar second mortgage, would you?" The salesman might have to be coached by you on this. "If I gave the seller a mortgage I'm holding on another property, do you think he'd be interested in

that?" Sellers will view outside paper in a different way than they view mortgages on what they are selling. But sometimes they don't know how to respond to the question.

4. *Does the seller know I want to own his property?* This is important. If the seller knows this, that is good. If the seller thinks you are *dying* to own the property, that is bad. If the seller is insulted that you have made a low offer and are trying to steal his pride and joy, then you have to do something to counteract this feeling. Usually it is a matter of reprogramming the salesman. "Look, I understand how the seller feels," you say to the salesman in a low voice that causes him to strain to listen. "You have done a fantastic job in finding us the very property we would like to own. We didn't fully appreciate its value and made a low offer, but please express our feelings that we love the property and wish there were some way to own it."

5. *Does the seller know that you will buy something else if you can't work out a deal with him?* This is essential: There must be some urgency on the seller's part. There is no need to tell the salesman this; simply ask to look at another house or two—even make another offer if you find something else in the meantime. The word will get back to the seller.

Let the Pyramid Offer Be the Face-Saver

"We're convinced of the value," you will say in essence, "but the deal has to be this way because it allows us to buy your house." When the pyramid is presented, make sure you have the backup on the "grass is greener" property to close the deal right then.

What Kind of Mortgage Should You Offer in a Pyramid?

Keep in mind that when you offer a pyramid, you are writing a mortgage against a property you own (in this technique) and the mortgage does not presently exist. This enables you to write a *soft mortgage*—a mortgage at an interest rate usually below the current market rate and at terms that suit your immediate needs and goals.

For example, earlier in this chapter when Charlie made the deal on the lot, he pyramided the seller off to a second mortgage on his three bedroom home. The amount was only $15,000; but as the security was excellent, Charlie may have gotten by with a 10% mortgage interest. In a current market of 16% to 18% interest, the 10% rate would have been rather soft; but as the seller got his price, the deal was cut without much argument.

In Mike's motel deal, he pyramided with a $315,000 first mortgage on some land. That mortgage could have been at 9% or 10% interest for a long payout of 20 years with a shorter balloon.

There are a thousand ways to make the mortgage, and *this is the area where you want to concentrate the final negotiations.*

If you can get the seller to accept the idea of the pyramid and can agree on everything else, then the final terms of the mortgage can be the easiest to work out.

Show the Seller How the Soft Terms Benefit Him

It is all a matter of economics. If the seller gets his price, you are closing down on the deal. I'm assuming you have gotten to the point where the seller is trying to get you to increase the interest rate on your pyramid, or shorten the terms. If you have played the pyramid properly, this is just where you want the deal to be. Here's why.

Interest paid to a seller is earned income, and he pays taxes on it at the highest possible rate, according to the tax bracket he is in for that year. On the other hand, the gain on the sale (capital gain) is taxed at a much lower rate for most sellers than the earned-income tax rate. This simple fact, when pointed out at the right moment, will show the seller it is far better for him to be getting the price agreed to, at a slightly lower interest rate on a part of the deal (the amount of the pyramid), than to take a lower price and get more interest.

As you have worked up in your offers, the salesman can honestly say to the seller, "I've got him up." This enables the seller to rationalize that indeed it is better to get a higher price (get the buyer up) and let Uncle Sam pay the difference by reduction of tax that the seller would have to pay on earned income (taking a lower price but higher interest), through the lower tax on capital gains.

Okay, you should have some idea about pyramids. They are exciting and full of benefits for both the seller and the buyer. In fact, the seller can use this buying technique to get rid of high equity and turn a difficult-to-sell property into an attractive buy.

I'll get into this and more about pyramids in the next chapter, which will cover pyramids on property you don't even own.

At the end of that chapter, I'll also give you all the *bad* news about pyramids.

24

The Distant Pyramid

THE GRAND PYRAMID, as described in the previous chapter, was based on the human tendency to see something we don't have as more valuable than those things we do have. This is often just an illusion, but it is a strong motivator nonetheless, and as such can be put to good use in buying property. Hence the technique of pyramiding equity into paper, which is used to buy other property. Yet techniques based on the pyramid concept go far deeper, as you will see in the twist described in this chapter, where you will promise to give a mortgage to a seller on a property *you don't own*.

This technique, called the "distant pyramid," is used when you are making two purchases at or about the same time. In this case, you will actually negotiate the seller of one property into holding a second mortgage secured by the other property being purchased. It is possible in fact to *double the distant pyramid* by setting up the purchase so each of the two sellers end up taking as a down payment the second mortgage on each other's property. In essence, you will make two deals without spending any of your own cash.

EXAMPLE: Phil wanted to buy an eight-unit apartment building and a small commercial building. His big problem was that he didn't have the cash requirement for both. He approached the situation with the use of the *conditional contract* and tied up the commercial building for 45 days. The conditional contract gave him several outs that in effect prevented anyone else from buying the property, giving Phil time to find out how to put the deal together.

Here are the terms of the purchase of the commercial building:

Price	$205,000
Existing financing Phil could assume:	
A first mortgage payable over 25 years	
at 11% interest	130,000
Seller's equity	$ 75,000

Phil was to pay this equity this way:	
Cash at closing:	$ 25,000
A second mortgage on another property	
acceptable to the seller	50,000
Phil matches the seller's equity	$ 75,000

With the contract on the commercial building tied up, Phil next went to the seller of the apartment building and negotiated the following deal, using a similar conditional contract (more on this later in the chapter):

Price	$200,000
Existing financing Phil could assume:	
A first mortgage	45,000
Seller's equity	$155,000

Phil agreed to pay this equity this way:	
Cash at closing:	$ 65,000
A second mortgage on another property	
acceptable to the seller	90,000
Phil matches the seller's equity	$155,000

Now, armed with these two deals, Phil proceeded to put his deal together. The first step was to find out how much new financing could be placed on the apartment building. This was quickly ascertained through a few calls to some loan officers at three of the local savings-and-loan associations he customarily dealt with. If the appraisal checked out, Phil could anticipate a cash loan of $160,000 on the apartments. The closing costs of the loan would total about $6,000, so Phil would net $154,000 at the loan closing. Since he knew he would have to pay off the existing first mortgage of $45,000, he could figure on having $109,000 left over. Of course, he would then give $65,000 to the seller, leaving himself $44,000 cash to play with.

The second step was to work up a nice *pro forma* on the *commercial* building and take it to the apartment owner. The *pro forma* showed the rents and other facts about the building as they actually were, but showed the projection for the future and a higher value based on the projection. The seller of the apartments studied the *pro forma*, looked at the building, and agreed to accept the second mortgage on the commerical building. In essence, the apartment seller agreed to hold a $90,000 second mortgage on the commercial property.

Phil then went to the seller of the commerical building and asked him if he would take a $50,000 second against the apartment building. The answer again was yes.

Phil arranged a simultaneous closing with both parties to pass title. From the loan proceeds on the apartment ($44,000), Phil paid the commerical-building seller $25,000. The $19,000 cash left over went into the bank to pay for the improvements Phil planned to make on both properties to quickly improve their appearance so he could increase rents.

In working a distant pyramid, the key is *control of the property you are buying.* You cannot effectively work the deal with less than a signed contract binding the seller to close on the deal if he approves the security on the second mortgage he is to take. The motivation on the part of each seller goes through a sudden transition the very moment a contract for sale has been signed, and this will work to your benefit if you understand it. Once there is a contract of sale, most sellers will psychologically let go of the property they are selling. Remember, up until the time they have "sold" the property, they are the owners and maintain 100% control. That period is one of constant mixed emotions for the sellers: to sell or not to sell. Now that the property is sold, the seller will wake up the following morn-

145

ing with what is commonly called "seller's remorse." This will happen to nearly every seller. Did I do the right thing? Did I get enough? Should I have held out for more? And so on.

When you are working with a conditional contract, you must make sure that your conditions extend beyond the usual period of seller's remorse.

There are several things you can do to help the seller over his bout of remorse, and you should anticipate this as a natural sequence for you to follow.

How to Help Cure the Seller of Seller's Remorse
(an illness that will kill your deal if you let it)

1. Make sure you have no direct contact with the seller during the conditional period. You are honest and don't want to be put into the position of having to avoid a question you don't want to answer. Your business is your business, so keep it that way. Avoiding the seller, however, must be done in such a way that the seller doesn't become worried about where in the hell you are. You don't want to see the seller (or talk with him directly) until you are ready to get his approval on the security of the second mortgage.

2. Be sure anything required of you in the contract is carried out promptly. If you are using an inspection of leases or of the mechanical apparatus of the building as a way out of your agreement (you have to have time to have them inspected, then to approve of the inspections), then be sure someone is actually inspecting the items in question.

3. Instruct those actually doing the inspections not to raise doubts about the inspections. You don't want the termite inspector, for example, to walk around shaking his head and stomping on the ground like he is killing insects. Likewise, the accountant or apartment manager you have looking over the leases should not comment *at all* on the condition of the leases. A smile, a kind word about something, will smooth ruffled feathers even if there are problems.

Keep in mind that if there is something wrong, you need to know all that's wrong before you attempt to adjust the contract in any way. In the meantime, the seller's motivations must be cared for and you want the seller to recover from that bout of seller's remorse. The big reason for this is that another seller's illness enters the picture.

Seller's Anxiousitis

Once the seller recovers from seller's remorse, anxiousitis sets in. "Okay, I've sold the property, now when are we going to close?"

Sellers move from one mental state to another. They've now made a deal, they will live with it; only when do they get their money, so they can go out and spend it? In fact, many sellers have lined up their next purchase by the time seller's remorse ends (it helps them get over it).

It is toward the end of anxiousitis that you want to plan your appointment to present the property on which they will hold the second mortgage. By this time the motivations are well in your favor and you can get an approval that you may not have gotten the day you presented the offer. You must be careful, however, as anxiousitis will revert to seller's remorse once again if you let it go on too long.

Phil's transaction was an extreme use of the distant pyramid. Frequently the technique is used in long-term-option properties, as in the following example.

Charlie had tied up a vacant tract of land two years ago on a long-term lease with an option to buy. He wanted to close on the property as it had appreciated tremendously, but he was going to be short on the cash he needed to tie up the loose ends to the deal. The reason for this was that, although the property value had increased from the $50,000 option price to $110,000, no lender wanted to make a loan on the vacant tract at terms that were realistic.

Charlie decided to look around for a property to pyramid with, to create a first mortgage for the vacant land. He discovered a nice $200,000 industrial building that was free and clear (without any existing financing). He offered to buy the property by giving the seller $100,000 in cash and a $100,000 first mortgage on the vacant land mentioned before. The seller accepted.

This allowed Charlie to go to a lender and offer the industrial building as security for a loan. The lender liked this kind of property and agreed to give him a total loan of $165,000.

147

Charlie financed the industrial building, netting out after loan costs $150,000. This gave him all the cash he needed to close on both properties.

It should be obvious that the longer you can benefit from appreciation without having to pay for the property, the greater your leverage in any form of financing tool. Charlie's option on the vacant land could have been part of another deal not connected directly to the vacant land at all. It is not uncommon to buy one property and at the same time ask for an option to buy another property from that owner. In leasing office space or commercial space, you will find that if you ask for an option to buy the building you are leasing, sometimes it will be granted. Sellers who are anxious to make one deal will frequently *offer* the option as an enticement to a would-be buyer: "Buy this and I'll give you an option on that." Look for these opportunities in every transaction.

The Drawbacks of the Pyramid

On the Buyer's Side

For the investor the drawbacks are few, and mostly centered around that symptom of "bad times"—too much debt to be serviced and not enough income to accomplish it.

The ease with which you will make 100% zero-cash deals will astound you when you use any of the pyramid transactions correctly. Your finesse in moving into the pyramid, and in some cases getting the seller to *suggest* the pyramid, will take practice.

"I sure would like to own your property, Mr. Jones, but as I've told you, I'm property-poor. I have several nice properties—why, you must have seen my home over on the Intracoastal, or the office building on Commerical Boulevard, and, on top of that, I've recently purchased over eighty acres of pine forest near Naples—but the one thing I'm short of is cash." A short pause as you show the eight-by-ten color photographs of your properties to the seller of whatever it is you want to buy. "And I've built up a lot of equity in these properties. The eighty acres, for example, is free and clear. I'd sell that land to buy yours, except I know it is going up in value too fast to sell now. I wonder if there isn't some way you could be protected in selling your property to me without my having to give you more cash than I can generate from the refinancing of your low mortgage?"

If you say this (in your own words, of course) you will find some bright seller responding, "Why not let me hold a first mortgage on that eighty acres?"

On the Seller's Side

In the right kind of pyramid, where the buyer has real equity in the other property, the risk of holding paper on a second property is less than holding it on the seller's property. Since risk is the enemy of profit, whenever you can reduce a lender's risk you can improve the chances of making the deal.

On the other hand, if there is no real equity in the other property and the buyer is trying to shove off a lot of risk on the seller, the risk has multiplied substantially.

And sellers (you'll be one someday) should approach the pyramid with caution. But do not avoid the pyramid, as it can save your rear end. In fact, for some sellers the use of the pyramid is the only way to get equity out of the deal and soften the debt service, enabling a difficult property to sell. Review the example of the seller's use of the pyramid in the preceding chapter.

In simple terms, the pyramid is a fantastic way to use a basic motivation of people, which is *to get a piece of something someone else has.*

25

Use Personal Property
as a Down Payment
(Your Junk
Is Another's Antique)

ANYTHING you own can be used to barter for real estate in lieu of cash. Many zero-cash real-estate investments are made by the buyer giving the seller something other than cash: In the last two chapters, for example, the buyer gave the seller notes or mortgages secured by other property. Many real-estate investors don't want to use real estate or cash as a means of securing the deal; instead, they make their deals using items of a non-real-estate nature. These items are called "personal property."

EXAMPLE: Bradford desperately needed to get his own place to live. He was sick to death of renting and was constantly being asked to leave once the owners realized that he loved dogs and had 12 of them. You see, dogs were Bradford's life—he raised them and was well known as one of the finest dog trainers in the southeastern United States. He had a good profession, but he couldn't hang on to money, so he was always short of cash.

He told his broker that he needed a home with a large backyard, but had no cash. The broker was smart enough to ask Bradford what *else* he had. Together, they made a list of his important possessions. The list included several blue-ribbon show dogs, but Bradford couldn't bear to part with them. Also on the list was some old jewelry that Bradford had been keeping in a safe-deposit box at his bank—some bracelets and rings he had been given by his mother before she died ten years before.

The broker suggested a current appraisal, and, sure enough, the jewelry was appraised at a substantial value. Bradford's first thought then was to sell the jewelry and use the cash to purchase the needed home. But the broker wisely told him that selling the jewelry would be a mistake—buyers of such merchandise would pay less than half of the appraised value; it would be better to exchange it for the desired property—in essence, use the jewelry as the down payment on the property.

Of course, many investors don't have a safe-deposit box full of valuable jewelry. But what *do* you have?

Take Stock of Your Valuables and
Examine Your Personal Wealth

If you have something you don't use, and you thus derive no benefits from its current value, use it to buy something else—real estate or personal.

Whether you're short of cash or not, whenever you are no longer getting the value out of something, consider using it instead of cash in the next purchase you make, or at least, as a substitute for some of the cash required.

The first step is to make a list of what you own. It isn't a bad idea to have a list of all your personal property anyway. You never know when some nut will break in and rob you, or a fire will destroy all your possessions, or your divorce attorney will want to know what you've purchased for the family over the last 20 years. So, make a list.

The best way to approach such a list is to first decide that you will not exclude anything. If you try to list only the "important" things, you'll find it too difficult and will probably overlook the very thing you would give up in an exchange. Thus, list everything.

How to Make a List of Your Personal Property

1.   Do it in one fell swoop—over a long weekend if you have a lot of stuff, one evening if not. But don't do it bit by bit, as that will screw you up. You will either overlook a lot of stuff or count things twice. Do your inventory in a marathon, however long it takes.

2.   First list everything in each room. You can transfer categorized items later on cards or sheets as you mark them off the room list. For example, like me, you may have lots of books. Mine are scattered all over the house, with the largest concentration in my office at home and at my real-estate company. If I tried to list "Books," I'd go from one room to another with a lot of wasted effort. In your case, you might have an art collection whose pieces are displayed in various rooms of your home or apartment. List first by room, then transfer to the category card.

3.   Give sufficient description of the item to remind you later what the thing was. "B.V.M." might tell you that it is the blue vase from the Ming dynasty, but five years from now you might forget that code. Therefore, I suggest you avoid too much shorthand and abbreviations in making the inventory.

4.   Put some current estimated value on the item or items, and the price you paid if it is recent, as well as the date.

5.   Subdivide the list into separate lists of those items you still need and use, those items you are keeping as investments, and those items you would just as soon not have.

6.   Add to each list as you purchase items, including date and price.

You will be shocked at the cumulative value of your personal property. Items add up—books, rugs, silver pieces, or just tools in the garage. They are all items of value—to someone, if not you. As you go about the task of packaging some of these items into real-estate transactions, don't work only from your list of things you can do without; the list of items you are keeping as investments is equally important. If you can improve an investment by letting its appreciated value allow you to buy real estate, then that is a decision you should consider. Investors will always exchange one investment for a better one if the real motive for holding the item is profit.

One buyer used $7,000 worth of sound-recording equipment as the down payment on a duplex. The seller happened to be a noted speaker who was motivated by the idea of making his own tapes to be sold at his lectures.

Another buyer gave a seller $50,000 worth of gem-quality opals for the purchase of a deepwater home in Pompano Beach, Florida. The seller, a wealthy man who was getting top dollar for the home and lots of cash (from the buyer's refinance of the home), was motivated to take the opals by the "King Solomon Syndrome." This is an illness that hits some people when you offer them jewels or jewelry and other riches. I've seen the toughest of all sellers turn to butter when the small sandalwood box was opened and inside, sitting on blue velvet, was the most beautiful of all yellow topazes.

Jim Wolf makes his deals with furs. You know, the mink or chinchilla that drives blondes wild. Well, Jim uses the furs he has obtained from another deal to buy real estate.

Mike Regas bought a car with a bracelet. Then he tried to give the car to someone as a down payment on a week time share.

The list of deals that can be made using personal property instead of cash is as endless as the kinds of personal property that can be owned.

The Reason Personal Property Works:
Sellers Want to Save Face

You are using basic motivation again. Sellers who want or need to sell, but cannot get their terms in the usual market, can become frustrated. They don't want to drop their price or compromise on the terms they feel they must have. They will, however, supplement things within that formula, so long as they end up pretty much at the same place they wanted to in the beginning.

This *"Please let me save face in this deal, but please buy my property"* is a major reason why some real-estate investors are able to make deals that astound other investors. In the first place, the average real-estate investor has his priorities wrong: Most investors think that the critical element in buying and selling real estate is the price. Nothing could be further from the truth. *Price is not the most critical aspect in making successful purchases or selling at the best benefit to you.* Price, in fact, gets in the way of your making a deal. Many buyers or sellers don't understand this simple fact: It isn't the price you either pay or get that is important, but the *benefits received.* You must look to the benefits.

The area of benefits, then, is where the seller can save face if you let him—and if you motivate him in that direction. A seller might think he wants or needs $15,000 cash down on the sale of his vacant lot, but in reality he is looking to some benefit that cash is going to give him. It might be that the seller feels he must get that much cash to secure the mortgage he will be holding on the balance of the deal. Another might be trying to raise the cash to pay for a vacation, or a doctor bill, or to buy a car.

As an investor, you must make an attempt to ascertain the reason for selling. The more you know about the seller and the benefits he wants to end up with, the better your opportunity to give him a benefit instead of cash. The seller then saves face by allowing himself to substitute items or benefits for cash. And because he doesn't have to "give in" on that part of the contract, there may be still other areas where you can extract another ounce of blood.

A writer friend of mine had twice as many books as I did. So many, in fact, that he offered to give one seller $4,000 worth as part of a deal. The deal was a big one, and while the books were of no real interest to the seller from an educational point of view, he did want to sell the property and $4,000 was only 3% of the total deal. It was, of course, 50% of the total down payment, and the seller could not in good conscience sell the property with only $4,000 as the down payment. The other $4,000 in books was a face-saver and made the deal. (The writer, by the way, didn't use any of his own cash in the deal—he borrowed $4,000 from his wife's father.)

Just as my writer friend did, you must make sure the values you place on the items of personal property are realistic. This means keep them as high as you can possibly justify.

Finesse in Personal-Property Deals

The way you make your personal-property deal is important. Frequently the best way to use personal property is in a counter-counter offer, after making an offer that didn't include any personal property at all. The down payment in your first offer might have been too low, and the seller realized that you were using some other technique to generate the cash and you weren't investing any real equity of your own. The seller then will make a counter, asking you to improve the deal you originally offered. The seller is telling you that he wants to sell, but you and he haven't gotten your mutual benefits clearly in view for the other to see.

Let's say you wanted to buy a condo apartment in Chicago. You offered the seller $100,000 for a property priced at $140,000. You might be using a pyramid technique, where you want the seller to hold a first mortgage on some land you own in an industrial area of Chicago while you refinance the apartment to generate $80,000 cash for him. This is a zero-cash deal for you, but not bad for the seller as he gets $80,000 cash but not the $20,000 pyramid mortgage on the industrial property. He wants a higher price, too, and counters at $120,000 with you securing the remaining $40,000 in paper over the next five years.

You have, in your personal-property list, a beautiful diamond ring, valued at, say, $20,000. You go back to the seller and say, "Okay, you've convinced me that the value of the unit is more than I've offered. I will pay you eighty thousand in cash at closing, and I will give you fifteen thousand over the next five years—and in addition, I'll give you this beautiful [and with this you hum the first three bars of "Diamonds Are a Girl's Best Friend"] diamond ring."

This technique won't work all the time, and in fact you might find that you have to go down your list of items to motivate a seller. If you have cash and do not want to go through this bother, then don't. But if you are out there trying to get your first deal, then stick with me on this, because it will work.

Advantages and Disadvantages of Using Personal
Property as Your Down Payment

In reality, there is no disadvantage to this technique from either side of the fence. Buyers will have the advantage of unloading personal property they don't need, or taking one investment and converting it into a more usable investment. The seller who ends up with the personal property will do so because he either wants the personal property or has substantially gotten his price in the sale and can "play" with the items offered.

As a buyer, the biggest problem you will have in using this form of purchase will be the offer itself. Investors who use brokers (I recommend you do, even if you have to educate them from time to time) may get some resistance from them and their salesmen. This resistance can be well founded, since the seller is apt to want the broker or salesman to take the personal property as all or part of the commission. For example, if Charles wanted to give the seller a two-year-old Mercedes as part of the purchase price, the seller may want to take the deal because of the other terms offered by Charlie. However, the seller might tell his broker that he will take the deal only if the broker takes the Mercedes as his commission.

It might be a good deal for both the buyer and the seller—and if it was always a Mercedes, not that bad for the broker. But from time to time there will be items offered that the broker just won't want to get involved with, and this reluctance on the broker's part can create an impasse up front. This is another reason why the personal property should be introduced in the counter-counter offer: It is too late for the broker to object; by then, he has invested time and labor and can be enticed into bending a little.

Some brokers, however, recognize that they might be able to do better in their profession if they encourage buyers to make offers of personal property. These brokers and salesmen know that if they can sell more real estate, they will make more in the long run, even if they take an occasional Mercedes or two. In fact, a Ford every now and then is okay, too.

Use your personal property as cash, then, to close the gap when needed—or just to clean out the garage.

26

Future Sweat: The Do-It-Yourself Down Payment

"FUTURE SWEAT" is a sweet way to make your cashless deals. In this technique, you will offer the seller your ability to improve the property as the down payment for your purchase. The seller gets the benefit of the improvements in two ways: (1) any increased rents during the improvements and (2) increased security on the deal should the buyer default on the transaction. To initiate this kind of deal, you would make an offer that explained that you wanted to buy the property but, due to its condition, couldn't unless that condition were improved. You would propose that *you* make the improvements and permit the seller to gain some benefit from those improvements, after which you would buy the property without any additional cash outlay on your part. The seller usually would take back a mortgage in the full amount of the agreed purchase price.

Using future sweat isn't for everyone, but it can be most useful when a property you are contemplating buying needs extensive repair and improvements, or when you would be remodeling the property for some other potential use anyway after you bought it. The technique works in its own right as a cashless transaction, as well as a way to reduce the total input of cash when used with other zero-cash techniques that generate cash from refinancing.

The flexibility and variation of this technique is very wide, thus this chapter will present several slightly different methods of using future sweat. We will also discuss adaptations that sellers can use to aid in the sale of their run-down property.

Examples of Future-Sweat Transactions

Fred is a carpenter by trade, and has general jack-of-all-fix-it-up abilities. There isn't much he can't do when it comes to building or repairing, so using future sweat is as natural for him as using cash is for a millionaire. Fred looks around for any kind of improved property that is either in gross need of repair or in fair condition but so ideally situated that a change of appearance would double potential rents. When he finds such properties, he "tests" the owner to find out if the property might be for sale.

Fred has discovered that many property owners don't have the time to look after their own interests. They may be businessmen or professional people with too many things on their minds to watch their own store. These people often let their property get behind on maintenance, and frequently let old tenants renew at rents that are too low for the current market. Fred has also discovered that many times these owners realize they probably should sell their property, but never get around to doing that—for much the same reason that they haven't painted the building in the last ten years.

Therefore, Fred never lets the absence of a "For Sale" sign stop him. "Mr. Seller," he'd likely start out, "you have a fine property which I know you'd be proud of if it were in the kind of condition it should be in." This is bound to get any property owner's attention. "I've made a list of all the work the apartment building you own over on Tenth Street needs. Mind you, this list is just from my inspection from the exterior; there is bound to be more work needed inside to put this property back in shape. What I'd like to do is to accomplish this list of repairs and improvements at my expense. I will do this because I would like to own the property, and the only way I can do that is to offer you these improvements as my down payment."

Fred will go on to show that his proposal offers the seller the benefits of whatever increased rents the seller can get for the remainder of the 12-month option period Fred needs to accomplish the full list of repairs. Fred promises, however, to have the major, most beneficial changes and improvements finished within the first three months.

Fred realizes that his approach must convey the impression that he is going in on this deal with all his ready cash tied up in the improvements, since this will spark the strongest of all sellers' motivations: *greed.*

You see, some sellers will view this kind of sale as a can't-lose proposition. First of all, if Fred does exactly as he promises—fixing up the building as the list of improvements outlines and later buying the property—the seller will have made a fair deal with little risk: The improved property should have sufficient equity over and above the mortgage the seller will hold to provide a buffer between the seller and default. Second of all, the seller realizes that *if Fred should default* at any time in the sequence of events, either on the option or by not purchasing for any reason, then the seller gets to keep his property with whatever improvements Fred has already made.

Fred, on his side, is careful to include as many of the improvements as possible in the list, and to be as familiar as possible with the rental market for the kind of property he acquires so he'll know how to improve not only the physical appearance of the property but its economic picture as well.

Fred's total investment consists mostly of his time. Naturally, there are some materials needed—paint, nails, lumber, bricks, etc.—but they represent only a small percentage (around 25%) of what the seller will have to spend if he wants to keep the property.

Lonny is a general contractor who, in the down periods of his profession, looks around for major properties he can fix up for later rental or resale. He is well known in the lending circles of town and combines future sweat with several other techniques to make his cashless deals.

In one method, he starts off much like Fred except that he offers the seller some cash as a part of the down payment. Lonny has discovered that, for him, location is the most important factor. He wants good sites and he knows that to get top locations he needs to be able to choose from a wide selection. To do this, he has to add some cash to his deals—not necessarily his cash, of course.

Lonny starts by finding a property, perhaps a run-down shopping center on a prime commercial corner. A center 25 to 30 years old, which has not had good maintenance for the past five years or so, is going to have rents well below the "like new" centers, and tenants whose leases are running or have run out. An ideal situation for a chap like Lonny.

Lonny begins his offer sequence by making a "lowball" offer somewhat within the realm of a bona fide steal should the seller accept. His *cash down* part of the offer is also very low—if, in fact, he offers any cash at all on the downstroke.

In the counters, when the broker (Lonny always uses one) attempts to negotiate the deal to a successful conclusion, Lonny allows himself to be worked up on the terms. The points the seller is winning, however, might be at the sacrifice of losing some points to Lonny. In the end, Lonny, if he must, will agree to spend considerable time, money, and labor, to improve the center during an option period prior to the culmination of the transaction. This option for the purchase of the property will not be exercisable by Lonny until the option term has run its course and Lonny has completed the improvements.

Lonny counts on the same seller's motivations that Fred does, and also on the factor of time. Tim is on the side of the optionee, and in this case the natural appreciation of the property, due not only to the improvements but to the time factor, will provide Lonny with a much better opportunity to finance the deal when he is ready to close on the option and to buy the property.

Susan isn't a carpenter or a general contractor, but she knows something about decoration and is a natural-born color coordinator. She looks for properties that are basically sound but present themselves in a bad light due to a lack of good taste in decor or style.

It is relatively easy for a talented person like Susan to cosmetically turn a dog into a gem. When she needs some heavy work done, such as carpentry or brickwork, she hires people she has gotten to know for that part of her future sweat. She has found that some real-estate owners are reluctant owners and are actually silently begging people like Susan to come around and enable them to sell their property. For Susan, the use of future sweat is a simple and far more profitable use of her time than her old job as a legal secretary. She used to make $300 per week; now, with half the effort, she makes $50,000 and more each year, buying and selling her own real estate.

Finesse in Using Future Sweat to Create Your Own Zero-Cash Deal

As you are developing expertise in the presentation of your offers with the previous techniques illustrated in this book, you should see the pattern of letting the other side win points by appearing to manipulate you into exactly the position you wanted to end up in the first place. You allow the broker to "get you up" as he wins points for and with the seller, and then you clinch the deal by allowing the seller to save face while he "gives in" to your ultimate demands.

This is the ideal situation, of course; in reality, it doesn't always work out quite that way. Nonetheless, in the use of future sweat, your own style of this fantastic technique will depend on your economic ability to back up the sweat with cash. Because some cash in the future-sweat deal gives you broader opportunities in property selection, the technique is often used along with other techniques that, on their own, generate cash. Investors who have cash and plan to use it in investing will be surprised to find that using future sweat will buy them the time to turn a good deal into a superb one.

In short, any investor who anticipates any improvement to a property has the opportunity to use this technique.

Some Sellers Are Doubting Thomases

"Mr. Cummings, with all due respect, what assurance do I have that you will make the repairs you say you will?"

I have several good arguments for this one. First, my past performance: "Look at my success here and there." This is sometimes enough. Second, I point out that I will lose my option to buy if I fail to do what I say I'll do. Some sellers will still balk, because they know that I might not live up to the letter of the contract *in their minds,* and that courts might be needed to settle that kind of dispute. Indeed, sellers wanting to avoid such potential problems will simply balk at *any* contractual agreement that doesn't cause me a sudden and painful economic loss.

Thus, when I know absolutely that I have to spend money on repairs, I might fall back on this: "I'll tell you what I'll do, Mr. Seller. I'll put up in an independent escrow account the sum of twenty thousand dollars to be used solely for those repairs. I'll present bills to the escrow agent which you can verify as being invoices for work or material used on those repairs I promised to accomplish. Naturally, I won't present a bill for my own time and labor, so I don't need to place that cash in escrow."

Future Sweat as a Seller's Tool

In developing your use of this tool, you will find that you can, as a *seller,* utilize future-sweat transactions to your advantage. Here's an example.

Harry owned three duplexes in an older part of town. The duplexes were showing their age, and the yards around them were overgrown with weeds. Harry knew he would never get full value out of a sale of these properties and that all he had to do was spend some time on the site with a few day laborers to straighten out the matter. But he didn't have the time, so nothing happened.

He then learned about future sweat and decided that the best thing for him to do was to set up a situation where a buyer could benefit. He ran an ad offering to sell one duplex to the right person for nothing down. The buyer had to be handy with carpentry tools and have a green thumb when it came to landscaping.

Harry found a buyer who fit the bill, and they set up the deal. In return for the opportunity to use future sweat as his down payment, the buyer would not only fix up the one duplex that was for sale, but, as credit on the sales price, relandscape and fix up the adjoining two duplexes Harry would keep for a while longer, then sell at a higher amount later.

Harry's benefit was clear and his ultimate profit increased due to the improvement not only of the duplex first sold, but of the two he held on to for a while longer. The buyer, too, got exactly what he wanted. He made a great deal on the purchase of a duplex—and on top of that, he improved the neighborhood (and thus the value of his duplex) by fixing up the adjoining properties. Best of all, he got paid for that (through credits at closing of title on the first duplex).

Not All Is Rosy in the World of Future Sweat

In fact, future sweat can be damned risky if you haven't selected your property correctly. If you are using future sweat as your down payment, not just to buy time, then the property you buy must be improvable within your means. The danger lies in anticipating that you can turn a property around with 100 hours of your own work and $1,000 of paint and lumber, only to find that a *thousand* hours of labor doesn't show any real improvement and you could spend thousands of dollars on materials just to fix the broken and run-down results of deferred maintenance.

It is all well and good to fix up property and make profits when you are able to do both. The problem, of course, in this quest for profit is that the real estate and the time don't always cooperate. The real estate can become a hole that will gobble up both your effort and money, and the time can turn a market from one of sure profit to one in which it's impossible to finance a new buyer into your pocket.

With this in mind, all investors contemplating any of the sweat-equity forms of investing should pay close attention to the potential losses they can suffer in attempting to improve real estate. Review the following checklist whenever you anticipate buying any real estate with the idea of "fixing it up."

The Prepurchase Checklist for Fix-It-Uppers

1. *Does the area warrant improvement to this property?* You don't want to take on a property that is already above average for the area. What you want is a property that can be improved to the point where it is still not the top property in the area but close to it. The spread of values in the area will give you some hint as to whether you are looking in the right neighborhood. If the price you must pay is not at least 50% below the prices of homes in the same neighborhood of similar size but in top condition, then you may not have much room for financial improvement.

2. *Is there a good seller's market for top-condition properties in this area?* Some nice neighborhoods just aren't in demand, so avoid them and look in the areas where buyers go to find their investments. You will want to sell for top dollar, and you need to be in a strong sellers' neighborhood for that.

3. *Have you done your "sold" and "available" homework?* In short, have you found out what similar properties have sold for in the past 12 months? If not, then do so. Your broker can help there, so use his services. Make a list of all properties sold that are either similar to the one you're contemplating, as it is now, or similar to the property as it will be when you finish with it. Check available properties as well: What is on the open market? How long? If they haven't sold in some time, try to find out why. Once you are up on what is going on in the marketplace, you can have more confidence in your judgment in buying selected property.

4. *Is the property you plan to buy structurally sound?* You may not be able to tell. I can't, so I hire an expert to check out the foundation and other structural parts of the building. But don't stop there: You want to know about the wiring, the plumbing, the heating, the boiler, the air conditioning, and, of course, one of the most important of all, *termites.*

Mind you, you generally won't find any of the structural or mechanical items in like-new condition. In fact, you should expect to find them in relatively poor condition, which will account for your good buy. However, it is important that you know just how bad "poor" can be. You don't want to get in over your head on repairs and find that you have to spend more than you have—only to lose your option and have the owner reap the benefits of the work you have done up to that point.

5. *Will time work for you or against you?* If you make your purchase option too tight, you will run into trouble. Investors using future sweat will typically anticipate that weekends of work on the property for a couple of months will be enough, only to find that 50-hour weeks for five months would just about do the trick.

6. *Will you have to hire everyone, or what?* If you can't do anything yourself and have to hire decorators, carpenters, etc., you might still do all right, but the spread between profit and loss narrows. If you are inclined to this kind of investing, then either move into it slowly or get some experience working within the building trades to learn what to do.

Despite the potential dangers of biting off more than you can chew, future sweat is still one of the more creative methods you can use. It is so adaptable that it can clinch many deals that start out with other techniques. It should be considered anytime there are repairs needed, or when you need to buy time.

27

The Slice of Pie

NEVER GIVE all of anything you own to buy something else when a part is sufficient to serve your needs. The concept here is to offer the seller (in the final analysis) a portion of something you own as an inducement for him to accept your proposal. This technique works as a solid zero-cash dealmaker on its own, or can be used as an adjunct to some other technique where you are attempting to develop this as a kicker to clinch the deal you are working on.

The mechanical function of this technique is to come up with something you can give the seller and still keep. As you will see, there are many different kinds of items you can use. The partial interest you give up may be temporary or permanent, depending on the kind of item involved. It is possible to actually divide some things, splitting the interest into 100% ownership of each portion of the original.

Following are several examples of buyers giving partial interest in various elements.

Mel wanted to buy a waterfront home. He and the seller had met on a fair price, and the seller had even agreed to accept a pyramid mortgage Mel was going to create on some vacant property he owned nearby. Mel had hopes that with the pyramid he could refinance the old mortgage into a new one, give the seller the cash needed to close the deal, and be in with zero cash. Unfortunately (as is often the case) the local savings-and-loan didn't comply with the plans and came up $10,000 short on the needed loan. Mel needed to make up the difference and was about to strike out.

Then he got a brilliant idea. He had learned that the seller was an avid sportsman and liked to hunt and fish. Mel owned a condo in the Abacos in the Bahamas, which he had traded into several years before. He didn't want to sell the condo as the current market for Bahamas property was about as low as anything could be, so he offered the seller use of the condo for any 20 months during the next four years as a part of the purchase on the waterfront home. All the seller had to do was let Mel know several months in advance when he wanted to use the facility and it was his. Anticipating the seller's potential objection, Mel put in the agreement that if the unit were sold or no longer habitable, Mel would owe the seller a *pro rata* portion of the $10,000 difference, which was the value Mel set on the use of the condo.

In essence, the seller was being asked to accept $10,000 less cash at closing in exchange for partial (and limited) use of the condo in the Abacos. The seller, who was not out of seller's remorse and into anxiousitis, saw this as a way to keep the deal alive and at the same time have some fun. There was no doubt that the use of the facility for 20 months was a good economic exchange for the $10,000, even if the seller used the facility only half the time.

Ruby and Bob owned a small citrus grove near Orlando, Florida, which was generating a good income for them. They wanted to buy some real estate, so they took stock of what they had to work with. They had some cash set aside for investing, but wanted to hold on to that if at all possible. They also had, of course, lots of oranges each year which just never seemed to get sold, or, at best, were picked for cattle feed at the end of each season.

They decided that they would have no difficulty "giving up" part of their orange crop each year, for some limited time, of course, to keep things simple. Therefore, they sought a seller who might be inclined to be a taker for their partial crop. Not wanting to spoil any of their usual buyers of oranges by offering the oranges on a real-estate deal, they crossed off the obvious takers for their oranges and looked elsewhere. A new market was a possibility, but so was a potential large user of their produce other than the vendor.

They ended up going to one of the state's larger real-estate developers and making a deal where they would supply that developer with sufficient boxes of fruit each year for the next five years to more than equitably match the down payment on that developer's condo they wanted to buy. The developer used the boxes of fruit as Christmas presents for preferred clients for those upcoming years.

Ron owned a sailboat that he used a few weekends a month, some months of the year; the rest of the time it sat there using up more of his time in normal upkeep. Ron didn't want to sell the boat, but, when it came time to make an investment, he had no hesitation in offering a part ownership in the boat as part of the deal.

Larry did much the same thing with his aircraft that Ron did with his boat. He simply realized that his social circle consisted mostly of aircraft people, just as Ron's centered around boat people. This gave him a natural opportunity to deal with people who would be receptive to what he might have to offer a part of. You will notice the same thing happening to you if you dig down deep.

Partial Ownership or Partial Use: The Pitfalls of Each

When you are about to give something to someone, make sure you aren't giving the wrong thing. There are two basic forms of partial interest: partial ownership and partial use. The basic and most important difference is that when you give up a portion of the ownership, it is permanent: The other party is now the owner of that portion of the property and has, in essence, become your partner. This means that as the value goes up, they participate in the profit; and as the value goes down, they take their portion of the loss as well. In the meantime, of course, your new partner in ownership will carry his load of maintaining the property. In a co-ownership of a home, boat, or aircraft, this can be substantial.

The main pitfall of sharing ownership is the possible difficulty in dividing the maintenance cost. In the condo or vacation home, it might be relatively easy to say you would each have equal time to use the facility and then simply split things down the middle. In theory, you can use this same formula for anything; but when you get right down to it, use will rarely be so equitably divided. Invariably, one person will get more use, no matter how well you plan things out. In fact, you will find that in shared ownership of something you use, having more partners will be more equitable than just two, because you can so severely limit use that each partner is more apt to use his time than not. This has given rise to a rising number of private time-share transactions, where several friends and acquaintances get together to own a vacation house, each taking a month of the year, renting out any leftover time.

The form of ownership with a partner you don't know can be very important if you plan to keep the property in its original shape. Giving up a portion of something you have will often be more practical if you divide the property itself whenever possible. There is no way to make a 40-foot sailboat into two 20-foot boats, but you can divide up a duplex, or a three-unit property where you give up only one-third. If you cannot divide a property, be sure you seek the advice of a good lawyer to properly form this joint ownership to your best advantage.

The advantages of joint ownership will depend on the deal you have just made. It is possible that the only way you can make your transaction is to give up a preferred interest in some real estate you own and will continue to operate or manage. Many real-estate investors like to do preferred deals, and they can be very enticing to both .ues of the fence. Indeed, this form of investing will work wonders for you as a buyer or seller, so make a special note to yourself that this is one of those big-boy techniques that will work for you on any level of your wealth-building career.

The Preferred Deal

Normally, the preferred transaction is viewed as a buyer's technique, so let's look at it that way first. Preferred buying is where the buyer comes in and says he will buy your property at a good price, but, instead of buying all of your interest, he only wants half. The amount of cash offered, however, is frequently more than half of what you might have taken if the buyer had purchased 100% of the deal. For example, if you wanted to sell a shopping center for $1 million and would take $250,000 down, the preferred buyer would offer you something like $180,000 cash down for only half the deal.

The advantage to the buyer is what happens next. The buyer will tell you that he wants you to stay on as manager of the property, for which you can take the normal management fee off the top of the income, but that out of the rest of the income he will be *preferred* a specific yield on his cash invested. Let's say the buyer in this case wants a 15% return on his cash to be preferred. Since he has invested $180,000 in cash, he will get a $27,000 return to match the 15% preference (15% of $180,000 equals $27,000). If there is only $30,000 of income left after you have paid all debt service, normal operating expenses, and your management fee, then this buyer will get $27,000 of it and you only $3,000. For you to share equally in the income, the property would have to have a cash flow of twice $27,000, or a total of $54,000.

Sellers often jump at transactions like this—sometimes out of desperation, sometimes out of good sound business sense. It all depends on the circumstances and the faith the seller has in the potential of the property to generate sufficient income to give each a good return and then some. It should be obvious that if the seller can get nearly as much cash selling only half of the project and still have the growing benefits of the other half, it is a good deal.

One reason buyers like this technique is that it can make an honest man out of a seller who has been puffing the income of a project. If the owner of the shopping center knew that the above deal would never make more than $30,000 for the next ten years, he'd refuse to go into such a transaction. If he did go into it, the buyer would have a lot of insurance that his return was protected.

Buyers also like the fact that there is a great incentive for good management. After all, the buyer's partner will not make a good return (above the management fee) unless the income of the property reaches double (or close to it) the preference income required by the buyer.

Okay, this is a brief look at the *buyer's* use of this technique. Now see how you can turn this concept into a different form by being the "seller" when you buy something else giving up part of the ownership in your property.

Bill owned an apartment house and lived in one of the units. It provided a comfortable income and required little management on his part. He wanted to get more real estate, but had little cash, so he found a seller of some industrial property that was grossly in need of repair and partially vacant. The remaining tenants were paying half the rent they should have been in the current marketplace—all due, Bill knew, to the lack of attention of the owner.

He went to the owner and offered him a preference ownership in the apartment building at a level of income return that Bill knew would be about equal to the income the owner was currently getting from the industrial property. Only now there would be no worry, and the risk of loss would be buffered by Bill's half of the apartment building. In return, Bill got credit for a substantial part of the seller's equity in the industrial property and gave him a mortgage back for the balance, ending up with sole ownership of the industrial property.

Bill could have approached this seller in any one of several different ways, and he had weighed several techniques before ending up with this one. The transaction suited Bill because he didn't have to leave his own apartment building. He got part of the appreciation of the building, which he knew was going to be substantial over the years, and with a cashless deal he ended up as 100% owner of the industrial property.

Giving Up Use, Not Ownership, Is the Other Way to Go

For some kinds of property, the use of it is more attractive than partial ownership. From the user's point of view, there is only enjoyment—no worries about maintenance or upkeep.

From your point of view, you keep the appreciation and only give up partial use, which, if planned carefully, won't be missed at all.

As a seller, you might keep this in mind and look for buyers who are owners of things or places you can use. Any time you can give an investor a cashless deal, you improve your chances of selling.

For example, I wanted to acquire a boat for charter in the Virgin Islands. I had the option of paying cash for whatever I wanted or going to owners of charter boats and offering something I owned as a trade. I ended up giving a boat owner part of some land I owned in exchange for ten weeks of charter. I got what I wanted, and the owner of the boat got five acres of land that he would never have bought with money but ended up with in a deal he couldn't turn down.

Finesse in Giving Up Partial Interest

There are several things you need to watch in using this technique. Review the list below.

1. Make sure you know what you have to give. You might find there are more things you can give up than you think. Piano lessons. . . ? Why not if you can?
2. Make sure you don't offer too much.
3. Make sure you offer only the interest necessary. Avoid giving ownership unless it is important and beneficial to you to do it that way.
4. Get legal advice in any partnership or joint ownership of any property.
5. Have everything possible written down about the costs and use of the property. Memories will not work as they are horrible when the repair bills come in.
6. Have a plan to either buy out or divide. Properties and partnerships have a tendency to become too valuable from time to time, and some formula is needed up front to cover possible disputes when you have joint ownership.
7. If you are giving use, make sure that use is specifically defined and some limitations and provisions for supplementations on your part are taken care of. If you want to sell tomorrow but have given up one week in January for the next five years, you may have a problem in selling. A cash-payoff figure built into the deal to cover lost time would be a key.
8. Seek sellers who are potential users or takers for what you have, then make offers.

You will find that this chapter has presented several interesting and varied techniques under the guise of giving up a partial interest. Like the preferred deal, the partial-interest technique will have wide appeal to many buyers and sellers alike. Use it to reap big profits.

28

Soft-Paper Option, Hard-Paper Sale

THIS IS one of those techniques that builds fortunes relatively quickly.

The technique uses two separate events to create the profit-making magic. The first is the option of soft paper. This is when the investor obtains an option to buy a property on easy terms. Contained in the terms of the purchase are factors that create soft paper, or low-interest mortgages, frequently held by the seller. Once the "buy" has been assured, the option allows the investor to restructure the deal in a new package, so he can offer the property for sale with different terms that create a profit.

This technique can enable the investor to buy a property and to shortly thereafter sell it *at the same price he paid for it* and make a substantial profit. Let's look at several kinds of transactions using this technique.

Warren found a home that was in poor condition but in a very good part of town. The yard was a mess, the shutters were hanging askew, the paint was peeling off, and there was a burned-out car in the carport (obviously the police had ordered the owner to get it off the street). Best of all, the seller was receptive when Warren offered a fair price for the property providing the seller held 80% financing at a rate slightly below the market rate. The price was good and, as Warren pointed out, the interest, while low, didn't upset the seller's income-tax situation. It was more important for the seller to get a higher price at the capital-gains rate than a lower price with higher interest on the mortgage, which would be taxed at earned-income rates.

The option Warren had negotiated gave him some time to do some fix-up work on the property. The seller had also agreed to this, of course, as it benefited him in case Warren backed out of the deal later. What Warren did was fix up the yard, paint the house, fix the shutters, hang a new front door, and remove the burned-out car. Then he put a nice, brand-new car in the carport (his own) and a "For Sale" sign in the yard.

He offered the property for sale at $2,000 above the price he had paid for it, and in the end profited by $20,767.53.

Look at the "buy" Warren had arranged:

Price	$70,000	
Cash down	14,000	
Mortgage Balance	$56,000	To be held by the seller for 25-year amortization with a 15-year balloon. Interest rate was 8% per year. Payments would be $432.22 each month until the balloon of $35,624.21 was due.

Warren spent $2,000 on the fix-up, which he added to the price. He then offered and sold the property on the following terms:

Price	$72,000	
Cash Down	16,000	
Mortgage Balance	$56,000	To be a *wraparound mortgage* held by *Warren* for a 30-year amortization with a balloon at the end of the 15th year. Interest would be at 10% per annum and payments would be $491.44. At the end of 15 years, the balloon would be $45,732.14.

Here's what Warren profits from:

Each month he collects $491.44 from the buyer and pays out in return $432.22 to the seller he bought from. He puts $59.22 in his pocket each month, or $710.64 each year (not counting any interest he earned on that in the meantime). If he holds on to the mortgage for the 15 years to the balloon date, he will collect $45,732.14 from the buyer he sold to and then pay $35,624.21 on the remaining balance of the mortgage to the seller he purchased from—pocketing in that sequence $10,107.93 to his benefit. As he got $710.64 per year for 15 years, he can add that total of $10,659.60 to the benefit in the ballooning of the mortgages to give him a grand total in this deal of $20,767.53. This is without ever closing on the house himself, and only expending a few thousand dollars and some time.

It should be obvious that if Warren had done what you will do—raise the price of the house—he would have profited even more. By the way, if Warren had invested the $59.22 he received each month at 15% per annum, the account would have totaled over $35,500 by the end of the 15 years—in addition to the balloon bonus.

Little things do add up.

Jim was into fixing up small income properties like duplexes and four-unit apartment buildings. He liked the manual-labor part, and it was easy to hire experts for the really tough jobs. He also discovered that high-school kids were good cheap labor on weekends and after school for painting and yard work.

He was building a sizable basis for a future net worth of millions. However, he was always short of cash, since his whole plan was to plow the money right back into the property. He used the pyramid from time to time to enable him to buy, and only rarely did he sell. When he did, he used the soft buy and hard sell—like this.

One interesting property was an eight-unit building rented to employees at a medical building a few blocks away. The owner of the building had kept the same tenants for nearly three years with no increase in rent. The property was in pretty good shape, but needed some tender loving care, paint, and new asphalt on the parking area.

Jim offered to assume the seller's existing first mortgage of $40,000 (which was at 8½% interest) and pay $50,000 cash down, provided the seller would take the $100,000 balance as a second mortgage against several buildings Jim owned across town. As the seller of the eight units was asking $200,000 for his property with some buffer for negotiating, and Jim was offering $190,000, the thought of holding the $100,000 second mortgage was not rejected. They negotiated for a day on the interest rate and term, and settled on a 10% interest rate on the $100,000 second to be placed on Jim's other property.

Jim had insisted on one more thing in the contract. He wanted 60 days in which to make some repairs to the eight units, and the opportunity to refinance the property if possible. If he failed to get the refinancing he needed, he could option out of the deal (walk away from the deal with his only loss being the repairs done to the property).

Jim knew he could remove all the tenants in the building as none of them had leases and were on month-to-month tenancy. Instead, he fixed up the building and went around to see each tenant personally. He told them he was buying the building and the rent would go up: Would they stay or leave? As he had anticipated, all but one agreed right away to pay the higher rent. In fact, when word got around that one had balked at the new rent, one of the tenants who had agreed to the higher rent called Jim and told him he had a friend looking for an apartment like that who would pay the increased rent.

Jim then offered the building for sale for $240,000 with $60,000 down. He agreed to hold a wraparound mortgage in the amount of $180,000 at 11% interest-only for ten years, with a balloon payment at that time.

The deal was a great one for the buyer, and Jim had no problem selling the property.

Here's what the whole deal looked like:

He purchased the property this way—

Price	$190,000
Cash Down	$ 40,000
Assume Existing	50,000
Pyramid from Other Property	100,000
Matches Price	$190,000

The mortgage he gave the seller on the pyramid was a 10% interest-rate mortgage. To make the calculations simple, assume the payout was 10% interest-only each year with a balloon at the end of ten years just like he sold the property (but with a higher-rate mortgage).

He sold the property this way:

Price	$240,000
Cash Down	$ 60,000
Holds a Wraparound	180,000
Matches Price	$240,000

The wraparound encompasses the existing first mortgage of $40,000 on the property. That mortgage pays out at $495.94 per month and is paid off in ten years (the reason why all the other mortgages are set at ten-year term).

At the closing, where Jim bought from one person and sold to another, he ended up with a net benefit on the down payments of $20,000 (paid $40,000, got $60,000). As Jim pyramided off on some other property, he will pay the seller (on the $100,000 mortgage) at the rate of $10,000 per year (10% interest-only, remember). While he will collect on the $180,000 wraparound at 11%, giving him a gross interest collected of $19,800 per year, he must also pay the first-mortgage payments he assumed when he "bought" then sold the units, which is $495.94 per month or $5,951.28 per year.

Interest recapitulations:

Jim collects on wraparound	$19,800.00 per year
But pays out:	
On pyramid to seller	10,000.00
On first mortgage he assumed	5,951.28
Jim is left with annual cash flow of	$ 3,848.72

At the end of ten years, Jim will owe $100,000 to the seller of the eight units from the pyramid mortgage as it balloons at that time. The first mortgage he assumed on their eight units will have been satisfied during the ten years so there will be nothing owed on that mortgage. The new owner of the eight units will owe Jim $180,000 as the purchase wraparound balloons at the same time. Jim's net on that swap of funds is a clear $80,000.

What is Jim's total profit?

Cash at closing	$ 20,000.00
Ten years of cash flow	38,487.20 ($3,848.72 × 10)
Balloon bonus	80,000.00 (180,000 − 100,000)
Total pretax profit	$138,487.20

All Jim did was spend a few dollars fixing up a property and offering it for sale at terms that were in reality better than any buyer could have gotten in the market. The pyramid portion of this transaction worked with the seller Jim bought from, since it enabled Jim to say, "Look on the other side of the fence and take that property as security." Jim knew his rental market, of course, and knew that he could support a higher value on the apartments not just because they were fixed up but because the fixing up would help keep the existing tenants in the property at a higher rent.

Monte took an option on a small office building he liked. Like Jim, Monte knew the rental market well because he made a habit of noting every rental sign in the area, frequently stopping in to talk to building managers, etc. He knew he could increase rents in the office building by simply telling the tenants to vacate if they weren't willing to pay a more realistic rent.

He gave the seller a check for $25,000 to be deposited within 45 days if Monte was able to find financing for the building. The price of the building is not important in this example because of the soft-to-hard-transaction bid. The deal, however, was at a fair price, based on the existing low rentals in the building.

Monte went to the tenants and told them he had a deal on the building and needed to know if they were going to sign a lease with him at the terms he was offering them. He presented the facts clearly and honestly: If he closed on the building, which he fully intended to do, they would be out if they were not willing to pay the fair and realistic rent he was offering them right then and there.

Monte was not greedy—he offered them a more than fair rent, knowing they couldn't find a better deal and that the aggravation and cost of moving wouldn't be worth the hassle.

Based on the new rental *pro forma,* Monte offered the building for sale at the same exact price he paid, with the buyer assuming the same exact terms that Monte had assumed with the first seller—

with just one difference: Monte kept the land by adding a land lease to the terms. In essence, Monte bought the building for $300,000, sold the building for $300,000, and, in the exchange, set a $10,000-per-year land lease on the building. This meant that Monte was now the owner of the land and would collect $10,000 per year.

This technique (sell the building and keep the land) is used nicely with the soft buy and hard sell. It worked for Monte just as it can for you.

Finesse in Soft-to-Hard Deals

The more you know about the other techniques in this book, the broader your application of this quick turnaround of property. Your use of combinations of techniques will constantly expand as you see new ways to adapt them to your own needs and desires. Practice will not make you perfect, only profitable.

The most important thing to remember in the use of this technique is *never let the Big "G" guide you.* The Big "G" is, of course, *greed.* It can destroy you and your deals faster than anything you can think of (except perhaps too much booze and women). Greed comes in when the soft-buy, hard-sell investor tries to buy too soft and can't ever make those deals jell, or tries to sell too hard and blows that side of the fence.

These transactions work nicely and reliably when the investor turns over the property quickly and at a modest profit. Let the cigar-chewing boys in the back room who have a hard time sleeping at night make the real nail-biting deals where everyone counts their fingers after the handshake at the closing. Don't get greedy.

Pitfalls in the Soft-to-Hard Deal

The pitfall in this kind of deal is your failure to make the deal jell on the selling side. It will be relatively easy to tie up property once you know your backyard. The key is to be sure you have been honest with yourself. If you become emotional about the property, you may not be able to set the harder terms that will enable you to sell. Your terms should be softer than those of the open market as this enables you to turn over fast—and fast is the name of this game.

You can, of course, lessen the danger by being ready and able to actually buy if you have to. If you run out your option and know you have a good buy but you haven't been able to find a buyer to take you out of the deal at a profit (due to the times), then it's helpful to have a plan to fall back on. One such plan might be to actually shop some financing, as Jim did where he had pyramided off with the seller. He probably could have found some local financing to enable him to buy the eight units himself. As long as he didn't go in the hole each month, he could wait out the tough market and then sell in better times.

As a seller, you might find that it is to your distinct advantage to encourage a buyer to take your property off your hands by offering him soft terms. After all, when you must sell, the major benefit might be to be rid of the property and to let someone else who can benefit from the property make a profit. I frequently recommend this technique to owners of buildings they have not been able to sell. By offering soft terms, they become "decoys" who attract (or seek out) those investors who see an opportunity to "take advantage" of these motivated sellers for a quick profit.

Your ability to buy soft and sell hard will depend on how well you become that decoy of a motivated seller to keep your price and to get the terms you need.

29

The Soft-Buy

Double Exchange

THIS TECHNIQUE has the same origins as the one described in chapter 28. Here, however, you use the option to purchase a property with soft terms, restructure the financing to your benefit on a sale at hard times, and then *exchange* (or sell) each element of ownership: The mortgage, the equity, and the property itself.

Let me break this technique down to its most basic elements. First there is the option to buy on soft terms. There are many ways to accomplish this, as you have seen in some of the previous examples. The objective here isn't to own the property but to turn it over. Because of this, there can be *cash* included in the purchase price, as long as you keep in mind that you don't plan on taking title yourself. To expand your market on the rollover, you will, of course, want to keep the cash side of the purchase light.

Second, you restructure the financing, usually with a land lease or wraparound mortgage. If you have pyramided the seller off to hold some paper on another property, your flexibility is increased as you have greater equity in the mortgage.

When you restructure the financing to a wraparound mortgage, you build in a future benefit. With the wraparound, you will have a surplus over the debt service on the existing financing. The surplus or bonus gives you increased equity in that mortgage, and this equity will be one of the elements you will use for exchange.

The third element is the appreciated value in the property. If you have optioned the deal for $60,000 but in reality you feel that it is worth $75,000, then there is a $15,000 appreciation to your equity. In essence, if you closed on the property for $60,000, you would benefit by this new value to the tune of $15,000. However, instead of this, you are rolling over the property and will sell or exchange this appreciated equity.

Those are the three elements of the basic "soft-buy, double exchange." Now let's look at two examples of this technique in action.

Harry found a vacant industrial building in a good part of the commercial side of town. The previous occupant had been in the building for over 15 years and had finally outgrown the building and moved across the street to a new complex. The owner of the building had all but forgotten about the place for 15 years, doing little but cashing his rent checks. Now the building was a worry, as it was vacant. Harry offered to paint the exterior of the building and fix it up for better rent-out—in return for which Harry would be given an option to buy the building at the end of the year.

The deal was structured this way: Harry would buy the building for $200,000 with $25,000 cash down, and the seller would hold the balance of $175,000 for 15 years, at interest-only payments of 10%. This meant Harry would be obligated to pay $17,500 per year in interest on the debt. (This, by the way, was equal to the rent the owner had been getting from the previous occupant.)

True to his word, Harry painted the building and then some. He added a fence to one side and some bushes along the front to make the property look nicer. Harry knew that even industrial users like their property to have some appeal. And sure enough, within a short time a user came along and wanted to rent the building at nearly double the rent the previous tenant had paid.

Harry then structured a new set of numbers on the building. First he decided that, based on the new income and expense figures, the property was worth $300,000. He set up hypothetical financing this way: He structured a wraparound mortgage in the amount of $200,000 (around the seller's $175,000) interest-only mortgage, putting interest at 12½% per annum on the wrap and a balloon in 15 years. He then offered the remaining equity in the building at this new price ($100,000) for exchange, requiring at least $25,000 in cash.

Harry didn't want to close on the property, but since he had plenty of time, he could be somewhat selective in what he got for exchange, though he was still very flexible. He was able to generate substantial interest within the exchange community and was offered many different kinds of deals.

He settled on some free-and-clear land for his $75,000 equity, balancing it off by receiving another $25,000 in cash. At this point Harry no longer had to worry about closing on the property, since, when he closed on the exchange, he exercised his option, paid the seller the $25,000 cash, and ended up with

1. the $75,000 of free-and-clear land; and
2. his equity in the wraparound mortgage.

Now let's look at the second part of this benefit Harry has developed thus far. He has a $175,000 mortgage within the wraparound. The face value of the wrap is $200,000, which gives it an equity of $25,000. The interest rate on the wrap is 12½%, while interest on the underlying mortgage is only 10%. As neither of these two mortgages amortizes any principal, we can see a direct yield on the $25,000 equity of 30% per year.

Remember: Harry pays 10% on the $175,000 or $17,500. He collects 12½% on the wrap of $200,000, or $25,000 each year, which means he pockets the difference of $7,500 ($25,000 less $17,500 equals $7,500). As the equity on the wrap is only $25,000, Harry receives an annual return of 30% (30% of $25,000 equals $7,500). Such a return is legal as long as there is risk to Harry on the wrap. (The IRS would like to close this down, however, so make sure it is still okay by checking with a good tax accountant.) Just about anyone would like to own a mortgage that paid 30% and was a fairly good risk. In this case it is a real gem.

When Harry decides to unload the wrap, he can exchange it with someone else. He does this at a later date, however, as there is no rush to make the exchange now that he has rolled over the property prior to closing.

Jake made a much smaller deal. He saw a vacant lot he knew was going to go up in value, so he tied it up on a lease-purchase basis. He leased the lot from the owner for a term of one year with the provision that, if he purchased the lot at the end of the year, the lease payments would apply toward the purchase price. The rest was reasonable and just about paid the seller's holding expenses for the year.

During the year of appreciation and contemplation, Jake decided how he was going to profit on this deal. He estimated that the value of the lot had gone from $35,000, which was his option price, to about $55,000. Based on this evaluation, Jake went back to the owner of the lot and asked if he would extend the lease for several more years. The owner agreed only if Jake would forfeit the future rent paid and not credit it against the purchase price. The rent was only $2,500 per year, but Jake hesitated so as not to let the seller know just how reasonable that was, and then agreed. In essence Jake now had a lease with an option to purchase whereby he could buy the lot for $32,500 (he would still get credit for the first year's rent). In the meantime, he would rent the lot for $2,500 per year. (The rent, by the way, was less than 7¼% of the purchase price, so that was a very, very good deal for Jake in a current market where interest on money was runing at 15% and higher.)

Jake now had two elements, each of which had a value.

1. *The leasehold,* whereby Jake had to pay $2,500 per year for the use of the property.
2. *An option to buy at a $32,500 figure,* which was well below the current market.

Based on this, Jake could keep both, sell, or exchange either— sublease the lot and keep the option. His flexibility in this transaction was ideal, as he had expanded his options. The fact that he had changed the lease terms to forfeit the rent didn't hurt much either, since the total rent would be deductible as a business expense.

Finesse in Using the Soft-Buy Double Exchange

Know your alternatives, study your options, and maintain flexibility—three important factors in *any* real-estate investing, to be sure, but even more important when you are attempting to set up a rollover prior to having to buy the optioned property yourself.

One factor, however, which stands out in dealing with options is to maintain the proper profile of an investor throughout the deal. If you go into one of these transactions telling everyone how you plan to tie up the property for a quick rollover, you will end up sitting in your corner with your thumb in your—well, never mind. Just remember, your business should stay *your* business. Never telegraph your plans for making a quick profit, because you might educate the other side of the fence to do the same. At best, no seller wants to make your profit for you by accepting the risk of time and the loss of a more genuine market.

Getting the upper hand in these soft-paper purchases and hard-paper transactions or splitting of elements to give you two avenues to attack and in which to profit will depend, of course, on your ability to spot that opportunity. The old grass-is-greener motivation, which can be used in your favor in the pyramid, will work against you in the planning of what and where you are to invest.

Many investors seek to own property outside where they live; they want to move up, away, to different surroundings. But the fact of the matter is that your own backyard is probably the single most important place for you to seek out your investments. It does you little good to worry about what is going on in the Salt Lake City market if you live in Washington, D.C., unless you plan to move to Salt Lake City. This should be clear in your mind. But confine it still further. Suppose you live in Miami—even more specifically, Miami Beach. Your market, then, is there, Miami Beach. Not Coconut Grove, though it is only ten miles away—unless you extend your backyard to include Coconut Grove by learning as much about that area as you know about Miami Beach.

Risk in investing is inversely proportionate to the amount of knowledge you have about the area and about the type of property in which you plan to invest. Know a lot and your risk is reduced. Know only a little and you'll chance losing your shirt.

You can gain this knowledge by following the hints and clues scattered throughout this book.

Pitfalls of the Soft-Buy Double Exchange

The only pitfall I can foresee is the possibility that you will take an exchange that turns out to be a real bummer. Barring that, as you are exchanging pure profit, what you are risking in these transactions is the amount of time, effort, and cash you have to expend to tie up the deal in the first place. As this is never fully lost (you do gain a tax credit and experience) even in a busted deal, you can only gain from prudent use of this technique.

30

The Three-Party Blanket

CASHLESS INVESTING, as I have previously demonstrated, can frequently be accomplished through a simple 100% financing with the seller holding all of the equity in the form of a second, or junior, mortgage behind the existing financing. To most sellers, the thought of selling their property and not receiving any security other than the equity in their former property just doesn't seem right. Yet when the seller is facing foreclosure, or has been transferred and needs to be relieved of heavy debt, he has little choice but to accept the best deal offered. Thus, in the absence of any other more acceptable offers, a 100% financed deal is often accepted.

The selection of properties available to you is expanded, of course, as you increase your repertoire of cashless-investment strategies. The blanket mortgage is an investment strategy that expands your field of sellers by enabling the seller to hold 100% financing without assuming extra risk. You will thus not need to look for "desperate" sellers only, and in fact you will be able to make cashless deals you never thought possible.

The use of the blanket mortgage involves offering the seller some other property as additional security on the purchase-money mortgage the seller is holding. In essence, you buy a property, give the seller a mortgage for his equity, and offer both that property and another property as the total security for the deal.

The Two-Party Blanket

The two-party blanket is the first and most basic use of the technique. Let's look at how it works.

Charles is attempting to buy from Bill, but Bill won't accept Charles's offer to assume Bill's existing mortgage and give Bill a second mortgage for the balance of the price. Bill does want out of the property, though, and doesn't want to lose a ready buyer. So he tells Charles he will take the deal providing Charles secures the second mortgage with some other property plus the property being purchased. If Charles has some property he isn't using and doesn't mind tying it up in this deal, he is apt to go along.

What makes this deal a two-party blanket is this: The deal involves only Charles and Bill, *two* people, *two* parties.

Move Up to the Three-Party Blanket

In introducing you to the three-party blanket, we are introducing you to a new element of real-estate financing: You don't have to own the property you are using as security in a deal; you can use someone else's property to make your deals fall into place.

In the three-party blanket, all that is necessary is a ready and willing property owner who will agree to allow you to tie up his property as security on your mortgage with the seller. You may have to pay a kicker for this "use of property," but, as the risk may not be too great to the owner of this other property, the kicker may be an acceptable cost to you.

Let's look at two examples.

Lawton had tried just about everything he could to make the deal he wanted on a small three-unit apartment building. The seller had agreed to a most attractive price, and Lawton liked the low-interest assumable mortgage. On top of this, the seller was willing to hold some paper. However, he wouldn't let Lawton make a cashless deal and leave him holding all paper to cover his equity. The seller's point of view was well taken and quite understandable: He simply saw no future in holding 100% of the equity in paper with no additional risk on the buyer's part.

Lawton didn't have any other property to pledge as additional security, so he had discounted the idea of doing a blanket. However, he remembered that his dad had a lot in North Carolina. Lawton then made a deal with his father to put the lot up as additional security on the apartment building. As a kicker, he offered his father a piece of the ultimate profit when the apartments were sold. The deal was set up so that the lot could be removed as the additional security once a set amount of principal against the total mortgages had been paid. At that point, the seller would have the security the lot represented, so it would no longer be needed in the deal.

Nevin, on the other hand, was trying to buy a lot in the Florida Keys with the idea of building a home someday in that part of the world. He didn't have the cash the seller wanted, but he was able to make a deal with the owner of the adjoining property (who was a friend of Nevin's and the reason Nevin wanted to buy there in the first place). The deal was simply this: Nevin's friend would put his lot and home up as additional security in Nevin's blanket mortgage to the seller. The friend would be able to use Nevin's lot as though it were his until Nevin decided to build. In addition, if Nevin sold the lot before building on it, the friend would get a piece of the action. The whole deal was then covered with Nevin giving his friend an option to buy the lot in the event Nevin defaulted on the mortgage, at a price equal to the mortgage balance at the time of the default.

In each of the foregoing two deals, the investor had to give up something to make the deal. The borrowing of this security from a third party made the seller more secure in giving the investor a cashless investment.

Finesse in Third-Party Blankets

This is a technique that few people develop finesse in, because it is often overlooked except by investors who are just starting out in their investment careers and may not have property of their own to use.

There are two areas you should pay attention to in order to gain the edge with this technique. The first is the way in which the approach is made to the seller, and the second is that a gain can come through being the third party in the deal.

In the first instance, there is no need to tell the seller that the property you are giving him as additional security to his mortgage isn't owned by you (unless that fact makes the deal even more secure for the seller). In most instances, the fact that you are giving as security a property owned by someone else might scare the seller! "That's so odd that I think I'll stay away from it." A more straightforward approach is simply to say, "In addition to the property I'm buying, Mr. Seller, I'll secure the mortgage with this beautiful commercial lot described in this brochure."

Some sellers have never heard of a blanket mortgage and must be carefully approached. Terminology is most crucial—never get technical without making sure that you are being understood. Real-estate terminology is not universal, and some people think a wraparound mortgage and a blanket mortgage are the same. (They can be, just like all the dogs in this room might be Dobermans, but not all dogs are Dobermans.) A first mortgage isn't a first mortgage just because the document says it is; likewise a blanket mortgage is what it is, not what the term calls it. Never assume that anyone understands any real-estate term you use; give examples to make sure. Because terminology can confuse people and the last thing you want to do is to confuse the seller, be careful to explain precisely *what is going to happen.*

"Mr. Seller, in this offer I want you to notice that, while no cash will change hands at the closing, you will have a large increase in the security behind the second mortgage you will be holding. As your property has an existing mortgage that is being assumed in the purchase, you will hold the balance of the price in the form of a second mortgage. Naturally you want to see additional security behind that mortgage, so this offer gives you as additional security on the second mortgage the property described in the attached report. In essence, if there were to be a default on your second mortgage, you would have the right to foreclose on both properties."

It is easy for a broker, in making this presentation, to point out the potential benefit to the seller in obtaining a good price in the deal with strong security. The need for cash is often far less than the need for security. The use of a broker in any transaction can be beneficial to the investor if the broker is a good one. In doing blanket or pyramid deals where there must be some discussion of some other property's value, a broker can discuss that value much more easily than the investor can. Sellers are biased against whatever someone tells them when that someone is trying to buy their property for nothing down. Use a broker who understands blankets and you will have a better closing ratio.

The second area I told you to pay attention to is the possibility that *you might want to be the third party*. You will recall that in the two examples cited earlier, both the third parties got something. If you have some unused real estate lying around, you can become a "silent" partner by lending your real estate to a security position from time to time. These situations don't just fall into your lap, however—you need to look for them. They are found through your broker, or through deals that start out as partnerships but end up this way.

For example, if a friend comes to you and asks you to join in a purchase with him, you might examine the deal to see if you can become a partner by simply lending your unused real estate to a security position. "Look, Brad," you tell your friend, "I'll take fifty percent of the deal. In fact, I'll show you how we can make the deal with you putting up less cash than you wanted to in the first instance [you leave out, for the moment, "and without my putting up *any* cash"], okay?"

Using the Blanket to Your Advantage

There are several elements of a blanket you need to know about and incorporate into your deals. The proper use of any blanket, both two- and three-party mortgages, will require that you include the following three *in the contract to buy*. They should not be left up to the usual "legal aftermath" that often occurs in normal mortgage situations. Blankets are not normal mortgages, so, to avoid trouble, use this checklist.

The Three-Point Blanket-Mortgage Checklist

1.   Describe in the contract the *position of security* that is being given up in the other property. It is possible to give a second position behind an existing mortgage, or to build in a *subordinated* position behind a future mortgage to be placed on the other property. In the subordinated position, the investor (or owner of the second property) is permitted to obtain financing in the form of a first mortgage on the property even though a blanket mortgage has been given.

2.   Provide for a release of the additional security. You don't want to lock up your property (or someone else's) for the duration of the mortgages. The seller can usually be convinced that, once you have established equity in the deal, there is no need for this additional security. If you don't provide for such a release, then you will lock up the other property until the mortgage is satisfied. A release provision is simply stated: ". . . and when the total mortgages on the purchased property have been paid down to a total outstanding balance owed of $45,000 (or whatever), the additional property as indicated herein, which is covered by this blanket mortgage, shall be released from this mortgage."

3.   Be clear on the form of amortization used. Most mortgage payments are a set amount each month and those payments include interest on the unpaid balance and some portion of principal. In some mortgages there is a third element, which is a combination of real-estate tax and insurance. The first two elements—principal and interest—are at times the culprits that can mess up any mortgage amortization if the mortgage is written differently than you intended it to be. For example, if a $50,000 mortgage is amortized over ten years with equal principal payments and interest at the rate of 10%, the annual payment would be $10,000 for the first year. Each year thereafter will have a slightly reduced payment. For example, by the fifth year the payment will be $7,500, and the final year only $5,500. On the other hand, if the payments were to be ten years of equal payments of principal including interest, each year would be $8,137.50. Some lawyers (and investors) like this first

format because it is simple to calculate. On the other hand, if cash flow is important, equal payments of $8,137.50 each year for ten years might be far more attractive, and is calculated using Table A and Table B in the Appendix.

Pitfalls in Using the Three-Party Blanket

From the seller's point of view, the use of a blanket mortgage aids in his security and reduces the risk of a cashless deal. All sellers, however, should be careful in accepting the other property to make a thorough examination of the title and value of this second property. There is no benefit or added security in taking a worthless or heavily overmortgaged property as part of a blanket.

One disadvantage to the buyer using this technique is that he gives up the freedom to use this other property to generate other financing.

If you are using another person's property in a three-party blanket, the owner of that property can lose a great deal if you default. Because of this, anyone considering becoming a third party in a three-party-blanket deal should first check into the amount of risk. As in every kind of real-estate transaction, if the risk is justly compensated for, the deal will be warranted, provided you can stand to protect your interest or lose your property.

Because of this, most three-party blankets will be made between an investor and a third party who are closely related or connected.

31

The Discounted Paper Swap

MANY INVESTORS have mortgages that they will gladly sell to you at a discounted value provided you give them cash. And frequently sellers of real property will take your newly acquired paper at its face value, as your down payment, provided their goals are met.

The "discounted paper swap," then, is a multiple event that enables you to generate instant profit and use this profit to buy something which you hope will increase that profit even more. The technique itself often involves the use of cash, and many investors who are heavy with cash will pick up mortgages at a discount and then use this technique to get extra mileage out of that cash. In this book, however, I will show you how to use this method to gain a foothold in real estate without any cash.

First, let's look at an example of the discounted paper swap in action.

Assume that you want to buy a $70,000 home. The property has an existing first mortgage of $22,000, and the seller says he will hold some paper if you give him at least $10,000 cash in the deal.

You know you can refinance this property with a 95% loan. This would give you $66,500 less the cost of the loan, approximately $2,000. Thus you would net $64,500, which still leaves you $5,500 short of making your cashless deal work.

However, as you know all about the discounted paper swap (in retrospect, of course), you have been looking around for investors with mortgages to sell. One such mortgage is a $34,000 face-value mortgage with ten years to go at 9½% interest. You have calculated the current value of the mortgage, if purchased by you for cash, at a 15% return, and have come up with a value of $27,270.25. You arrived at this amount through use of the discount formula and checklist supplied in this chapter. The owner of that mortgage needs cash, and if you were ready to pay him the $27,270.25, he would give you the mortgage.

You tell the owner of the mortgage that you are about to do a deal and ask if he'll sit still on the paper for a few days to enable you to firm up the home transaction. The mortgage owner, anxious for cash, is willing to wait for a while.

Before going to the homeowner, you survey what you have. You know now that if you give the mortgage owner $27,270.25, you can become owner of a mortgage with a face value of $34,000. This difference would give you an instant equity of $6,729.75. You also know that you can borrow 95% on the house and end up with net loan proceeds of $64,500. Looking back over the rest of the deal, you decide as follows:

If the seller of the house will take your about-to-be-acquired mortgage at face value of $34,000, and you pay off the existing mortgage of $22,000, you can give him $14,000 cash.

House seller gets the mortgage you will acquire	$34,000
Then you will pay off existing finance	22,000
And then give the seller cash on balance	14,000
Matches price of house	$70,000

That looks simple so far. But just how did you do this without spending any of your own cash (which you don't have anyway)?

In this transaction, you actually made money in the end by buying the discounted mortgage, which you used as a form of pyramid, refinancing the balance of the deal through a local lender to generate the cash needed to pay off both sellers. The two sellers were

You will get a new mortgage on the house of	$66,500
But you have to pay:	
Loan cost of	2,000
This leaves you with a net loan proceeds of	$64,500
Out of this, you pay the mortgage owner the	
cash you agreed to of	27,270.25
This leaves you with a remainder of	37,229.75
From this you pay off the existing mortgage	22,000.00
You are then left with	15,229.75
Then you pay the seller the balance owed	14,000.00
And you have enough left to have a housewarming party	$ 1,229.75

each motivated by cash, the mortgage seller getting about 80% of what the face value of the mortgage showed, and the home seller getting $14,000 and selling the home.

There are many fine points to dealing with mortgages you will want to buy in your investment career. Using them in this kind of buying technique is just one of many opportunities to profit through discounted mortgages. Because of the great flexibility you will have in dealing within the mortgage arena, it is important for you to have a quick and easy way to calculate the value of a mortgage at any rate or term. I will show you the key points to look for in the actual value of a mortgage later in this chapter, but first let's look at the actual discount of the mortgage itself.

Constants are a simple shortcut to discounts. To find a mortgage discount, you must either have in-depth knowledge of the mathematics of finance or have a simple "constant" table such as the two provided for you in the Appendix of this book. Tables A and B both show constants in a column under the term of a mortgage and alongside the interest rate for which the mortgage is contracted or demanded. Multiplying the constant rate by the actual balance of the mortgage will give you the total amount of the annual payments. Dividing that by 12 (in the case of table A), will give you the monthly payment.

For example, under the column for ten years at 9½% interest, you will find the percent shown to be 15.528. If the mortgage in question is $10,000 of principal over ten years at 9½% interest, multiplying the constant (15.528%) by the mortgage amount ($10,000) will show the total annual payments to be $1,552.80.

(Don't forget that multiplier, a percent, must be converted to a decimal by moving the period two places left.) If you divide the annual amount of $1,552.80 by 12, you end up with a monthly payment of $129.40.

The thing to remember is that you can find the annual payment of any mortgage (and then the monthly payment) by knowing the interest rate, the years to term, then finding the corresponding constant and multiplying it (as a decimal) by the mortgage amount. Remember that table A relates to *monthly* payments, however, and the annual amount must be divided by 12 to end up with the correct figure. If you were dealing with a mortgage that had an annual payment—that is, one payment per year—you would use table B. You cannot take the annual amount from table A, divide it by 4, and come up with an accurate quarterly payment. To find quarterly or semiannual payments, you would need tables designed specifically for that. You can, however, estimate the payments using either table A or B, by selecting table A for any schedule of payments up to but not including semiannual payments, and table B for the longer spacing of payments.

This is the specific function of the "constants" table, but understanding this function will enable you to do many other things with these tables. One of these things is to calculate very easily the discount of a mortgage.

The Formula for Finding the Discounted Value of a Mortgage

The use of constants will enable you to arrive at a value for any mortgage, based on the return you would demand for that mortgage. In essence, mortgage values are a function of the return that the mortgage will show the holder of the mortgage, and the goals that mortgage will fulfill. Let's look at the economic side of the picture first.

The contract rate on any mortgage is the interest the mortgagor pays by virtue of the original loan agreement. While this interest may fluctuate, the *contract rate* will always be a rate that is described in or a function of the original or modified loan contract. The 9½%-interest contract rate previously mentioned would have been considered well below market in the mid-1980s. A lender would demand a much higher rate, and 15% would be considered more acceptable. To "force" a 9½% mortgage to return you 15% over a term of ten years, you would have to pay less for the mortgage than the current unpaid balance. How much less? You must take the following steps to find out.

Five Steps to Finding the Discounted Value of a Mortgage

1. *Ascertain the demand rate to which you want to discount the mortgage.* This means simply decide what yield you will be willing to make if you pay cash for this mortgage. You may find that your offer may not be accepted and you will end up with a lower rate of return than you hoped for, but if some of the other, noneconomic circumstances are right, you may well accept a slightly lower rate than your initial demand.

In the case at hand, we are assuming your demand is 15%. As you want to make 15% on this (or any) mortgage and you know the term of years, you must now go to step two.

2. *Find the constant rate for your demand rate.* You want to find the constant rate for the remaining term of years of the mortgage you want to discount, at the demand rate. Since the mortgage in question has ten years to go, and your demand rate is 15%, you look in table A (assuming we are dealing with a mortgage of monthly payments), go to the ten-year column, and follow it down till you reach 15%. The resulting constant percent is 19.360.

3. *Find the constant rate for the mortgage at the contract rate.* In the same column (ten years), look for the interest rate that matches the contract rate of the mortgage. As the mortgage in question has a contract rate of 9½%, you will find that the constant rate—which represents the actual annual payments this mortgage now has (and will have for the remaining ten years)—is 15.528%.

4. *Find the current unpaid balance of the mortgage.* Usually you, or the mortgagor, will know this by examining the mortgage amortization schedule. If this amount is not known, you may have

to reconstruct the events dating from the start of the mortgage. This involves having a copy of the mortgage contract to know the exact starting time, the original principal, and the number of months that have passed.

For example, if you read the mortgage document and see that the mortgage is at 9½% interest for 12 years of equal monthly payments, you can look at the 12-year column next to the 9½% interest to see a constant of 13.997%. This amount multiplied by the beginning loan amount (shown in the contract) of $37,718.94 would give an annual payment of $5,279.52, which when divided by 12 gives the monthly payment of $439.96 that the mortgage will carry for the full 12 years. A quick check on this will prove out by matching the payments you might have been given. Remember, however, that you are using principal and interest payments here and some mortgages will add taxes and insurance and other items to the total payment. You must discard all added figures and work solely with the principal and interest portions. Once you find the original constant, you can then go to the constant closest to the present time. As a buyer of discounted mortgages, you will select the half-year point already past if you cannot fall right on a time span shown in the tables. In this case, however, you notice that exactly two years will have gone by from the original start of the mortgage to the date when you would become the owner.

As you are trying to find (or test) the actual remaining principal outstanding, you locate the constant at the actual current date— which you did in step three. Since you know, or have calculated, the actual mortgage payments, you divide the annual payment by the constant.

ORIGINAL ANNUAL PAYMENT $\left\{ \dfrac{\$5,279.52}{.15528} = \$34,000 \right\}$ Remaining Balance
Divided by CURRENT CONSTANT

The $34,000 then is the *remaining balance of the mortgage*

Whichever way you have found the current unpaid principal, you can check it with the other way.

You are now ready to move to step five.

5. *Calculate the discounted value.* The discounted value can now be found by using the formula shown below. You have all the necessary elements to put into the boxes.

$$\frac{\text{CONSTANT RATE FOR CONTRACT RATE}}{\text{CONSTANT RATE FOR DEMAND RATE}} \times \frac{\text{UNPAID BALANCE}}{\text{ON MORTGAGE}} = \frac{\text{DISCOUNTED VALUE}}{\text{OF MORTGAGE}}$$

$\dfrac{.15528}{.19360} \times \$34,000 = $ Discounted Value of Mortgage

$.8020661 \times \$34,000 = $ Discounted Value of Mortgage

$\$27,270.25 = $ Discounted Value

By following this formula you can arrive at a discounted value for a mortgage. It is also possible to discover the actual yield from a mortgage offered to you at a discount in a similar way.

Let's assume you are trying to buy the same mortgage in this example. You know the current principal outstanding is $34,000 and the annual payment totals $5,279.52. In the negotiations, you make a lower offer than the seller wants, only to find you are able to buy the mortgage (if you want) for the reduced sum of $25,314.00. You know that this will yield you more than 15%, which was the discounted sum the seller offered. But what yield?

You need to find out what constant is represented by this amount. In short, you divide the annual payment by the price you are able to buy the mortgage for.

$$\frac{\text{Annual Payment}}{\text{Price You Pay}} \left\{ \; \right\} \frac{\$5,279.52}{\$25,314.00} = \text{The Constant for the Term at the Demand}$$

This will give you .2085612, which, when represented in a percent (by moving the decimal over to the right two places), gives you a 20.85612% constant rate. As we are dealing with a ten-year mortgage in this case, you simply go down that column (the years remaining) to the closest possible constant. You find that 20.856 corresponds to 17%. This mortgage at this price, then, would return approximately 17% on the $25,314.00 paid.

This is a lot of math just to set the stage for this technique, but it is essential because you will never be able to effectively negotiate for mortgages unless you can properly discount them to current values. You will find, however, that the actual math is very simple and that the cheapest of all electronic calculators should do the calculations effectively. One note of caution: You must make sure you are using a calculator that does not round off decimals to three or four places. Test this by multiplying .1234 by .1234. If you don't register .0152275 as your answer, it could be that your calculator is dropping the 4 or even the 3 from the multiplication problem. This kind of calculator will be of little use to you in finance.

Other Factors to Evaluate in Mortgages

There are several factors that contribute to the value of a mortgage and make the discounting of mortgages very profitable to those people who know how to evaluate these factors. Understanding these elements will better enable you to know when to keep the mortgage being offered to you at a discount and when you should simply use it as an element in the discounted paper swap. These factors are as follows:

The Four Noneconomic Factors of Mortgage Values

1. *What is the mortgage's loan-to-value ratio?* This is a key factor in any mortgage situation. What is the value of the property, and what is the total loan circumstance? If the property is conservatively valued at $100,000 and the total loans on the property are $80,000, there is an 80% loan-to-value ratio. The amount of equity the owner has in the deal decreases the risk on the part of the mortgagee. Low loan-to-value ratios are therefore better than high loan-to-value ratios.

2. *Where is this loan in the total picture?* It is possible the property has more than one loan outstanding. If you are buying the first mortgage, you want to know the loan-to-value ratio as it pertains only to the total loans but not including any loans behind, or junior to, this one. If there is a first mortgage of $20,000 and a second mortgage of $60,000 and a total loan-to-value ratio of 80%, but only a 20% loan-to-value ratio for the first mortgage, it is easy to see that the second mortgage is riskier than the first.

3. *What do you know about the owners of the property?* This will tell you a lot. If the owner is anticipating an addition, or a possible refinance of the total loan structure, or a sale of the property, these elements can cause a sudden and premature payoff of the loan. This creates a bonanza, as you will see.

4. *What do you know about the property itself?* Examination of some properties will show that they are ripe for redevelopment.

Trends in the area might dictate that only the foolish would hold the property in its present status for very long.

A study of these four elements will often reveal a potential early payoff of a mortgage. You should be aware that it is rare for any mortgage to run for more than ten years, no matter what the original contract. The need for funds, a new buyer, redevelopment, additions, etc., all cause the property to be refinanced. The advent of new federal savings-and-loans provisions in their first mortgages, requiring adjustments or refinancing in the event of a sale or other disposition of title, will trigger early payoffs of junior mortgages.

The Profit in Discounted Mortgages Due to Early Payoff

Let's look at the mortgage you bought in this chapter for $27,270.25. Originally you tied up this mortgage with the thought of using it in the discounted paper swap—but then you realized the owner of the real estate was going to pay off the mortgage. Perhaps you discovered this when you went over to look at the property securing the mortgage and noticed the "For Sale" sign being taken down and the new buyer told you he was going to remodel the whole property. Remember, the face amount of the mortgage still outstanding is $34,000. If you can buy the mortgage for $27,270.25, and within a month or so have it paid off for the full $34,000, you will profit to the tune of $6,729.75. This is a healthy yield of 24.67% if it took a full year for this to occur—and that would be in addition to the interest yield you would earn. But if it happened within one month, it would equal a 296.13% annual return. Not bad, not bad at all, and it shows some of the potential in discounting mortgages.

Making the Discounted Paper Swap Work

Getting back to the technique at hand, you will find that sellers of real estate will allow the pyramid to work for you in this kind of deal because of that grass-looking-greener-on-the-other-side-of-the-fence syndrome I've talked about before. The fact that you will give a seller a mortgage at its face value when you have bought it at a discount doesn't matter: You aren't offering an alternative, for one thing; and if the seller doesn't find that the totality of your offer does something for him, he will turn it down.

The motivation of the seller to sell and get a good price is the major point for you to work on. You must never allow yourself to get caught in the trap of making comparisons between what you are offering and what the seller wants. The only comparison that is valid for either you or the seller is to compare what you are offering to what *has been offered* and *what is currently still open*. In essence, you compare what you want to do with all the options open to you.

Many sellers turn down the first and best offer they will ever get, only to take something less later on. Time works against many sellers who are motivated by the need to make a deal as soon as possible. Their need for cash makes this and any real-estate deal easier if you make use of the techniques offered in this book that enable you to generate cash (none of it yours) to the seller.

Pitfalls in the Discounted Paper Swap

There is no pitfall to the investor who ties up some paper at a discount and then uses the appreciated value to generate the cash or equity he needs to make a deal. This kind of transaction creates pure profit up front. The equity you obtain in the deal is yours to work with and is the same as cash when the seller takes at face value the mortgage you bought at a discount.

The pitfalls for the seller can be many, however, and all sellers taking any mortgage paper must follow business prudence in making sure that the mortgages are sound, that the security isn't over-evaluated, and that the real risk of having the loan wiped out in a foreclosure of a senior mortgage is low. This will require that the seller taking such paper examine the situation carefully. The pitfall can be a sudden and drastic loss of 100% of the value of the mortgage in a foreclosure that cannot sustain the values of the debt outstanding.

Proper evaluation of such risks, however, will enable sellers to use this tool to their advantage. There is nothing wrong with a seller taking good paper providing the total picture is worthwhile. If the cash the seller is getting is sufficient, and the total price on the property is above what the seller might have been forced to take had time eaten him up, then the total goal of the seller might be well serviced.

In fact, many such sellers find that taking discounted paper where they don't get the advantage of the discount is not only no chore, it is downright rewarding.

32

The 1031 Gold Mine:
The Real-Estate Exchange

THE Internal Revenue Service gives and takes away—mostly the latter. The "1031 gold mine" is one of the few "gives" they have; and if you use it properly, it can help you not only make cashless deals but save on taxes at the same time.

First of all, let me set the record straight. Not all exchanges you will make will qualify under the Internal Revenue Code 1031. This doesn't mean that those exchanges will not be of benefit to you— *any exchange that moves you closer to your goal is a good exchange.* The benefits of 1031 exchange are basically that you can postpone or even avoid altogether any capital-gains tax you might have to pay in the event of a sale. When you use the 1031 exchange, then, you will save on the amount of the tax you would have had to pay. At times this fact will work for you in enticing a seller to "take" your property in an exchange because of the tax *he* will save.

Real-estate exchanges are simple to accomplish, but most people never get involved with this exciting part of the real-estate profession or end of investing. There are several reasons for this, and it is important, I believe, that you recognize what these reasons are so you can cope with them both in yourself and in those buyers and sellers (and agents) you will be dealing with.

The Six Reasons People Avoid Real-Estate Exchanges

1. *Because they don't understand them.* It is human nature to avoid something you don't understand. But remember this about your "comfort zone"—it works both for you and against you. As a real-estate investor, you must strive to expand all those areas that can increase your profit potential, and one such area is that of real-estate exchanges. When you know the techniques of this kind of investing, you no longer can use this excuse. But in dealing with people ignorant of exchanges, you will have to go slowly to avoid giving the "sharpie" look to what you are doing.

2. *Because they believe that one party to an exchange gets the raw end of the deal.* I won't say this doesn't happen from time to time, but it can happen in anything you do. How many sellers feel they got the most they could? How many buyers feel they paid the lowest price possible? The client of mine who tells me that he will make one offer and it will be a take-it-or-leave-it would be most chagrined if the seller said, "Okay, I'll take it." That buyer would forever wonder if he hadn't offered too much.

The more you know about exchanges, the more you will realize that for some people the exchange is more beneficial than a sale. In fact, some sellers will accept in an exchange a property they would not have purchased (given a wide selection and the cash to make the purchase), because the exchange was offered to them and the cash was not.

Your use of exchanges will show you that both sides of the exchange can and most often do come out smelling like a rose. The biggest proof of this is that most exchanges occur between members of the real-estate profession—brokers and salesmen exchanging real estate in their own portfolios with other brokers and salesmen. These exchangers form clubs and networks where they deal with one another. The slipshod or shifty dealer is quickly recognized and is "dealt" out.

3. *Because they believe that people who exchange set two prices: one for exchange and a real one for cash (which is much*

lower). Now this point is often true and is to me one of the drawbacks of the exchange side of investing, unless you know how to deal with it. The basic reason for setting prices this way is that most people don't understand that since exchanges can save you tax money, the exchange should be at a lower value than what the sale would have to be to end up at par after paying the tax. After all, I'd rather have a $40,000 lot in exchange (if I wanted the lot) than $45,000 in cash with a $9,000 tax to pay. Other people set higher prices on exchanges than on cash sales out of defense. Personally, I like to quote one price and then stick to it like glue to glue. However, you can easily counter the double standard of pricing by never asking someone the value of the exchange, but, instead, always asking what the price is for sale. Work from that evaluation every time.

4. *Because they believe that if you are going to exchange, you must end up with exactly what you want.* This is downright silly. You don't end up with exactly the cash you want when you sell. If you truly understand your goals, you will have an easier time with this negative view of exchanges. A clear view of your end goal will enable you to see when the exchange is taking you closer to that goal. You do not need to make the jump from San Francisco to New York in one exchange. Not mind you that such an exchange isn't possible, only that you are far more likely to get to New York if you take Phoenix, then St. Louis, then Washington, D.C., on your way to New York. When it comes to real-estate exchanges, you have to be willing to give up something that is not doing for you what it should, or what you need to progress toward your goal, in exchange for something that will. Remember: *any exchange that moves you closer to your goal is a good exchange.*

5. *Because they can't accept the thought of taking something they don't want at all as an intermediate step.* This is often very difficult to explain, though it appears simple enough. The professional exchanger will frequently take a client through a multileg exchange to end up with a beneficial exchange. For example, if I want to acquire a duplex, I might offer the owner of the duplex cash (which I'll get from refinancing the duplex) and some vacant land out of my Armadello Ranch near Naples, Florida. If the duplex owner doesn't want my vacant land, the deal could die right there. But it probably won't if I explain (and I will) that he doesn't have to keep the vacant

land—that we can exchange it for something he does want or is willing to take if he will allow me the time for the extra legwork.

If he agrees to allow the deal to be tied together (binding us both to the exchange if I can dispose of the vacant land for him by bringing in something he will take), then I can work out the rest of the deal. He might say he would take a vacant lot, but only if it were in the Florida Keys. I might find a lot he would take, but that owner doesn't want the vacant land in Naples, Florida. I keep going until I find someone who will fit the slot and make the whole jigsaw go together.

I'm not sure what the world record is of legs to an exchange, but I know of one that had over 25 different steps before it was finally put together. Patience and a determined broker are essential to exchanges.

6. *Because people believe you have to own something to make an exchange.* The answer to this is simply that you can exchange property you don't even own. How? Wait until chapter 33 for that answer.

Real-Estate Exchanges Are Prime Options
for Buyers or Sellers

The fortunate thing about real-estate exchanges is that you will have the opportunity to use them as both a buyer and a seller. Your ultimate benefit, of course, is not to be a buyer or seller when using exchanges but to be an exchanger.

As a Buying Tool

When you learn the motivation of the seller, you often realize that the exchange might be your way to do one or both of the following things:

1. *Get rid of something you don't want to keep.* If the seller of what you want is highly motivated, he is apt to be willing to take as part or all of this equity something you have in exchange.

2. *Motivate the seller because of tax benefits.* The seller hang-

ing on the fence might be motivated by the tax savings you can show him through the exchange you are offering.

As a Selling Tool

As a seller, there will be times when you have to dig deep down to the bottom of your soul and come up with some powerful tricks. After all, not all real estate will sell itself; sometimes you have to find a "taker" for your property, as that is often the start of a deal.

Offering your property, or part of your equity, for an exchange will broaden your market. There are buyers out there trying to find what you have, only they don't have money. Try to show them how to make a cashless deal that will solve your needs.

In finding "takers" for your property, you generate additional options for yourself. When someone says to me, "I'll take your property and assume the new mortgage I can put on it (giving you 80% cash) if you take this lot for your remaining equity," I now have cash and a piece of land, which I can keep, exchange, or offer out on the same basis (I'll hold the mortgage and take something for 20% of the lot's equity).

I've made million-dollar exchanges in which only a small portion of the transaction was property taken in exchange while the majority of the deal was cash and mortgage. One such exchange arose out of my desire to sell a large tract of oceanfront land I controlled in the Vero Beach area. My marketing program simply didn't produce a buyer, no matter what I did. Then I decided to open the property up for exchange. Not, mind you, that the exchange was either the most desirable or the most practical thing to do because of the nature of my partners in the ownership of the property. Nonetheless, I knew finding a "taker" was essential.

Shortly after placing the land on exchange, the offers began to come in. A large villa in Spain, an orange grove in Florida, other proposals that didn't get to the writing stage. Then an offer to take some vacant land, free and clear of mortgages, for the equity in the oceanfront land. This offer came from a highly qualified "buyer" who thought of himself as an exchanger. Through heavy and long negotiations over four months (nothing else was happening on the property anyway), the deal was concluded. The exchanger saved face by giving up some vacant land, and we got cash and mortgage for the balance. What started out as an exchange with no cash ended up as a lot of cash and very little exchange.

When you find a taker for your property, you have the choice of moving on your own property or moving off the exchange property. For example, if I offered you a small duplex as part of a deal to buy your motel, you might say: "I'll take the deal if I can find a buyer or other exchange for your duplex, as I don't want it."

If I'm motivated to take your motel, I'll sit still for a while and let *you* go in two directions. I can't stop you from making a deal without me if someone else comes along to buy or exchange for your property. I'm at the mercy of your intent to try to move off my duplex onto something else. I can, of course, try to find a buyer to take the duplex out of the picture and give you cash.

All sellers should investigate their opportunities and examine the value of an exchange. Even the seller who says "I can't exchange, because I need cash" might find there are no buyers for what he has to sell and that his only way out is to exchange for something that is sellable.

The Mechanics of Making Exchanges

There are several essential mechanical aspects of making exchanges. The first is the *balance of equities*. The others relate to *presentation* and the *maximizing of gains*.

Balancing Equities in Exchanges

All exchanges must have a balance of equities. There are three ways to achieve this balance.

The Cash Balance

Assume that you own a duplex worth $75,000 and owe $50,000 in a first mortgage against it, so your equity is $25,000. You want to exchange for Peter's apartment building, worth (to you) $200,000. Peter has a first mortgage of $130,000 on the building, giving him an equity of $70,000. You want to make the exchange and will balance the equities with cash, as shown in table 3.

TABLE 3
Cash Balance of Equities

	(YOU)	(PETER)
Property given up	$75,000	$200,000
Less outstanding mortgages	− 50,000	−130,000
Equity	25,000	70,000
Cash balance—who gives cash	45,000	0
Balance of equities	70,000	70,000

The Mortgage Balance

If you don't have enough cash to balance the equities, you might try a mortgage balance, as shown in table 4.

TABLE 4
Mortgage Balance of Equity

	(YOU)	(PETER)
Property given up	$75,000	$200,000
Less outstanding mortgages	−50,000	−130,000
Equity	25,000	70,000
New mortgage owed to		(45,000)
Balance of equities	25,000	25,000

In balancing equities with a mortgage, you add an additional mortgage to the property you are to take. In this case, you give Peter a $45,000 mortgage against the property you are taking from him, or some other property you already own.

The Combination Balance

In the combination, you might give Peter $10,000 in cash and $35,000 in the form of a mortgage. Or you could augment your equity by adding other properties. Nothing will keep you from offering Peter the duplex, a gold watch, and seven partridges in a pear tree in addition to some cash and a mortgage.

Presentation

The key to all exchanges is the presentation to the other party. Does this sound familiar? It should, because so much of your success in real-estate investing depends on the tone set at the time the original offer is presented, and how well the pressure of the deal is both maintained and accepted.

If you are dealing with a real-estate broker who has not dealt in exchanges, you are apt to have some problems from the very start. For the same reason, however, it is very difficult for you to make your own exchanges. So your first step is to acquaint yourself with someone knowledgeable in exchanges in your area. I'd suggest a call to the local board of realtors, or a look in a newspaper for a real-estate-exchange column, or just calling several brokers and asking them whom they would recommend you talk to. Since having the best representation won't cost you any more commission than the worst—and the worst can be more expensive in the long run—try to find the best *in your area.* I stress this last part because finding a great buy 1,000 miles away won't do you a dime's worth of good.

In the presentation of any offer, there are seven things that should be avoided.

1.   Never ask the other party what the exchange value is of their property. You only want to know the sale value.

2.   Never presume the other party will turn down anything. Only soothsayers are good at presumption, and even so, look where they are.

3.   Avoid too much talk. Simply say, "I want to buy your property, Mr. Seller, and I'll give you five acres of pine woods and ten thousand dollars as my deal." Sounds much better this way and won't upset a never-before exchanger.

4.   Never present an offer without documentation for the other property in the exchange. Have some backup package on what you are offering, too. If you let your broker go off without a package, you will lose the edge.

5.   Be persistent with your offers. Make them until you are blue in the face, but don't be too conciliatory too quickly. "Look, Mr. Seller, I'm very interested in your property and will keep coming back to you if I can think of something to make this deal work." No genuine seller will want to turn you down too flatly, as you are demonstrating that you are a taker—and you might come up with something.

6.   Never be too set on what you will do. Exchanges are a new, wide-open game for many people. You might be turned on by an

offer for an around-the-world cruise on the *QE2* as part of a deal, and who in the world would have thought of that? Options that are opening up to you will be exciting. Live with them for a while.

7.   Never close doors too hard. It is all right to ease them closed: "I'll say no to this, as it doesn't solve my problem, but I do appreciate your interest and I hope we can work something out."

The Benefits of the 1031 Exchange

The IRS Code 1031 says that if you make a like-for-like exchange, you don't have to pay the gains tax at the time of the exchange. This is true as long as you have done everything properly, have not received any boot, nor had net mortgage relief. Let me explain. "Like for like" simply means "investment for investment." You can't exchange part of your inventory as a builder for an investment, or part of your parking lot for an investment, and have a 1031 exchange. Investment for investment is the major thing for you to remember.

"Gain" on property is the sum of everything you get in a sale (or exchange) less your adjusted cost. Your gain, or profit, is thus the price you get less the price you paid, after the latter has been adjusted for depreciation or improvements.

The basis is like book value. When you buy a property, it has a value. You can add to the value by building something on the property. You can take away from it by certain deductions, such as removing part of the improvements, or depreciating the assets over the years as allowed by the IRS.

In the new tax law of 1981, most of the depreciation rules were revised drastically to make real estate a major tax shelter for investors. The law also revised the calculations for adjustment of basis. In essence, when you depreciate a property you artificially reduce its value, and reduce the basis accordingly. In reality, of course, depreciation has little effect on actual value. The IRS allows depreciation to be treated as an actual expense (even though no money was spent) and, as such, in the year-end tax accounting it will reduce actual earnings or profits. As earnings are automatically reduced each year, you pay tax not on actual earnings but the reduced amount.

For example, if I earn $100,000 this year, but I have depreciation of $100,000 from my real estate, my taxable earnings are zero. Of course, in this example, I actually received $100,000 in earnings and I actually didn't spend the depreciation of $100,000, but as far as the IRS is concerned I did, so I won't have to pay any tax.

Along with the new depreciation schedules, there has been a change in the accelerated-depreciation rules. In short, now if you take any form of depreciation faster than straight line (15 years at straight line would be one-fifteenth each year, or .06666666667 of the present value less salvage value each year), that depreciation cannot be used to create capital gain, and the gain equal to the accelerated depreciation will be ordinary gain.

This means that if you had a building worth $150,000 and a $20,000 lot cost and depreciated that building on the straight line over the 15 years allowed, you would have $10,000 of depreciation each year. At the end of five years, your adjusted basis would be $100,000 plus the lot cost of $20,000, or a total basis of $120,000.

If you sold the building and lot for a total price of $220,000, you would have a gain of $100,000 and it would be taxable as a long-term capital gain (six months' ownership in an investment will qualify you for long-term capital gains).

On the other hand, if you had taken the maximum accelerated of 175% of straight line right off on this building, you would have a depreciation totalling $77,935 in five years, giving you a depreciated building value of $72,065 to which you add the lot of $20,000 to end up with an adjusted basis of $92,065. However, as you sold the total package for $220,000, you would have gain as follows:

Sales price:	$220,000
Adjusted basis:	92,065
Gain	127,935
Ordinary gain*	77,935
Long term capital gain	50,000

* The amount of the accelerated depreciation which will be taxed at your normal ordinary tax rate rather than the more favorable capital gains rates.

"Boot" is the part of the exchange that will be taxable even in the best-set-up 1031 exchange. Boot is anything other than real estate. If you get $10,000, it is boot. If you get a gold watch, it is boot. A car, boat, airplane, diamond ring—all are boot and are taxable. You can qualify for a 1031 with receipt of boot, but you will still be taxed on the boot portion.

214

Net mortgage relief is something else to look for. When you exchange one property for another and they are both free and clear of any mortgages throughout the exchange, there is no mortgage relief in that there are no mortgages given up. However, when you deal with properties encumbered with mortgages, you need to look for the situation referred to as "net mortgage relief."

Assume you have a property worth $100,000 and you owe $55,000 against it. If you exchange for a property worth $45,000, making an even swap—your equity for theirs—you will be relieved of $55,000 of mortgage obligation. You now own a $45,000 property without mortgages. You have had an exchange without any boot, but you have a recognized gain of $55,000 (the amount of the mortgage). You will have a taxable exchange if the mortgage relief is greater than your realized gain by the amount of the mortgage relief. If there is any gain at all, and you have net mortgage relief, you will have some tax in this exchange.

The reason for this should be simple to understand. Assume for a moment that today you own the same $100,000 property and it is free and clear. You go down to the local savings-and-loan and borrow $55,000 in cash, which you put into your pocket tax-free. A day later you make the exchange shown above, getting a free-and-clear $45,000 property. As you now have net mortgage relief, you may have a tax because you have already received the $55,000 cash without paying any tax on that revenue.

Calculating the Taxable Gain in Exchanges

I will borrow from my book *The Complete Guide to Real Estate Financing.* In its chapter on how to use exchanges in financing real estate, there is a table showing the tax calculations of the following exchanges:

Smyth and Greenbalm are our two owners. *Smyth* owns 100 acres of land. Its value is $200,000. He owns this land free and clear of any mortgages and his basis is the $100,000 he paid for the property. The other $100,000 in value is appreciation over 12 years of ownership. *Greenbalm* owns a 15-unit apartment house. Its value is also $200,000, and it, too, is free and clear. Greenbalm's basis is $140,000 (he paid $180,000 but has taken $40,000 in depreciation). Smyth and Greenbalm make a trade with no cash paid between them and no mortgages swapped or assumed. It is an even-steven exchange.

In the second exchange, the two parties are Jones and Blackburn. *Jones* owns 100 acres of land valued at $200,000 with a first mortgage of $50,000. Jone's basis is $100,000. *Blackburn* owns a 15-unit apartment house valued at $300,000. His basis in the apartment house is $125,000 and he owes $200,000. Jones has an equity of $150,000, while Blackburn has a $100,000 equity. In order to make the exchange, Blackburn must balance his equity with Jones's. He will do so with a $50,000 cash payment to Jones.

Table 5 shows the tax calculations in these two exchanges. In examining this table, you will notice that in the Smyth-Greenbalm exchange there will be no resulting tax, as the recognized gain for both Smyth and Greenbalm was zero. But look what happened to Jones and Blackburn.

You can use the numbers of your own exchange in place of those shown in table 5 to see just where you will stand in the case of a potential tax. The tax, of course, will be calculated on the taxable-gain portion by using the current capital-gains calculations. As these are apt to change from year to year, consult your tax accountant for the current method. Under the new 1981 tax law, the maximum capital-gains tax is 20% of the gain. Yours, however, may be less than that. The taxable gain is to be added to your income and your total adjusted income applied to the tax tables for your year.

Getting Into Exchanges

The only way to get into exchanges is to make exchange offers. You don't make exchanges by sitting on your rear waiting for someone to come around and ask *you* if you want to exchange. The best way, I believe, is to find an exchange-minded salesman and then go through a learning process with him or her. All investors who expect to make profits over a long haul, and to reduce or eliminate as much risk as possible, will be continually learning. I know that I feel slighted if I don't learn something every week I am in business. Fortunately, I never feel slighted, as I usually learn something every day. All that learning doesn't always keep me out of trouble, but it sure keeps me from being bored.

TABLE 5
Calculations of Taxable Gain in Exchanges

	Jones	Blackburn	Smyth	Greenbalm
Value of Property Received	$300,000	$200,000	$200,000	$200,000
ADD THE FOLLOWING:				
Cash Received	50,000	0	0	0
Other Boot Received	0	0	0	0
Mortgage Relief	50,000	200,000	0	0
SUBTOTAL	$400,000	$400,000	$200,000	$200,000
SUBTRACT FROM SUBTOTAL:				
Basis at Time of Exchange	$100,000	$125,000	$100,000	$140,000
Amount of Mortgage Assumed	200,000	50,000	0	0
Amount of Cash Paid	0	50,000	0	0
Amount of Other Boot Given	0	0	0	0
GAIN REALIZED	$100,000	$175,000	$100,000	$ 60,000
TO COMPUTE AT THE TAXABLE GAIN:				
(1) Total Mortgages Relieved	$ 50,000	$200,000	$ 0	$ 0
(2) Less Total Mortgages Assumed	200,000	50,000	0	0
(If [2] is greater than [1] put 0 Amount)	0	$150,000	$ 0	$ 0
Less cash paid	0	50,000	0	0
Subtotal	$ 0	$100,000	$ 0	$ 0
Plus Other Noncash Boot Received	0	0	0	0
Plus Cash Received	50,000	0	0	0
RECOGNIZED GAIN	$ 50,000	$100,000	$ 0	$ 0

Taxable Gain is the lower of Gain Realized or Recognized Gain. Note below calculation shows the Gain which is not taxed by virtue of the exchange.

	Jones	Blackburn	Smyth	Greenbalm
GAIN REALIZED	$100,000	$175,000	$100,000	$ 60,000
Less Taxable Gain (Recognized)	50,000	100,000	0	0
GAIN SAVED:	$ 50,000	$ 75,000	$100,000	$ 60,000

The Pitfalls of Exchanges

Frustration is the enemy of the exchanger. There is a lot you can get frustrated about when it comes to exchanges. You will be dealing with people who think you are out to take them—or, at best, will pretend they don't understand anything. You will have to deal with double-pricing situations, with hotshot salesmen who will tell you that a five-story building is a seven-story high-rise. You will get turned on only to find that what was described as a beautiful home by the sea just washed out at high tide.

But, as Elbert Hubbard once said, "There is no failure except in no longer trying." When it comes to exchanges, you have to keep trying. Your day and the right deal will come along.

From an economic point of view, you need to watch your tax laws and your own tax situation when it comes to the exchange at hand. It is possible that you will be better off making a sale and then purchasing, accepting the tax liability in that year, rather than allowing your old basis to carry over to the new property. You see, if your old basis in that $200,000 property is only $25,000 you would have a $175,000 gain in that year. Even with a 20% maximum tax on capital gains, you would have a $35,000 tax to pay. However, if you also had a major loss in the same year—say $175,000 worth—you might prefer a sale in which your losses would offset the gain. You could then step up your basis in a new property, beginning fresh rather than passing along a $200,000 value with only $25,000 of basis.

My suggestion is that you don't try to be an expert on tax ramifications (unless that is your business of course) and that you hire the services of a professional in tax law and taxes.

33

The "It's Not Mine but You Can Have It" Exchange

WHEN you find a seller who will approach an exchange as a beneficial move on his part, or a seller who will take an exchange as a part of the deal, you are on your way to building equity for yourself prior to the deal and making a cashless transaction. You can do this *even if you don't own the property you are going to exchange.* In fact, you can make more exchanges at greater profit if you don't own the property in the first place.

What you are going to do is this: Find out what the seller wants or will take in the form of other property; then go out and locate something that is similar to or exactly meets that requirement and borrow it for a while until you make the deal.

Let's say you are interested in buying a small office building you have located in your town. The property is offered at $300,000 and has an existing first mortgage of $110,000 and second mortgage of $55,000. You know you can refinance the building, generating around $210,000 net after mortgage costs.

The seller started the negotiations saying he wanted all cash to the existing financing, but in the end game agreed to take a minimum of $100,000 cash and hold some paper. The seller confided to you (or your agent) that he needed the cash to buy some vacant land on which to build some apartment buildings.

Armed with this knowledge, you now see a possibility of finding some apartment land and making an exchange. You search around for a few days and find a tract of land that is zoned for business and commercial use, but can also be used for apartment sites. The property has not sold as a business site because it is a poor site for that kind of use, but it's ideal for apartment construction. The property owner will sell the land for $75,000 on easy terms.

The fact that the land is not labeled "apartment property" (it's zoned for business) causes many investors to forget that labels in real estate mean very little. It is what you can do with the land that is important, not the specific category of the zoning. Most zoning (get to know yours) comes in grades: business, industrial, commercial, residential, etc., in varying orders of classification. In many parts of the world the building regulations permit a "down use": for example, the right to build apartments on a business-zoned property, but not the right to build a business on apartment land.

Okay, you have an owner of some vacant business land who can't sell it, but wants to sell it. You then offer him a "soft deal" that ties up the land so you can make your exchange on the small office building you wanted in the first place.

You set this up by telling the owner of the land that you will buy the land giving him $5,000 down and a $70,000 second mortgage on the office building across town. You tell the owner that you are about to refinance the office building and it will have a new first mortgage of $215,000. You set the interest on the second mortgage lower than the market rate because the seller of the vacant land would rather have some cash coming in than keep the cash-eating land.

You now go back to the seller of the small office building and tell him that you will do the following:

1. Give him $25,000 cash.
2. Take over his existing financing—subject to your obtaining the new financing mentioned.

3. Give him the apartment land (which can also be used for commercial and business use as a bonus). The value of this land you peg at $100,000.
4. Give him a personal note signed by you in the amount of $10,000.

If he accepts this, you will then apply for the loan you want of $215,000, which, less $5,000 in loan costs, will net you $210,000. You will use this to pay off the existing mortgages on the small office building, a total of $165,000 (a first of $110,000 and a second of $55,000). This will leave you with $45,000.

But wait, you have to pay the seller of the land $5,000, so that also comes out of the $45,000, leaving you with $40,000. You then take another $25,000 from that and give it to the office-building owner. You end up owning the small office building and have $15,000 left over for fix-up—or for further negotiations if this deal didn't fly on the above-described offer. In short, you have another $15,000 to play with to make your cashless deal work.

Even if you had not been able to increase the value of the vacant land, you were putting yourself in a far better economic position than by trying to buy the office building with the usual financing. The landowner, after all, was willing to take soft paper, which enabled you to maximize your leverage of the office building with some mortgage at below-market value.

Finesse in the Use of This Technique

Every time you buy real estate, there are four things you should do to ascertain whether the seller can be enticed into this kind of transaction.

1. *Get to know the goals of the seller.* In the previous example, knowing that the seller wanted to build apartments was what started you off on this tangent.
2. *Take a quick look around the marketplace to see if you can help the seller meet the desired goal.* Sometimes the seller has picked out exactly what he wants to buy. If you can find out what it is and then talk to the owner of that property, you might find you can still do the "soft paper" deal shown in the previous example. You do not want to be hunting for pie in the sky, however. Some

sellers set unrealistic goals—and since even they won't find them, why should I spend my time looking for them?

3. *Tie up the "borrowed property" before making the offer to the seller of what you want.* You must have control of a property before offering it in an exchange. If you have only a loose deal based on a handshake, it may not survive to the closing. Remember, good intentions are offset by many things, and greed is the number one cause of death of real-estate deals.

4. *Understand that "ideal" doesn't exist, so don't overlook other alternatives.* Perhaps the seller would build office buildings instead of apartments. If there aren't any apartment sites you can tie up to use in an exchange, try something else. Any property owner can and will take *something* in exchange. As long as you can "buy" a property on soft paper and move that paper onto the property you are going to buy, you have something to exchange. In this way you can generate a "cash" equivalent of property equity. You might tie up a North Carolina lot by agreeing to give the owner $20,000 (full price) in a soft mortgage on the $75,000 duplex you are buying. If you can give the seller of the office building the $20,000 lot as your total down payment, then you've just made another cashless deal.

Pitfalls of the Borrowed-Property Exchange

The usual pitfalls—lack of control over the property you are dealing with being the major one. Another is that the opportunity to make this cashless deal can move you into heavier debt than the property will support, but this is less of a danger here than in some of the other techniques we've examined. Using a soft mortgage deal as a part of the total financing structure will aid you in the economics of the buy, but that may not be enough. You must watch your *pro forma* carefully and not kid yourself about what you can do.

34

The Moon (The Future-Event Down Payment)

FOR MANY SELLERS, the thought of taking a future event as a down payment might be just the thing to make your cashless deal work. This technique can be used when a buyer plans to have something in the future that can be offered now to a seller. A developer getting ready to build a condominium can easily offer a seller a future unit in the building as a part of the down payment. A home builder can do the same, giving the seller an opportunity to own a home in a project to be built.

As happens with many of the other techniques, the ability to move some of the purchase price (seller's equity, really) off to another property enables the investor to get maximum use of cash generated in financing. Sometimes, moving all or a portion of the seller's equity to this future event enables you to give him cash in addition to that event.

EXAMPLE: Simone is a top builder in South Florida. She and her husband used to build high-rise condos; now, after her husband's death, she concentrates on low-rise, garden-type condominium apartments. Usually she has several projects going at the same time, and she finds she can offer sellers of land sites future units in her developments as a part of the deal. She and other developers who use this technique have long since recognized that sellers will frequently take a future unit on the site they are selling rather than an instant unit across town. They do so out of sentiment for the site they owned.

One such deal looked like this. Simone needed a site for around 50 units. Her broker located a nice site in the Tampa area at a price of $500,000. As this was only $10,000-per-unit land cost, and as the units were going to sell for an average of $100,000, the ratio of land price to selling price was well in the profit range for Simone's development. In fact, for sites like this she has been known to pay as high as 15% of the end price of the units.

Like most builders, however, Simone doesn't like to tie up cash in the land. The deal she would work out with the seller, then, would have to be as highly leveraged as possible.

The broker, knowing how Simone operated, structured the deal with a local lender to place a mortgage on the land in the amount of $350,000, with the seller getting this cash and taking two units in the completed building to make up the balance. The two units would be worth a minimum of $200,000, which is a premium of $50,000 to the seller of the land. However, as the apartment building would not be completed for nearly three years, the $50,000 bonus really amounted to interest of about 14% per year compounded.

Because the broker had brought in a lender to lend the $350,000 on a mortgage instead of the seller, and as the seller was getting $350,000 in cash, the deal worked out nicely for everyone. Simone was able to pay a higher interest rate on the $350,000 mortgage than she might have otherwise (which enticed the private lender into the deal in the first place), and Simone got in on a cashless deal. Had the seller taken *three* future units, Simone could have kept some of the cash herself. As it was, the seller got a lot of cash, but none of it was Simone's.

Giving a future, then, is an ideal way to start out your negotiations if you are a dealer in future events. Land developers turning farmland into residential subdivisions can frequently make the same kind of deal. Their futures are vacant residential lots, which, if tied up early enough by the tract seller, can prove to be excellent investments.

Page owned 100 acres of flatlands in Georgia. Along came a developer, ready to make a deal to turn the land into golf courses and homesites. Page didn't need cash, so he decided it was better to take 25% of the total value of the 100 acres in future lots—at a discount of 15% off the average sales price of the first ten lots sold to the public. Since Page was going to hold what would amount to 100% financing until he got his lots, he insisted that the buyer blanket the mortgage with some property owned near Atlanta. The developer made a cashless deal, Page made a secure deal with ample value behind his mortgage, and the future profits and annual interest on the mortgages Page held were to be substantial.

Finesse in Making the Future-Event Deal Count Big

Nothing is better than resting on your laurels when it comes to making future deals work for you. The success of your past performance will give a seller some idea of what can be expected in the future.

If you are just starting out, you can overcome much of the seller's objections by using the blanket-mortgage approach to secure the seller's 100% mortgage. In this way you give a future but secure the balance of the deal with a blanket mortgage. If you screw up and blow the "future," at least the seller has some other property to look to as security on what you owe him.

The presentation of this kind of deal is very important, so you must spend a lot of time in its preparation. If you are using a broker, you will be ahead of the game as the broker can tout your past performances, whereas, if you did so, you'd sound like a braggart. Modesty is important to some people, and one thing that will turn off a seller quicker than anything is the guy who tells everyone how important he is. "When I say I'll deliver, that's good enough—you can count on my word. . . . A handshake from me is like gold. . . . I'm so important that just doing business with me should impress you. . . ." This kind of person makes me as sick as he does you (unless you use this technique and have just finished patting yourself on the back).

If you have a good record of past performances, let your broker document them. A package of your sales brochures; some photographs; a history of what has happened, showing, best of all, the list prices of all the units on opening day and what those same units are selling for now, years or months later. If you have made "future" deals before, it might be interesting to show how the sellers in those other transactions came out—assuming they came out on top of the game.

If you have to fall back on a blanket mortgage to cover a lack of past performance, then make sure you have well documented the property the seller is going to get as additional security. If as a developer you are in need of some land released from any mortgages to begin development, make sure you cover this with the blanket approach, too. You are making a cashless deal here and need to cover all your bases.

The Six Keys to Making "Future" Deals Work

1. *Never offer the future deal until you have tested the seller's motivation.* This means sticking your foot into the water to see how cold it is and whether you really want to swim after all. When it comes to negotiating your deals, you must invest some time and force the seller to invest some of his time as well or you will find the "no" given far too easily. It is possible that there are other forms of buying that will be better for you than this technique—and if you want the property, you want to buy it at the best terms for you—but the seller will never say yes until he is motivated to do so.

2. *Get some press coverage on your past abilities.* I don't mean you have to have actual media coverage, but if you have some past clippings from the newspaper, use them as part of the package your broker gives to the seller. (If the article is about your release on parole, then forget it.) Remember, never talk about yourself—have others talk about you. Place an ad if you have to, however, to get into the paper.

3. *Give yourself ample negotiating room in the "future" offered.* You don't want to promise something in two years that you won't be able to deliver for five years. It's always possible to get caught in some delay so be sure you have covered yourself at the outset by having a "buyout" provision where you can substitute cash for the future event. It is a toss-up as to whether you should make that a unilateral event with the option going to either you or the seller.

4. *Make sure your price or discount for the future event is fair to you and the seller.* At this stage you aren't worrying about the seller; but if you have a buyout provision and the seller wants to take cash, you can be trapped into losing on something you had planned on making a profit on. On the other hand, if you are offering a future unit and set a price now for that unit and have delays in building, you might find the unit costs twice as much to build as you presold it for. It's best to give a discount on the average of the first few sales to the public as a tie to actual market value at the time you actually start selling. The seller taking the "future" will, of course, want to have a fixed price set now.

5. Use the blanket-mortgage technique to lock up wishy-washy sellers. Review chapter 30 on blanket techniques to refresh your memory of how they are used. There are many other ways to bring the seller in line with your future deal by connecting the future to some other event—such as an exchange, a pyramid of another mortgage, and the like.

6. *Think Options and Alternatives.* This is a must with every kind of technique you will work with. Your final deal and the technique you use may not resemble any of the examples I've shown in this book. Your own unique situation will require you to adapt the technique or techniques to fit the mood and motivations of the seller with your needs and abilities. Almost all the techniques in this book can be used in conjunction with each other.

Pitfalls of Using Futures to Make Your Deal

From the investor's point of view, there are only two real pitfalls to watch out for. The first is pre-fixing the value of the "future," and the second is giving too much of a blanket.

The first is simple—I've already discussed the importance of making sure you don't get caught giving the seller a future that ends up costing you far more than you anticipated. Keep in mind that some futures can come from other properties and not the one you are buying. If you are building across town, you can offer a unit there—or perhaps it isn't a unit at all but a percent of the profit when you sell something. Futures are anything that hasn't happened yet. Just be darned sure you don't have to reach into your savings later to cover something you didn't count on.

The second is a real danger if things go wrong. The blanket mortgage you may have to give the seller to entice him into the "future" deal will tie up some other property you own. In this way the seller is covered and if there never is a future (because he has foreclosed on your project and you, too), he will not be left holding the bag. You don't want to tie up a million-dollar property just to blanket a $500,000 property you want to buy with a "future" deal. Try to match the security requirement to the needs of the seller. If you feel you can make the deal fly with only a $100,000 additional security, then put one-tenth of the million-dollar property up as security. Always keep the "release provision" in tip-top review in making your blanket mortgage. This provision enables you to release the extra security from the blanket when you do something spelled out in the mortgage. That something might be a payment of part of the money owed, or simply completion and delivery of the future event as promised. These release provisions are essential to you in working a wrap, so don't overlook them.

35

The Plant Sale

"FOR SALE, two oak trees, five elm trees, and one hundred assorted bushes and shrubs. U'dig'em."

The first time I heard of this technique I was in Jacksonville, Florida, giving a seminar on creative real-estate investing. The investor who told me about this technique had apparently used it successfully half a dozen times.

"It's quite simple," he said. "I look around for properties in the older parts of town. You know, where the landscaping has matured and what trees that are there are full-grown and valuable. I make sure the property is sound in value and that I can do something with the buildings on the site. I make as good a deal as I can, trying to keep the cash down as low as possible, or the cash I need to close at a minimum. I then sell the landscaping for the cash I need, closing on the real estate at the same time."

His explanation of this technique was so simple and clear, I could think of no way better to give it to you. In the examination of the technique, however, there are many elements that need greater study, as this opportunity often slips by many investors. In fact, I've seen what should have been smart buyers end up having unwanted or unneeded trees removed at great cost when those same plants could have brought a profit.

Let's take a look at two examples of this technique, where each investor will use the plant sale for a different result.

Harper was a house buyer who fixed houses up then sold them. His whole philosophy was to find property that was run-down but in a good part of town. He knew that most buyers associated small, young trees and shrubs with newness. He also knew that many properties in the older parts of town were so overgrown with older trees and shrubs that he would have to cut out a lot of them just to paint and fix up his newly purchased houses.

Knowing all of this, Harper gave high points to properties that had landscaping which was (1) removable and (2) salable. Harper knew that at worst he could get a trade-off at the local plant nursery when it came time to relandscape the refurbished property, but at best he could sell off some of the better and rarer plants at a profit.

To make sure he didn't overlook any prime opportunities, Harper visited several leading landscapers in town. He selected them after phone conversations with about two dozen listed in the Yellow Pages. He wanted to be sure he was dealing with large-scale landscapers for major developers, hotels, hospitals, airports, and the like—clients who wanted the finished job to *look* finished, not like something that would have to grow for ten years to look good. Such landscapers would need larger, mature plants, not the potted house-plant variety.

In visiting these landscapers, he found out what kind of plants they could use, making a list of them and, if possible, taking a photo of the plant itself. He also got an idea of what the landscaper would pay for a matured plant. He was then ready to start looking for a property. Of course, plants weren't the primary criterion for his real-estate transactions: If he couldn't fix up a property and make a profit, he didn't buy it, plants or no plants. But the sale of the plants helped Harper make greater profits, and that he liked.

Harper was able, on some occasions, to make cashless deals because he recognized the value of the plants. He knew whom to call when he saw a display plant that would look fantastic in the lobby of a hotel under construction across town.

Evan, on the other hand, was using every dime he had or earned to make ends meet. He was plowing rents from the homes and apartment buildings he was buying back into the fix-up of these properties, not with the idea of selling them but with the idea of increasing the rents on the properties. This was great, but it kept Evan property-poor and constantly out of cash.

His need, then, was to buy without cash, so cashless forms of investing were the most important part of his program. He wasn't interested in the fast turnover that Harper looked for, so could take properties in less-than-prime areas and look for a longer-haul picture. If he could rent a property for enough to cover the mortgage, pay the expenses, and put a few dollars aside for the property's improvement, Evan would more than likely buy the property.

Thus, for Evan, the idea of getting some instant cash out of a property, to use as a down payment on the very same property, was not only ideal, it was fantastic.

He took a night course in landscaping at the local public high school, and even took out a city occupational license as a contractor and landscaper. This cost him about $25 a year, but allowed him to buy supplies and plants to fix up his buildings at builders' and landscapers' prices, which were often well below the price the public would pay.

In going through this course, and in later dealings with the landscapers in town, he learned, as did Harper, what plants the landscapers would pay premiums for and how to go about selling them.

In selecting properties, Evan looked first at the area, to see if he had any interest in owning there. His primary concern, of course, was the rental market: If there were a lot of vacancies in the area at what he felt was market or below-market rent, then he didn't want to touch the area unless the price and terms of the property would allow him to grossly undercut the vacant rental offerings.

The next thing he looked for was plants. When Evan saw a property whose front and side yards were filled with salable plants, he knew he had a gold mine. He would use the promised cash from the landscaper as part of the down payment even if he had to split-fund the deal with some of his own cash up front (he'd not pay a creditor for a month to get that cash), then repay himself when the plants had been sold.

Finesse in Using the Plant Sale

There are five key elements in this technique that you need to keep in mind.

1. *Know your plants.* When you start out in this technique, you will not be as familiar with the plant market as you will be later on. It will help if you cultivate (excuse the pun) the friendship of a landscaper and have him take a look at an intended purchase you think is full of valuable plants. Look also for local courses in horticulture and landscaping as additional ways to add to your knowledge of plants and the marketing of them.

2. *Learn what plants you can do without on the site.* Unknowingly selling off valuable plants can cause your newly purchased property to go down in value—and that's cutting off your nose to spite your green thumb. In this age of high electric bills, that well-placed shade tree might mean far more to the building you are buying than the cash you will get in selling it. However, thick trees blocking the cool summer breeze will have to go, and why not at a profit, too?

3. *Learn which landscapers you can trust.* This is sort of like finding out which heart specialist will have the highest success in your own open-heart operation in advance of the operation, but it can be done if you simply ask around. Make sure you are dealing with the guy who does a lot of expensive work, because he can afford the expensive plants.

4. *Don't overlook the grass.* Today, sod is very expensive, and sod growers have machines that will pick up a whole yard in a few hours. If you are putting in wood decks and stonework and that sort of thing, or if you anticipate that workmen going around the property for a few weeks while you fix it up will kill the grass, then sell the grass first. Granted this is sometimes more difficult than selling the plants, but it might mean another couple of thousand dollars, and that might put you into the profit range earlier.

5. *Don't try to move plants yourself.* If you don't have the right tools and know what you are doing, you can easily kill a plant—and dead plants don't bring in any cash.

Of course, the real finesse is in tying up the property so that you can get a price on the plants. You don't ever want to spend much time fooling around with any property you can't tie up first.

Once you have made the seller an offer that both he and you can live with, you can move ahead. Your offer, by the way, will have some provision permitting you to inspect the grounds to ascertain what plants must be moved to accomplish the needed repairs, remodeling, and improvements. It will take you about a week to ascertain the potential profit, if any, from the plants—or at least what a landscaper will do for you in exchange for the trees and plants you want to get rid of. Do *not* tell the seller that you need a week to find out how much you can get for the plants. The seller may have a sentimental attachment to the apple tree in the front yard (just where you want to put a new driveway) and if he thought you were going to sell it or cut it down, he might find some reason to object to a term or condition of the agreement. Remember, George Washington may have sold the cherry tree he cut down— for the dollar he used to throw across the Potomac.

Okay, step one is to tie up the property. Step two is to get a quote from two or more landscapers on buying the plants you want to sell. Step three is to tie the closings of both sales together so you can get the cash you need out of one for the other.

This often is very difficult. The seller doesn't want to give you the property until he has gotten his cash, and the landscaper doesn't want to give you cash until he gets the plants. If you can do what Evan does and simply not pay someone else that week to get the cash for the other, then that's okay—if you don't get caught on the short end of the stick. The best way, of course, is to tell the seller that you would like to start with the landscape work before closing. Naturally you will assure the seller that you will pay for the work done (that needs to be paid for). If the seller balks at this, then try to get the landscaper to put some cash up front. Once you have a working relationship with the landscapers, they will be more inclined to do this. The first deal is always the hardest.

You might try a short-term loan. . . .

The Pitfalls of the Plant Sale

There are only three pitfalls to watch out for. But they can get you if you're not careful.

1. *The mortgage that covers the plants.* Most mortgages do not cover landscaping, but as the plant-sale technique gets around, you will find lenders getting smarter. Read the mortgages on the property carefully to be sure they do not encumber all improvements to the buildings and land. If they do, you will have to get approval from the mortgagee to relandscape the property. Have a simple sketch drawn up showing what you are going to do to the site. As you will be planting new (but much smaller and cheaper) plants in the right kinds of locations, you don't have to worry about the sketch looking barren. The person who reviews the sketch and gives the final approval probably won't even look at the property. A few photos showing how cluttered the existing landscaping looks won't hurt, though, just to make sure the guy doesn't drive by and fall in love with the live oak you are going to sell for $1,500.

2. *The landscaper who digs a hole you fall into.* "*I know I said I would give you fifteen thousand for all those trees and that yard of grass—but that was last week,* and now I'm just not sure I can afford more than three thousand. Take it or leave it.*"*

This kind of conversation can make your stomach turn over, and unfortunately it can happen. The bigger the landscaper, the better your chance of making a sale, but anyone can run into a tight situation and fail to live up to an agreement. A deposit from the landscaper at the time you agree to sell the plants to him might help, but you need some insurance. Your insurance is a quick closing and an out if something goes wrong. Since time works against you in these deals (the landscaper no longer needs the plants), you should be ready to move fast. There is no room for hesitation in this kind of deal, and if you are the softhearted kind, then it's best to move on to another technique.

3. *A black thumb and no plant smarts.* In selling anything of potential value, it is essential that you have some idea of that value. A while back I went to a football game—the Dolphins against Pittsburgh in the Orange Bowl. I went down with a friend at the last moment, without a ticket but anticipating I could buy one at the stadium from a fan who had an extra one. (The night was dark and rainy, and that usually causes wives to chicken out.) Instead, I found tickets being scalped for $75 and up. I decided to wait until the kickoff and positioned myself out in the VIP parking lot, away from the crowds. As people ran past, I simply asked, running alongside, if they had any tickets, holding the exact price in my hand ($14.00). I

had two offered in the first three minutes. One seller, anxious to get into the stadium and not miss the kickoff, was willing to take only half the price of the ticket (I gave him the full price as I knew I would be sitting next to him). The ticket was on the 50-yard line.

This is an example of knowing what was going on. I knew the market. They didn't. I was willing to wait until the last minute before the kickoff, at which point sellers were anxious to get into the game and didn't want to haggle.

You should not try to play the landscaping game until you invest some time in learning about plants—what they are good for, which are valuable and which aren't. You don't want to be caught with extra tickets (plants) and the game (real-estate closing) about to start and not have any room to negotiate.

When you acquire some expertise, you can turn that black thumb green.

36

The Home-Loan
Down-Payment Caper

WHEN INVESTING in real estate, you will find that the easiest mortgage to obtain is the home loan. This goes for new first mortgages as well as second mortgages. Because of this, many investors find that when they need to generate cash to make a worthwhile investment, this cash can often be obtained through the financing, or refinancing, of their homes. This is important, of course, if you have a home that you can refinance. But even if you don't, it is possible to include a home in your investment portfolio *for this very purpose.*

Therefore, I will approach this technique from the standpoint of both the investor who has a home to use and the investor who does not presently have a home, to show how the technique can benefit both.

First the investor *with* a home.

Ginger is a flight attendant for one of the international airlines. She loves her work and has enough seniority to pick and choose the flights she wants so that she can have sufficient time to work at fixing up her real-estate purchases. She has a live-wire salesman working on her behalf, scouting out properties for her to buy, and she is constantly making offers. Most of the time Ginger is able to make cashless transactions by using pyramiding and refinancing of the properties she buys. But sometimes she finds something that she wants to have and a seller who won't respond to her usual techniques.

One such example was an industrial complex that backed up to one of the local private airports. She realized it would be an ideal place for the many pilots she knew to store their small weekend aircraft. The seller, however, wouldn't take a pyramid, and the existing mortgages on the industrial building were at such low interest that it would not benefit Ginger to refinance them. So she looked over her portfolio to see if there were any other properties she could refinance. She found that the only property she owned that didn't already have a maximum loan-to-value ratio was her own home, but she had worked hard to pay off the mortgage on that property and had sworn to herself that she would never have a mortgage on her own home. Many investors feel this way, and, for some, it is a sound way to go. But Ginger had a better use for the capital she had tied up in her home, and when she tried other ways to get the industrial building, she soon realized that the only way to get the needed cash was to put the mortgage on the home.

She didn't need as much cash as she could generate from a new mortgage, so the loan-to-value ratio was going to be less than 50/50. This meant that she would have some bargaining power with the lender to cut the right kind of mortgage. In essence, she was able to make a better deal than she had anticipated.

The story, of course, has a happy ending. Once she owned the industrial building, paying the seller cash to the mortgage on that property, she was able to rent the building out to the airline pilots after she formed an aviation club specially for them. As the rent on the building was far more than the old tenant had paid, the value of the new property went up quite fast. The best part of the story is that Ginger was able to pay off the mortgage on her house in short order (in the loan negotiations, she had insisted on a clause permitting early payoff without penalty).

237

When you finance your home or obtain a new mortgage on the property, you want to gain as much leverage on the terms of the mortgage as possible. Savings-and-loan associations are, of course, your primary source of funds for this kind of loan. Your local savings-and-loan is a business much like any other—they have a lot of rules and regulations governing the way they act and controlling much of what they do. But one thing many investors overlook is the fact that these institutions are in a very competitive business and will thus make concessions and offer deals that the competition may not. Because of this, it is essential that you shop your loans, going to at least three loan institutions in the attempt to get the best deal.

You should approach a savings-and-loan association with a clear understanding of what you want in the way of loan amount (net to you after loan costs), interest on the loan, and term of years. Your desire for prepayment rights without penalty must also be clearly stated in your loan request. This loan request should be presented to the loan officer of the savings-and-loan association. It should follow the outline given you in this chapter and must be brief and concise. The association will have its own loan-application forms and financial statements, which you must also have filled out and attached to the loan request.

It is helpful to have some rapport with a loan officer at each of the savings-and-loan associations you plan to deal with. This is best established well in advance of a need for their services, and I recommend that all investors—as well as real-estate brokers and salesmen—maintain a rapport with these lenders on a permanent basis. It doesn't take much effort on your part to stop by a loan association and meet some of these loan officers. Tell them that you are going into real-estate investing and hope to use their services in the near future. In the meantime, you would appreciate their explaining the policy of their institution so you will be familiar with the applications and procedures for obtaining a loan. Loan officers will be pleased to have the opportunity to set up what might be a good account for them in the future. A frequent phone call or occasional visit to each will maintain that rapport until the time when you need their assistance. When you do make the professional call and present them with your loan request, they will have a personal stake in your success with the loan committee.

It is a good idea to use the following outline when you make any loan application. This outline is as effective for a multimillion-dollar loan as it is for a $10,000 loan. Remember, however, that the greater the loan amount requested, the more detailed the backup data should be.

Outline for Mortgage Loan Request

I. Description of the Property
   A. General description
   B. Legal description
   C. Location
   D. Location sketch
   E. Location benefits
   F. Aerial photo
   G. General statistics
      1) Demographics
      2) Average rent
      3) Traffic count
   H. General site data
      1) Size and square feet and land and site coverage
      2) Use of site
      3) Zoning
      4) Available utilities
      5) Access
      6) Sketch of lots sharing building location
      7) Survey
   I. Site disadvantages and drawbacks
   J. Land value
      1) Estimated value of site
      2) Comparable land sales and values

II. Description of the Improvements
   A. General description of the improvements
   B. General statistics
      1) Date built
      2) Year remodeled
      3) Type of construction
      4) Other structural and mechanical data
      5) Floor area: living, covered, garage, balcony, etc.
      6) Parking available
      7) Other general data
   C. Sketch
      1) Show sketch for each floor.
         (a) If income property, show apartments and rents.

        (b)   If residential home, show appointments in construction.

        (c)   Draw to approximate scale and show only basic dimensions.

   2)   Building plans (for new construction or as backup on refinanced property)

D.   Personal property in building
   1)   Inventory of mechanical personal property.
   2)   Inventory of furniture and fixtures which are personal property
   3)   Values in a summary

E.   General statement of condition of improvements and personal property

F.   Replacement cost of structure
   1)   Original cost
   2)   Replacement cost

G.   Comparable sales of improved property of similar nature

H.   The economics of any income-producing improvement (actual)
   1)   Income
   2)   Expenses
   3)   Net operating income
   4)   Economic value
   5)   Rent roll
   6)   Sample lease
   7)   Past records of income and expense

I.   Opinion of the economics
   1)   Relationship to average square-foot rent for area
   2)   Average current rent per square foot in the building
   3)   General opinion of income and expenses
   4)   Estimate of future for type of rental

J.   Change in income as result of loan (if loan is being used to make changes in the building)
   1)   Change contemplated
   2)   Effect on income
   3)   *Pro forma* of income and expenses after changes
   4)   New evaluation of value based on increased income

K.   General summary of value
   1)   Land value
   2)   Replacement value
   3)   Personal-property value
   4)   Estimated present value
   5)   Economic value at present income
   6)   Economic value at projected income

III. The Person
    A.   Name
    B.   Address
    C.   Occupation
    D.   General data
    E.   Net worth
    F.   Supporting documents
        1) Association's loan application
        2) Association's financial-statement form
        3) References
        4) Position of employment
        5) Verification of salary
        6) Estimate annual earnings
        7) Previous year's IRS form 1040
        8) Credit report of applicant
        9) Other forms requested for applications by S&L
IV. The Loan Request
    A.   The amount of loan requested
    B.   The term of years requested for payback
    C.   The interest-rate maximum
    D.   The other terms and conditions of the loan requested

When you use this outline, do not be tempted to expound in great, superfluous detail. Often this information will take little more than five or six neatly typed pages—not including the sketches and backup data, of course. If there is something in the outline that simply does not apply to your situation, leave it out. If you're not sure whether it applies, put it in.

A Loan Is a Loan Is a Loan?

No, it isn't. All loans are different, but they do share the same end result when they are not paid back. Thus, while you should not refuse to consider financing your home, you should choose the option most economically beneficial to you. If you can borrow the needed cash at 14% on your home instead of 19% on the building you want to buy, the choice should be clear.

Using the Home Loan When You Don't Have a Home

This gets a little more tricky, as you might imagine. First of all, if you are trying to buy a property such as a vacant lot or a vacant industrial building, or some other difficult-to-finance property, you might want to tie that purchase to the purchase of a single-family home at the same time. This is one of those situations where it is sometimes easier to buy two properties at the same time than one.

Assume you want to buy a nice vacant lot as an investment. You know that, due to its commercial use and prime location in the path of growth, you will see a great rise in value over the next few years. The owner of the lot says he will take the price you have negotiated him down to, which is $50,000. However, he will take this price only if he gets $15,000 cash and can hold the balance in a purchase-money mortgage on the lot. This is great, except you don't have the $15,000 cash.

So you look for a free-and-clear house that will fit into your investment portfolio. You find one and, after some preliminary negotiations, learn that the seller of the home will take $75,000 for the property and will hold some paper, but he must get at least $25,000 in cash. Of course, you don't have the $25,000 in cash, either, so do you give up? No. In fact, you've just made the deal go together, because:

1. You know you can finance the house for an easy $60,000 through any of several savings-and-loan associations. You know this not because you are clairvoyant but because you have called some of your loan officer buddies and have picked their brains and have the up-to-date scoop on what their associations will do on this property.
2. You have tied up the two properties with subject-to-financing agreements and have some control over the destiny of the property owners.
3. The economics of the deal work if you make one change—which shouldn't be that hard to do. What you need to do is go back to the lot owner and ask him if instead of holding the $35,000 mortgage on the lot you are buying, he wouldn't prefer to hold a mortgage on the home you have (you don't add "under contract") across town. You show the lot owner a photo of the home, even drive him over and show him the place. You can say someone else is living in the home now but you will be moving in soon (or renting it to someone else). If the lot owner takes the switch, then you are all but set.

Next you go to the home owner and tell him that you will give him a $50,000 mortgage on the vacant lot and since it will be a first mortgage, wouldn't he like that better?

If each of these sellers will allow this switch of security, you don't have to offer anything else and you still have some cash up your sleeve. You are going to borrow $60,000 on the house, so, even with $2,000 of loan costs, you will have $58,000 to work with. So far you have to give the lot owner $15,000 and the home owner $25,000—a total of $40,000. The remaining $18,000 will go into your pocket if you have made the mortgage swap without any further cash outlay. To make the swap, however, you might have to give the lot owner another $5,000 cash, and the homeowner another $10,000 cash at closing. You still have made a cashless deal and have $3,000 in your pocket.

When making the above deal, follow the rules.

1. Never tell the other party that you have just contracted to buy this property and will give him the mortgage on it.
2. Use a broker to do your negotiating so you won't be confronted with direct questions you don't want to answer.
3. You can fall back on the blanket and give the remaining holdout a blanket mortgage on both properties.

The Pitfalls of Financing Your Home—The One You Have or the One You Are About to Get

There are no more pitfalls than usual. In fact, if you use the motivations of the sellers, the deal is pretty easy to do. You don't have the fluctuation of choice in any kind of cashless deal that you have when you walk in with all cash, but in these transactions the idea is to *generate cash* to give you added flexibility of choice. Since this is the objective, use it to your benefit by buying something you want but can't get.

37

Barter Your Craft in
a Cashless Society

LONG BEFORE money was invented, people did things in exchange for other benefits. Today, as in ancient times, the barter of one's craft is an ideal method of cashless investing. A craft, by the way, is a job you can perform for someone rather than some merchandise you might manufacture. The doctor or dentist has a craft that is frequently bartered within their own professions for like services. The plumber (sometimes a more highly paid professional than the first two mentioned), because of the realty orientation of his profession, might find more opportunities for cashless real-estate investing.

As I go through this chapter, you will find that you not only can barter your own craft, *you can barter someone else's craft* for your cashless real-estate deals.

First, your own craft.
Peter is a carpenter. He works about 45 hours a week at his job, but is free on the weekends. He used to work from time to time for

Evan (remember him?), who bought property to be fixed up for a fast turnover. It was here that Peter got the idea of going into real-estate investing for himself. However, as is frequently the case, Peter didn't have enough cash to make that move.

In a conversation with Evan, Peter learned that cash wasn't necessary. To prove the point, Evan told Peter he would sell him one of the properties Evan wanted to turn over—*for no cash down.* All Peter had to do was agree to work sufficient hours over the next year to pay the down payment. Evan would hold on to the title to the property until Peter had fulfilled the agreement, and then pass the title to him.

Peter thus bartered his craft of carpentry to Evan for some real estate. And once Peter had the property, he could spend some more of his own time and effort to continue to improve the property and enhance its value.

Margo is a tax accountant. She had been renting her office from the same landlord for six years and wished she could buy her own building, but she just never had the cash she thought it would take to buy. Then a developer built a condo office building across the street from where she rented. This was the ideal moment for her: If she could scrape up the down payment, she could own for less than the monthly rent she had been paying. Better to make mortgage payments and build up equity than make rent payments. Besides, she had a strong working knowledge of the new tax laws and knew that she'd be better off owning than renting.

She was able to raise some cash, but in the final negotiations to buy she fell short by $6,000 to meet the total payment. In desperation, she told the developer that she would have to bow out of the deal despite the fact that she wanted to buy very badly.

The developer thought about it for a few moments and then told her that they would work something out. It seemed that ne needed a tax accountant to wrap up the year-end for several of his corporations, and if she would do that work for him and become his tax accountant on a consultant basis, he would let the $6,000 shortage be the retainer against her future fees.

In this way she made her deal. And while it wasn't completely cashless, the important thing was that she bartered her craft and made her investment.

* * *

Alvin is a landscaper who has worked with different developers around town for several years. He is expensive, but the best. He needed a condo to live in, so he offered a new condo project his services on a barter basis. He got the job, even though his actual bid was a lot higher than the next guy's, because Alvin didn't want or need cash—instead he wanted an apartment, and that wasn't cash out of the developers' pockets at the very time they had to count every penny being spent.

Make Side Deals with Your Craft If You Have To

If your craft isn't in demand with the local real-estate sellers, look around for what is and make a swap with them. Let's say your expertise is in the field of hospital development and you want to make a barter deal with a condo developer. You might find that, while the condo developer has no use for that expertise, you can go to someone who uses your services and see if they will swap some of their services to the condo developer.

In this way a dentist might trade his services to the owner of a lumber company for credits on lumber and building materials for a housing developer who has no kids or teeth.

If you have a craft of any kind, you should be in a position to make some kind of barter, either direct or indirect.

"Okay, okay, Cummings, so I'm a cabdriver in Asheville, North Carolina. What can I barter for?"

"What do you do?" I'd ask.

"I told you. Drive cabs."

"But what exactly is it you do? You drive people from place to place. Like a chauffeur, right?"

"Yeah."

"Then perhaps you can barter time as a private chauffeur."

You might find it tough to find a barter, and if this technique looks like it will be harder to make work for you than some of the others, then read the other chapters over for clues. Or change crafts.

How to Barter the Craft of Someone Else for Your Benefit

Okay, cabdriver in Asheville, try this on for size. It is possible that you are still learning what will be a worthy and valuable craft in the future (safecracking, brain surgery, electronic eavesdropping, etc.), but right now you—and many young people without a truly barterable craft—might find it easier to barter with another person's craft. Remember the scrip transactions? Well, much like those, you can make a deal for someone's craft and then exchange that craft or service for what you want.

Sylvia was still a student at the University of Michigan when she decided to buy a duplex. She didn't have much cash, and what cash she had she wanted to use to fix up the property. She negotiated with the owner of a nice property and got the seller to hold a major part of the sales price in the form of a purchase-money mortgage provided that Sylvia did actually spend the money she said she wanted to spend on fixing up the duplex. However, the seller insisted on $5,000 in cash.

Sylvia didn't have an extra $5,000 in cash, so she did some homework. She discovered that the seller owned a company that built schools for various school boards in the state. Sylvia had no craft that would be of economic interest to the seller, but she knew of many jobs that the seller must utilize on a consultant basis.

She checked around and found a very well-recommended structural engineer who had done some work on school projects from time to time, and she offered to buy on "soft paper" some of his time.

Essentially, what Sylvia did was contract for a certain number of hours of consultant time at a rate equal to the usual payment the engineer was accustomed to receiving, except that Sylvia would pay for those hours in the form of a personal note with a spread of payments instead of cash. From the engineer's point of view it made sense, too. The business Sylvia would bring to him would more than likely be business he wouldn't get otherwise, and things were slow enough that he could use the opportunity to strike up new clients who would lay cash later on.

Joel did much the same thing that Sylvia did. Joel discovered that the seller he was dealing with was a mortgage broker who handled

247

several large mortgage bankers. Joel knew that this kind of business uses real-estate appraisers from time to time, so he made a deal with one large appraisal firm whereby he would act as an agent for their time, provided they would take as payment his notes payable over two years at a low interest rate as the time was used.

Clayton was negotiating with a builder to buy a model home and ran into trouble raising the cash to make the down payment. Clayton went out and "bought" some carpenter time from a local carpentry company and bartered that time to the builder. Clayton then paid the carpenters off on a spread-out schedule.

Bartering your own craft or the craft of others gives you the opportunity for maximum leverage in transactions where you have a minimum of cash.

Finesse in Bartering a Craft

The fine points and the pitfalls of craft bartering can be lumped together.

When you barter *your own craft*, there are four things to keep in mind.

1. *Never sell your craft short.* If your usual wage is $30 per hour, then barter it at that same amount. If your services are profitable, then you are dealing at par with the seller: He, too, has a profit in what you are getting.

2. *Don't barter time that you can easily convert to cash.* It would be silly for you to give up actual paying time to barter for something else. If you can convert that time to cash, then negotiate with cash. You will get a discount when dealing with cash.

3. *Do attempt to barter with persons who will need more of your craft than you are offering.* In this way you will have room to negotiate and the opportunity to develop a new client who will pay cash later on.

4. *Don't be too anxious.* It's unwise to take on something you don't want or don't feel comfortable with just to make a barter deal. Make your deals count.

248

When you barter with *another's craft*, there are two things to keep in mind.

1. *Never make your barter offer until you have tied up the craft.* If you want to make a deal with a builder, go around to some of the building trades or suppliers. Tell them you want to use their time services to buy real estate if they will "sell" you those services on soft paper. If they say yes, get that in writing before you go to the builder to make your offer.

2. *Make sure you have sufficient outs in both agreements.* You don't want to have to spend money to supply the craft if the craftsman backs out of the deal. If the builder has agreed to sell you the property with the craft service as part or all of the down payment, and the tradesman or craftsman then goes belly-up and leaves you high and dry, you might have to dig into your pocket. You can protect yourself by having an agreement that you assign to the developer. In essence you have contracted for a craftsman's time, and the agreement between you and that craftsman is for a specific time in work. You assign that agreement to the seller of the real estate you are buying. If the work doesn't get done, you don't have to pay, and the seller has no claim against you—unless you somehow are also at default in the agreement.

38

Float Your Down Payment

PEOPLE who own their own businesses know all about the float. "Float" is the money owed to you from the normal course of your business enterprise. As all of us deal with someone else, there are times when we owe other people. It might be the American Express bill at the end of the month, or the gas company bill, or any of dozens of other monthly bills that come into your mailbox at various times of the month.

The normal outstanding bills many of us have each month add up to a great deal. If the would-be investor has a high monthly payable, it is possible that the needed cash to make investments can come from payments you would normally make on your bills.

Let me explain. It is all a matter of priorities and simple economics. If you need a couple of thousand dollars to complete a real-estate transaction and you have several times that much in monthly payout on bills (both personal and business), you might be able to put some of these creditors off for a while and use that cash to make your deal.

EXAMPLE: Charles ran a nice publishing business. He was expanding his business each month and, while he wasn't making much money, he was paying off his equipment and could see that in a few years he would be on easy street. His monthly payables for supplies, services, rent, electricity and other utilities, and miscellaneous payments—not including his employees' salaries—totaled over $21,000 per month. Part of this was the $3,000 monthly rent for the building he was occupying. Charles knew that he would be far better off if he could buy a building and move into it instead of paying rent.

He found a nice building and, applying some of the techniques shown in this book, nearly made it as a cashless deal. But hard as he tried, he just couldn't quite make the transaction go together with the cash he had. He needed another $5,000 of cold hard cash to entice the seller into taking the other terms offered.

Charles studied his monthly payout and decided he could push several of his creditors to the tune of $5,000 that month. In short, he let the creditors carry the float of $5,000 for a while longer instead of paying them on time.

Now before you cringe and think I've lost my mind about sound investment techniques, let me tell you that many people do far worse to their creditors. I've even know several noninvestors who stopped paying their creditors in favor of playing the horses. The idea isn't to get into the habit of pushing off creditors, only to know what to do if all else fails.

Sometimes the need to own some real estate, as in Charles's case, overshadows the temporary benefits of being an on-time payer of your bills. If the picture in the relatively near future seems to be beneficial and you have a promising economic year ahead, the chances are this technique can be useful to you.

How to Determine Which Creditors Not to Pay Now

This is the tough part of this chapter because the answer is very simple: The creditor you will push will be the one who is least likely to press you when he isn't paid right away. It might be the creditor you have been using the longest. It might even be your best friend. But most certainly it won't be the guy who will slap a high interest rate and credit charges on your account if you are five minutes late with your payments.

Take a look at your monthly flow of bills. If you notice that there are several creditors who are regulars each month and one or more of them (on the monthly basis) will total up to the cash you need to make a deal go together, then consider these creditors as likely choices.

Do You Make a Mortgage Payment?

Sometimes you can find that the lender actually has a heart of semisoft matter. Savings-and-loan associations are well-known softies—they *hate* to foreclose. After your mortgage has gone close to the end of its grace period, you can always send them a check (drawn on a bank in Alaska) to meet the deadline. In this way you will never be in default and can get a month or so behind, using the savings-and-loan to carry your float.

If you need more than one month, or have a short grace period in your loan, you might want to call the loan officer and have a chat. "Frank, I've purchased a building across town and am going to be up against it for a couple of months. I won't be able to meet my payments during this time, but I promise I'll catch up later on. Can we work this out?"

Overlook what he says next, as it is apt to verge on profanity, and then, more softly this time, say: "I understand your point of view, but I am simply under the gun. Is there someone more understanding I can talk to—like the president of the institution for example?"

Are Your Renting?

Rent might be the best bill to forgo—but be sure you know the exact terms of your lease and the penalty for default. If you are going to move out soon anyway, you may not have to worry about being thrown out on the street, but you don't want to incur any heavy legal expenses for the landlord.

To Tell Them or Not to Tell Them—That Is the Question

Should you level with the creditor or not? You could just call him up and say, "Bill, I'm going to be a little short this month—in fact, I won't be able to meet my payment to you at all. But I promise that I will before the end of next month." This is the tack some of you will take no matter what the reason for being short of cash at the end of the month. If, on the other hand, you are absolutely using the cash to buy something—like the building you are to occupy—and to expand your business, then it is better to say: "Bill, we've made a big step this month and I wanted to let you know that we've bought the building over on Main Street. We will be growing bigger and bigger because of this, but we've extended ourselves a little much this month. We want you to know we appreciate your service over the years and hope you will be patient for about four weeks until we can catch up on our payments." Now doesn't that sound better?

Of course, keeping your business to yourself might be a better way for some of you to go. In short, keep your mouth shut about what you are doing and what is going to happen—which is no payments for a month. When the second notice comes in, you can choose to ignore that one, too—waiting out the month then making the payment just one full month late. This works sometimes, and, if you anticipate catching up in a very short time, it might be best to say nothing until pinned against the wall.

Don't Be Intimidated

Some creditors will be on the phone with you the instant your check is five minutes late. If your contract doesn't term minor lateness a default, there is little they can do except try to collect the amount due them. No creditor in his right mind is going to sue you without trying to collect the amount owed him on his own first. Collection companies and lawyers will take too much from the amount collected.

This brings up an interesting side fact. One investor I know (but haven't done business with) pushes off all his creditors and then has his brother-in-law (or someone like that) call up the creditor and offer to make the collection for the low cost of only 15%—and guaranteeing collection within 30 days. This is a real neat game these guys have, as you can calculate. The only problem is, it doesn't allow one to build up any longevity in the community.

253

Finesse in Using Your Float

Don't make a habit of it. It *can* be habit-forming, and, once it starts, it is tough to catch up. Use this technique only as a stopgap measure when all else has failed—and use it sparingly.

Pitfalls

Push the wrong guy too far and you might end up with both legs and both arms in a cast. I'm sure this has happened to some people who aren't around to talk about how well they almost played the game.

39

The Syndicate

WHAT if I told you that you could make all the cashless investments you ever dreamed of anywhere in the world, have any kind of
property almost at your beck and call? Would you be interested?
You might be when I finish this chapter, or you might be turned off
forever to dealing in syndicate territory.

Syndication is an event where you put an investment package together and get others to put up the money. Your reward can vary
from a commission to a healthy percentage of the deal. Your ultimate profit depends on how the property was purchased, how your
percentage was set up, and *time*.

Take a look at two separate syndications.

Guy was from Canada and had been living in south Florida for
about seven years. He went back home from time to time, and each
visit brought new requests from his former business associates for
Guy to locate an investment for them. When I met Guy, he was
sure he had a gold mine but didn't know how to put the gold into
his pockets.

The first thing I told him was to gain control over the situation by
getting the package together and then offering his friends and associates the opportunity to join in. Guy had experienced the result of no

control in the past by telling his friends he knew of something good and having them blow the deal because they could never agree on its potential or make up their mind on what to do. This time, following my suggestions, Guy located a fine investment property and together we wrote up an offer to buy. Guy gave me a check for $1,000 and it became the deposit on a property selling for $350,000. Guy couldn't understand how he could tie up a $350,000 property for only a $1,000, and, on top of that, get the $1,000 back if he was unable to syndicate the property within 45 days. I knew an explanation would not suffice, and the proof was simple explanation enough.

Guy now flew up to Canada, taking with him a package showing the location of the site, the projections for the future, and other data that was accurate, factual, and showed he was serious about his intent to buy this property.

"Fellows," Guy said to his friends, "this is a property I've purchased. I don't close for a few months [90 days, in fact—and only *if* he completed the syndication, but the "fellows" didn't know that] and"—he paused and smiled—"you have always wanted to come in with me on something down in Florida, so here is your opportunity. I've broken this down as shown in the data I've given you. If you want in, let me know by the end of the week."

Guy lost sleep for three nights, but the deal did go together. He didn't put any cash into the deal, and ended up with a piece of the action.

One of my syndications was a 60-acre tract of land in Delray Beach, Florida. The land was purchased for around $700,000 and a few years later sold for around $2 million. My piece of the action was a simple 10% of the profit. Not bad, and, for a syndicator, somewhat conservative and modest. I've seen syndicators take 25% of the sales price right off the top, plus other goodies at the same time. Your ultimate benefit will be whatever the investors will pay, of course—and take it from someone who has been through a lot of headache with syndications: The investors who gripe the most and the loudest will usually be the guys who have nothing to do but find a cause to campaign against, no matter how much money you are making for them.

On the other hand, some people are real gems, and when you are dealing with investors in a big and continual way, you will come across both kinds.

So syndications are the up and down of real-estate investing. They put you into partnerships or other forms of legal encounter and can tie you down, or up, depending on your point of view. But you can make a fortune with them. More on that . . .

How To Put a Syndicate Together

Objective. You must have an objective before anything else. Simple, you say? Not so in reality. Your future goals differ from mine and from those of just about everyone else you will meet. If you are profit-motivated, you will (or should, at least) have a healthy regard for money—not just the making of it but what it can buy, what it will cost to get, and what it will cost you once you have a lot of it.

Far too many energetic people waste their energy on the wrong goals and priorities. Far too many successful people have beat their brains out to get something that in the end, once they had it, they found of no use to them.

Therefore, your objective is crucial to *your* application of any tool of investing. Use any tool wisely and you can build something. But will you like it when you're finished? Only if you chose the right objective.

Do you want to build equity, a bankroll, or income? These are just three of the many economic questions you have to answer prior to putting a syndicate of your own together. Whatever the property is that you decide to syndicate, you will find that your ability to make the deal fly will be increased a millionfold *if the investment fulfills your primary objective or moves you closer to it.*

Couple this concept with one more and you will see my point. *Your comfort zone should never be violated with a syndication.* Invest your partners' money just as though it were your own. That means don't experiment with their money by moving out of your own comfort zone.

Now that you can see the foundation of beginning the syndication, take a look at the syndication checklist and go from there.

The Syndication Checklist

1. Have you clearly identified your objective in doing a syndication?
2. What is it? Write it down and see if you can accept the concepts without trying to kid yourself.
3. Do you know your comfort zone? Write it down and make sure you are not bragging to yourself. Once you understand what you are comfortable with, you can take steps to expand that zone by first learning the fundamentals of new areas and then learning about the market of those new properties in those new comfort zones.
4. Do you understand the natures of the "partners" you plan to seek money from in the formation of a syndicate? Are they compatible with your objectives and your comfort zone?
5. How much *cash* do you think those would-be partners can generate for a down payment? Are you comfortable with that amount?
6. Will your comfort zone produce a property that will
   A. be accessible to you with the cash available in the syndicate?
   B. be within your partners' objectives?
7. Have you reviewed the area in search for that kind of property?
8. Have you made comparisons between the selected property and others both in and out of your comfort zone?
9. Have you made an effort to purchase the property on the most favorable terms to meet your objectives?
10. Have you firmly tied up the property so it cannot be sold out from under you?
11. Are your ready with a solid and well-documented package to show your would-be partners?
12. What time is your first appointment?

Syndications do not have to be grand multimillion-dollar ventures. In fact, some of the best for people to begin with are simple three- or four-people investments. Pick something that won't take more than $5,000 per investor for the down payment and raise $20,000 to buy a run-down duplex that you plan to fix up and resell.

If you are running the show, you don't have to put cash into the deal—your time and effort are enough. If the others don't agree, they don't have to give you the money.

The Legal Forms of Syndication

I won't go into a lot of detail on this matter for two reasons. First, your state might have different laws with respect to the legal forms of ownership than Florida or the other states I'm used to. Second, laws change, and you need to be sure to get the most current data and apply it to *you* and your objectives. However, it is a good idea to know some of the common forms of holding title and to have some conversational comfort with them. They are:

Partnership

Just about what it says. You and I are partners. We are in this mess together, and if I screw up, it is your rear end just as much as mine. If we both pull it off, then we will reap the benefits on the percentages as stated in the partnership agreement.

General Partnership

As in the regular partnership, you and I are general partners: We pull strings the same, speak the same language (to debtors and creditors), and have the same liability. We are brothers who will eat off the same plate if we have to in hopes of finding the rainbow on the other side of the mountain.

Limited Partnership

A separation between general partners and other kinds of partners. The limited ones are just that—limited in the scope of their liability. The general partner is God and will be held accountable for the bad and usually not given credit for the good. The limited partners do not have much say, if any, over what goes on in the partnership.

Trust

I can hold title to your property in trust for you. If I form a land-investment trust (legal in many places), then you have a beneficial interest in a form of joint venture but I hold the title to the land. Your interest as an investor is usually considered personal property, not real property, and that has some advantages as well as disadvantages. The transfer of a trust with many beneficiaries can be complicated if a dissenter wants to make life miserable for the others. On the other hand, it is a very simple form of partnership with a minimum of exposure to the investors.

Corporation

You and I form a corporation. We issue stock and take the money and buy a property. I'm the president because I own 51% of the stock. You can yell and scream all you want but you only own 49%.

If you just want to put money into something and you have full faith in the future of the corporation, then this is the way to do it.

Joint Venture

A form of any of the above where two or more people get together to do something. Each party might be one of the above, joined together in one of the above. For example: a corporation formed by two corporations, or by a partnership and a corporation.

Pitfalls of Syndications

The main pitfalls are the law, the SEC, the state Security and Exchange Commission, and so on.

The laws governing the formation of syndicates will vary from state to state, but all are overseen by the Federal Security and Exchange Commission. If you run into one of these agencies, you may wish you had never heard of the word "syndication"—not because you have done anything wrong, but because they will treat you as though you have.

It is nearly impossible to do a syndication in full compliance with all of the laws and regulations that govern or restrict syndications— unless you elect to go through a full-blown registration of the venture with the proper governing agencies. For most investments by small syndicators, this is not economically possible or feasible. Because of this, the laws generally offer some exemptions for the small syndicator. If you fall within one of these exemptions and adhere to the rules of that exemption, you *may* be okay. Then again, you may not.

Still, *don't avoid syndications out of fear of the law.* The laws are basically designed to protect the investors. Take a look at some of the full-blown registrations (get them from your local stockbroker) and see how they are put together. The name of the game is honesty and full disclosure.

If you are sincere about what you are doing, and have invested some time (a couple of hours) with your local syndicating lawyer, you will know just where the thin ice lies. There are also some fine courses and seminars on forming syndicates, books on the topic, and accountants who will aid you willingly (if you use them later on).

But watch out for these four no-no's.

1. Never have a retired elderly person as a member of your syndicate unless you have rocks in your head.
2. If you have rocks in your head, make sure the retired elderly person has a lawyer and accountant who have examined the proposed investment, asked you questions, and given you a letter stating that they advise their client and that their client is capable of making a decision.
3. Never buy a property for syndication that you would not buy for yourself (if you had the money, of course).
4. Never run a syndicate according to the rules of a democracy. Dissenters will create anarchy in a hurry, and you will be the first they send to the guillotine.

40

Incorporate for the
Down Payment

WHY NOT simply issue stock and give the stock to the seller as
your down payment? After all, the idea of incorporation is kinda like
the American dream. IBM issues stock whenever they need to generate new capital, so why not you?

This technique is akin to the technique of syndication discussed
in the previous chapter, in that a corporation is one of the forms of
ownership sometimes used in that form of dealmaking. However,
you should understand that incorporation and the issuing of stock as
a method of making your down payment is not in itself a method of
syndication.

Let's look at some examples of the use of incorporating for a
down payment.

Edwin was a single-family-home builder who liked to build
around a dozen expensive, custom-designed homes a year—about
one a month. This made for a comfortable life without many worries. Then along came the hot deal that Edwin didn't feel he could

turn down. It was a great opportunity, if he could come up with $150,000 in cash within a few months.

Like many builders, Edwin had a lot of his cash tied up in his building projects. He would have as many as nine homes under construction at any given time, and that meant a lot of capital out in the field in the form of materials and labor.

So Edwin packaged five of his homes into a corporation and sold 30% of the stock for the capital he needed to make his $150,000 investment. The homes were all within six to seven months of being ready to be sold, so it was unlikely the incorporators (investors) would have long to wait until they got their money back. The incorporation ate into Edwin's profits, of course, but the cost was well worthwhile as it enabled him to make the other investment without having to give away an even larger portion of that deal to get the capital. Edwin used his past success to form the base for the corporation, yet didn't tie up his whole organization. Only five homes were at risk in this very limited use of the corporation.

Glenda, on the other hand, was a hot-blooded down-to-business gal from London who knew more about business than any solicitor or lawyer she had ever run into. She liked to incorporate the future and would give away (as she put it) up to 45% of her future ventures as long as the investors would put up the capital needed to carry the projects through from start to finish with ample cash in reserve. She, too, liked to rest her case on her past performance, and as it was rather impressive, her attempts at generating capital through this means were fruitful.

Of course, many of you reading this book won't have the opportunity to use this technique right now. You will have to build some past successes to allow those laurels to carry you on to other (and, with luck, more profitable) deals. But even if you are just starting out, you will still have some use for the incorporation techniques to nail down those deals where you can't quite close the gap in the cashless deal you began with some other technique.

For example, assume for the moment that you are trying to buy a home in a nice part of town. Since you know the value of the area and feel you can fix up the property—even change its current use to a duplex (the zoning allows it)—you know you are in for a nice profit down the road. But first you have to buy it.

Here's the deal. Price, $70,000. First mortgage, $35,000. The seller tells you he wants a minimum of $15,000 in cash and will hold a second mortgage of $20,000.

This looks like a simple pyramid job and a refinance of the existing mortgage. So you get him to hold a second mortgage on another property you own and discover you can borrow $56,000 on the property. That loan will cost you $2,000, netting you $54,000 in new money. After you pay off the existing loan, you will have $19,000 cash left over. You can pay the seller his $15,000 and still have $4,000 to make repairs and the like to the house.

This is fine, except that the remodeling and repairs you want to make turn out to be much more expensive than you thought they would be. By the time you get all the bids in, you find that if you close on this deal you will be short of cash. The work the contractor bids on will cost $12,500, and this is the very minimum remodeling you want to do.

If you incorporated the house into a single-event venture, you could then offer the seller $9,000 in stock in the corporation as part of the cash offered earlier. I've added $500 to cover the cost of the incorporation, and the rest of the deal will balance out.

Your obligations in this deal are:

To pay off the existing mortgage of	$35,000
Give the seller some cash	6,000
Pay for incorporation	500
Have cash for remodeling	12,500
Pay for loan costs	2,000
Total cash obligations	$56,000

As the cash is generated out of the loan proceeds, you can easily see the deal made, provided the seller will take the $9,000 in stock and the pyramid of $20,000 to some other property. Of course, you now have a stockholder who is into you for a piece of the action. This stockholder is going to want to profit out of the deal, so be ready to back up that obligation to him.

The percent of profit or piece of the action will naturally depend on the percent of the corporation you had to give up to make the deal work. That is between you and the seller and depends on the motivations of both of you.

Finesse in Making Corporation Deals Work

There is one single key to the use of this transaction. The *seller*. This deal will be far more palatable to some sellers than others. Remember, we deal in a complicated society where some people seek the simplest way out. Here you find a seller who is motivated to make a sale. He isn't interested in some truly complicated situation and wants to do what is normal. There is nothing more normal than a stock deal. (Notice I said "normal," and not "usual.") Americans wake up in the morning and read the "stock report," we live and profit by the "stock market" and the Dow Jones average of the top stock companies.

Use this familiarity when dealing with a non-real-estate, highly stock-oriented person as it will be more comfortable to him than any other technique you can dream up.

The motivations of the seller are critical. You can manipulate him into asking for a piece of the action if you handle the situation properly. This gives you a distinct edge in closing the deal as you wanted to in the first place.

How to Get the Seller to Suggest the Stock Deal

You've made your series of offers, each one slightly different from the last: different, but not necessarily better, to avoid direct comparison between your offers and to keep your ultimate "highest offer" hidden. As you progress in the attempt to buy the property, you might discover that you are unable to make the cashless deal without some participation on the part of the seller. The thought of seller participation opens up several alternative forms of buying, of which the incorporation is one. Syndication in one of the formats shown in chapter 39 is another way to offer participation, as would be the land lease.

Assume for the moment that you feel the best way for you to go with this seller is to give him a piece of the action in the way of some stock in the corporation you plan to form for the deal. If you came out and asked the seller, "Would you like some stock in this venture?" you might get a yes. "Yes—say about fifty percent of the deal, okay?" Far more than you want to give.

Instead you work on the seller, never giving any hint that you will take a partner into the deal. You build up "effort" points between you and the seller. These points might be scored directly between you and the seller or through the broker dealing on your behalf. (This is one of those times when you, the buyer, should be paying the broker, as you want to keep the entire edge in the deal.)

After you have made what looks like a firm deal, you later elect to terminate the deal through one of your "outs" in the contract: You simply didn't get the financing you had planned on, or whatever. The fact of the matter is the deal isn't good enough for you the way it is structured and you can't close this deal on these terms. So you tell the seller: "Gee, Phil, I really wanted to make this deal. I've done a lot of work and have invested a lot of time and money into this project already. I'm confident of the profit potential once I've remodeled the building and quite frankly I'm disappointed that the financing fell through."

This would be a good time for a third party—say your broker—to say to you, "Say, Mr. Buyer, if Mr. Seller were interested, would you give him a piece of the action if we could hold the deal together?"

You look at the seller, he looks at you, you both smile, and you know you are on your way to making a deal.

Pitfalls in Making Stock Deals

There are several pitfalls you have to watch out for.

1. *Laws of your state dealing with stock offers.* Never make this kind of an offer unless you are sure you know the ramifications. You can do it, but there are limitations. Learn what they are from any lawyer.
2. *Sharing the profit.* Never offer any participation unless you have examined alternative ways to make a deal without giving up a part of your hard-to-be-earned profit.
3. *Offering too much.* Don't offer too much of the action. Offer 5% even if you are ready to go to 45%. Keep in mind that you can balance the rest of the equity in mortgages and offer only a token piece of the action. Sometimes that is enough.
4. *Loss of control.* Never give more than 49%. A fifty-fifty deal is noth-

ing but headaches, and losing control is not fun either. Better to find another deal than give up too much.

5. *Too many partners.* Don't deal with a lot of stockholders. Don't give the lawyer a piece of the action, the broker a piece of the action, and the seller his piece, too, or you will be in for a lot of sleepless nights.

41

Profit from Your Name

NAMES are big business, as you can tell from television and radio commercials. The name of the guy who is standing there drinking that beer is what's important, not so much the taste of the beer.

Your name can be big business to you, if you have a recognized expertise in real estate. The degree of expertise is relative: All you have to do is be more "lendable" or more "credible" than the person who needs to use your name to make his deal work.

EXAMPLE: Emery had dabbled in real estate a little. He owned his own home, a vacant lot he purchased on a contract for deed,* and a condo he inherited from his mother a few years ago. The condo was rented out, the lot didn't cost much, and his house had tripled in value in the past five years. Emery was a real-estate tycoon, however, in comparison to Jake, who had more theoretical knowledge about real-estate investing (having read half a dozen books on real-estate investing and taken several seminars on how to make it big in "fix-it-uppers") and all the ingredients of a self-made man, but didn't have a dime in his savings. Jake did have a lot of guts and determination, however.

* On which he paid a little down and so much per month over a relatively long term of ten years but didn't get the deed until he paid off the entire portion owed. He contracted, in essence, to get a deed at the termination of the payout.

Emery liked Jake a lot for those last attributes. So much so, in fact, that when Jake found a small apartment building that Jake was sure he could fix up and rent out for double the existing rents, Emery was receptive to going in with Jake.

Emery wasn't going to put up any money, only assist in obtaining the financing. Emery took a 20% position in the investment without putting any cash up. What Emery did was let Jake use his name in the deal. The seller of the property liked the fact that Emery was in the deal, the savings-and-loan liked Emery on the mortgage, and Jake liked the whole setup because he couldn't have swung it without Emery, or someone like Emery.

The fact of the matter is that there are a lot of Emerys out in the world looking for Jakes. You, of course, can profit from either side of the coin. As an Emery, you can pull the strings to put deals together, allowing the hardworking Jakes to make your fortunes even larger than they might now be. As a Jake, you get your opportunity to become an Emery.

How to Get to Be Important Enough
to Get Paid for Your Name

In thinking about this one, the first factor I thought of was "have a good credit rating." Giving this further thought, however, I was reminded of the many developers who had gone bankrupt only to spring back in good favor with lenders. Good credit is only one of several desirable assets, and often not the most important one. The following list will give you some idea of what makes for a "good and valuable name" in real-estate participation, and will guide you toward the things you can stress in your future real-estate dealings.

Your name will be valued if:

1. You have a net worth greater than the other partners to the deal.
2. You have greater knowledge in the venture than the other partners.
3. You have a record of success in similar ventures.
4. You have a well-known and respected name in the area.
5. You are politically "in."
6. You are associated with the upper economic strata of the community.

7. You speak out loudly, clearly, and not maliciously.
8. You are the big cheese in town.

How to Lend Your Name and Maximize Your Profits

"There is everything in a name. A rose by any other name would smell as sweet, but would not cost half as much during the winter months."—George Ade.

Your name will have its time, and if you don't take advantage of it, then shame on you. You see, there is no shame in capitalizing on what others need if they, too, will profit. The benefit is thus mutual. The deal may not always be mutually beneficial from your point of view, however. This is the major area where people get into trouble in lending their name, and I will dwell on this in the "Pitfalls."

We'll assume for the moment that you have examined the proposition brought to you and have recognized that the deal, as presented, will increase your wealth and that of the other party, without causing you greater *risk* than you wish to accept. Risk, of course, is an ever-present, inescapable element whenever there is potential for profit. Never be led into believing there is *no* risk when you lend someone your name. Even if any financial loss from the venture will not come out of your pocket, the very fact that someone associated with you has lost money will reflect back on your name.

Therefore, never lend your name unless you have examined the pitfalls below so closely that you are positive that either they don't exist or that you are so slippery you can slip out of their sharp teeth. (I'll bet on the trap every time.)

Pitfalls to Avoid: Seven Traps in Lending Your Name

1. *The would-be partner you have known forever, but not very well.* He may have gone to kindergarten with you, and you've seen him a thousand times over the past 30 years, but only to say hi to. You are sure he has been doing well, because he always drives a nice car, dresses well, and gives his regards to your wife when he bumps into you (even though he hasn't met her). To your embarrassment, you frequently forget his name, and he prods you along with a statement like "Why, remember when our English teacher used to single

me out with her 'now you there, little Charlie Wodsworth, quit pulling those girls' hair.' "

This guy is a potential trap when he asks you for your name in a venture. He is a trap because you have been lulled into "remembering" him as a good guy, when in fact you hated his guts in school—and would now if you could see what was about to happen to you. It is far better to start a new relationship with someone you have never met, and to check them out with a fine-tooth comb.

2. *"Look, there isn't one ounce of risk here."* There is always risk, and if the would-be partner doesn't understand risk, he's no businessman. Take a close look and point out where the risk lies. If he counters unsatisfactorily, back off.

3. *Any transaction that has no defined and limited liability that you can accept.* A general partnership, in which, it appears, all you have to do is to lend your name, might put you into one heck of a mess later on when 500 limited partners come after you (they know your name, remember) to get their money back after the other general partner skips to Rio. You avoid this simply by knowing what the liability is. See your (very good) lawyer to explain that to you if you aren't sure.

4. *The enormous profit deal that will make you a zillionaire overnight.* "Just put your name here, Charlie, and we will own an entire island in the Bahamas [covered with cannabis] and we will charter flights to and fro [carrying the maryjane] and make millions [and do about ten years in the slammer]."

5. *Allowing yourself to be dazzled by glamorous offices, sharp-looking gals at the front desk, sharper-looking guys moving around, and the would-be partner who says, "We like to bring local people into each of our many ventures."* Be sure to count your fingers after you shake this guy's hand.

6. *Allowing your comfort zone to be put on the back shelf for the time being.* Remember what I've said about your comfort zone: You should never invest out of it no matter how "riskless" the deal seems to be. The less you know about the venture, the less capable you are of recognizing the risk. Say, "I'm sorry, this sounds like a magnificent deal, but to be quite honest with you [you are being so with me?], I'm frightened to death of anything I can't understand, and that's out of my comfort zone. If I had the time and inclination, I'd expand my comfort zone and learn about your venture. But as you need the answer by midnight tonight, I'll pass."

271

7. *Becoming part of a crowd.* This is one of the easiest traps to fall into. "Say, Charlie, I've got a deal that is dynamite, I mean *dynamite*, and Brad Whatshisname and Phil Whoever are both putting up statements to make the venture look even stronger. You know what I mean? All you have to do is the same and we're home free, rolling in bread forever and ever, amen."

Of course he has just said the same thing to Brad and Phil, and when one signs, the others fall into line.

These seven traps won't usually stand out as clearly as I've presented them. They come sneaking in behind the mask of good intentions and well-meaning deals. Often the proposal comes from a person who simply hasn't thought out the deal as well as *you* should. Play the advocate and question the deal looking for the defense attitude, or—and this you will bet on—the confident, well-homeworked answer that shows you that the would-be partner knows what he is talking about.

There is one more pitfall, or trap, I've left out of the list: your own good nature or generosity. There is little I can do to stop you, but you should at least recognize it, and maybe someday someone will found an organization like AA that will enable you to call in the middle of signing a deal and have three former name-lenders rush over and drag you off to a bar. I'm talking about the guy who will give his name out of compassion, pity, and sorrow. "Oh, my God, Charlie, I'm about to lose my house, car, clothes, and stereo! I can pull it all back together if I buy this industrial building, and it's a bargain, too, because it is vacant, but I can rent it up, I know I can, despite what they all say, only I need you to cosign on the note and mortgage. I'll take you out in a few months, I promise. I will. Really."

You sign—you sentimental fool.

42

The Keep-Some,
Sell-Some Technique

IN THIS TECHNIQUE, you make a deal dependent on your ability to sell off part of what you are buying to generate the cash needed to close. The degree of "sell-off" will determine the percentage of interest you retain in the original investment, as well as the future capital you might have to invest. You might, for example, sell only enough to give you the money for the down payment. Or you might sell enough to give you a fully paid interest in the remainder of the property without any cash investment on your part. Let's look at some of the variations.

The Keep-the-Plus-and-Sell-Off-the-Negative Method

You find it prudent and desirable to buy a tract of land consisting of 100 acres. You don't really need the entire 100 acres—it's the road frontage of about 40 acres that attracts you. You know, however, that the price you have negotiated of $5,000 per acre for the whole 100 acres is well below the price for smaller tracts, and you can't pass up the bargain. Moreover, of the $500,000 total purchase price, the seller is willing to take only 10% down. And on top of that, at the closing, the seller will release five acres in the far rear of the property, farthest away from the road. The five acres, now released from the balance of the mortgage, will be yours and you can sell it. All you have to do, then, to generate the cash you need for the down payment is sell off these five acres at $10,000 per acre, closing on them at the same time you close on the 100 acres.

This transaction would work as long as an investor could be found at $10,000 per acre. However, you might have to introduce another technique or two to solidify the deal and make it more secure. One way is to add the pyramid, if you have another property off which you can pyramid.

In buying the property for $500,000 you give the owner the $50,000 cash down he wants, and, of the remaining balance, you give him some of the mortgage in the form of a pyramid. In this hypothetical case, assume he took $100,000 in paper against some other property you own and $350,000 in a first mortgage on the property he sold you. In this deal, he now releases 15 acres instead of the original five, since he has only a $350,000 outstanding mortgage on this property and thus needs less security on the mortgage. This gives you more flexibility in selling off the land, as you can offer terms. Naturally, if you had to, you could drop the price to $8,000 per acre on a "bargain all-cash deal" and generate a total of $120,000. This would give you the down payment you need at closing and could also reduce your debt even further. (Or you could have a ball with the extra $70,000.)

In this example you have sold off some of the negative property. This back land was of no real use to you, but, as the package deal came in the form of 100 acres, you had to make the bulk purchase. This allowed others to come in and buy the frontage from you at a good price for that kind of property.

You might have done the opposite, as in the next example.

Keep the Negative and Sell the Positive

What would have happened if you had sold the 40 acres fronting the road for the full price of $500,000 and ended up with the remaining 60 acres free and clear and without any capital investment on your part? This is called "coming out smelling like money (to heck with a rose)."

You might have sold that front 40 acres in 5-acre increments at $62,500 each (8 tracts × $62,500 equals $500,000). This might have been very possible had you introduced another investment technique into your bag of tricks: the *time delay*. If you had optioned the property with a long option, or even leased it with an option to buy, you could have capitalized on some event you knew was coming—a beneficial event that would increase the value of the property multifold. It is a good feeling to watch something you don't own yet going up in value when you have locked in the price at a much lower level. Ah, the sound of money in your pocket.

It should be obvious that it is often far easier to sell off what is presumed to be the *positive* than to sell the *negative*. Because of this, you might look for investments that have a positive that isn't (for you) and a negative that is your positive. Sound confusing? Here's an example. You are buying a home in a New England ski area. Actually, you don't like to ski, but you'd enjoy the place in the summer. This is an ideal situation, because you can sell the "positive," and end up with your own summer place without spending a dime of your own money. The summer is your positive and the winter your negative—but the money people see it the other way around.

Selling Just Enough for the Down Payment

You are buying a place in the Florida Keys—Key Largo or Key West, whichever turns you on—and you don't want or need 100% use of the facility. It is a simple matter of selling off part of the time in the property to make your initial down payment.

Assume that your villa in the Keys is priced at $120,000 and can be purchased for $30,000 down. You will owe $90,000 in mortgages and have an estimated annual cost of $11,106 in debt service (30 years at 12% interest) and another $6,000 in estimated taxes, insurance, and maintenance on the property. (Total carrying cost, then, is $17,106 per year.)

Assume you just need the down payment of $30,000 and you decide to do a private time-share. You will take this property and divide it into time increments, which can then be sold to others. In this format you can actually sell ownership (rather than lease rights to use) and you divide the total time up into 11 months of *use*. The twelfth month you set aside for repair-and-maintenance or rent-out time. However, as you are going to get some time for your effort, you will *actually divide all the cost of the facility over ten months*. The total price of buying a one-month share is now $12,000. In the breakdown, that means a buyer will make a down payment of only $3,000 and pay a $1,710.60 annual carry for expenses.

When you sell all ten months of time, you will end up with the eleventh free.

You should be sure to include *all* costs of upkeep—including furniture and fixture replacement.

Developing Finesse in Picking Your Investments

You will not haphazardly make effective use of the techniques we are discussing in this chapter. You will have to plan carefully the kind of investment that will lend itself to a partial sale at sufficient return to carry the total purchase, or provide the desired up-front capital. In selecting a property there are five things you need to look for:

1. *A forced purchase of excess property.* If a seller is forcing you to buy more property than you want, examine the possibility of a partial sale to increase the investment potential of this purchase. It is far better for the seller to require the additional purchase than for you to try to negotiate for the additional property. The reason for this is that you can frequently reduce the price and soften the terms, usually gaining some edge at least on the down payment. The seller may want out, but without breaking up the tract of property. Use that as an edge to gain time, get a reduced down payment, and easy interest costs. Make sure, however, that the property meets other criteria for a potential investment.

2. *New roadwork on its way.* You should be on the ball gaining knowledge of your backyard, and thus broadening your comfort zone. If you haven't paid a visit to the road department in the last three months (or phoned them, once you have made contact), then you are losing your edge and should go back to selling encyclopedias. Don't limit your research of future events to road departments, either; any government office is a potential source of interesting

data. If you hear of something about to happen that will make the property more valuable, verify it. If you can't verify right away, then tie up the property until you can. Once you are sure of the upcoming event, capitalize on that by selling off some of the property to cover your investment.

3. *Sales of similar properties in smaller chunks at multiples of the value.* If five-acre tracts are selling at three to four times the price of the 100-acre tract you're considering, then you have a potential to sell the property at a large profit. This can be mitigated by the costs of making those sales and the time elements involved, however. If you can make a fast turnover at triple the price, and the cost is small, then you are all right. But don't be misled by simple multiples of values. If you have to put in asphalt or concrete roads, water, sewers, electricity, and provide fire protection, or must give the state or county some of the land for hospitals, parks, schools, and a vast multitude of other pots to be filled, then you *must* sell in multiples of four to six times the raw land to come out with a healthy profit to offset the risk. Learn of the costs and go from there.

4. *Property that has no governmental restrictions against subdividing.* Such a property might be a gold mine, since many "in vogue" areas are cluttered with regulations and restrictions that make it impossible or very costly to subdivide. The environmentalists have tied up so much of the desirable land that in some places development simply is not economically feasible. I'm a realist when it comes to nature. Cities like Fort Lauderdale, Miami, New Orleans, San Diego, San Francisco, St. Louis, and New York would have had a very difficult time becoming what they are (for good or bad) if they had to live up to the environmentalists' procedures and regulations of today. So look out for restrictions and look for property that is unique to the area because it has few or no restrictions governing its use.

5. *A plus factor you can sell off.* This plus factor, as I've mentioned, is ideal if the other side of the coin appeals to you more. In this way you get to keep what you wanted in the first instance and sell off at a profit the unwanted portions.

Pitfalls in Partial Sales

The biggest pitfall you need to look out for is the form of ownership and the method of accounting for expenses and sharing of costs. Friends will become enemies, relatives will stop talking to each other, divorces and separations will abound in the dispute over who broke and must now pay for the water heater.

I've found that the tighter you make the deal from the standpoint of (1) expenses, (2) mortgage payments, (3) taxes, and (4) replacements and the like, the better everyone will like it—in the beginning. "Mr. Would-be Partner, this deal is damn tough on the guy who defaults on his obligations. I know this point is important to you because you and I both want to make sure that the other guys in this deal *with* us live up to their obligations like we will." Mr. Would-be Partner will emphatically agree, even though he may later be the first to default and be eased out of the deal because of it.

If you have tied up a bargain and you offer out part of the deal for a percent of the action or to cover your down payment, then there is little risk on your part. However, you might have a gold mine that you're ready to give away for too little. Keep your values up and don't let anyone try to get too much of a good thing unless you truly have no other option open to you.

43

The Sliding-Mortgage Technique

"AND NOW—the sliding-mortgage trick! You will razzle and dazzle seller and lender alike, as, with one smooth movement of the hand, you create magic that you never thought possible!"

In the sliding-mortgage technique, you will move the mortgage from one security to another. In doing this, you maintain, or only slightly alter, the format of the existing financing. You thereby ease the total debt as it pertains to *the property to be purchased,* creating greater equity (for you) in the new property and enhancing its ability to support new and greater financing. At the same time, you decrease equity in the "other" property, which now serves as security for the mortgage.

Robin, for example, owned several interesting properties and was constantly on the lookout for other investments. He found a nice duplex on land that permitted up to seven apartment units. Robin had a builder friend of his look at the property and they decided that, with around $30,000 capital outlay, Robin could convert the two garages in the duplex into four additional units, and could add onto the existing building, bringing the property up to seven units in total.

The seller of the property wanted $60,000 for the building, and still owed $9,000 at 8% on a very old first mortgage that had only five years to go, and $40,000 on a second mortgage at 9½% interest-only for another seven years with a balloon payment at that time. The second mortgagee was the previous owner of the duplex who a few years earlier had sold it to the seller Robin was now dealing with.

Robin negotiated the following deal:

He would give the seller cash payment at closing	$ 5,000
Assume the existing first mortgage	9,000
Assume the existing second mortgage	40,000
Give the seller an unsecured note for	6,000
Matching the full asking price of	$60,000

The interest rates and terms on the unsecured note were agreed to by the seller. The deal had one further condition, however: Robin had a period of 15 days to negotiate with the holder of the second mortgage to slide it to another property.

Robin didn't want to pay off the second mortgage; he wished only to "transfer" it to another property. If the mortgagee would agree to replace the security of the duplex with one or more of Robin's other properties, then Robin could effectively remove the mortgage from the property. He would therefore increase his equity in that property by the amount of the mortgage. Remember, Robin needed $30,000 to accomplish all his remodeling and another $5,000 to give the seller at the closing. Knowing the outcome of the ultimate deal and the agreement of the second mortgagee to transfer the mortgage over to another property by modifying the mortgage itself, Robin could easily borrow more cash than he needed to accomplish the cashless investment.

He and his accountant worked out a *pro forma* showing the duplex as it would be—a seven-unit apartment building. The income potential and final estimated value would support an appraised value of $95,000. Based on this, Robin (before he closed on the deal, of course) went to several lenders and made the best deal he could live with to borrow all the cash needed. He would have to pay off the existing mortgage, so he needed a minimum of $44,000 ($30,000 + $5,000 + $9,000 = $44,000), but as he would have mortgage costs and needed some safety factor to cover costs not contemplated, he asked for and got $55,000 in new loan proceeds.

With this money, the deal was closed, and everyone was happy.

The sliding-mortgage technique is often used in exchanges where one property in the exchange has a mortgage that can be slid over to another not involved in the exchange.

Charles wanted to exchange his equity of $50,000 in his home for a small office building. The other party had $50,000 in equity in the office building subject to a first mortgage of $30,000 and a second mortgage of $75,000. In making the deal, Charles worked out a slide of that $75,000 mortgage over to some other property Charles had so that he could improve the income picture of the office building by reduction of the debt service. Charles wasn't concerned with the debt service on the $75,000 since he planned to sell or exchange the other property that was now the security on that mortgage.

In essence, this exchange and sliding of the mortgage aided Charles in disposing of this other property, because reducing his equity in that property made it easier to sell.

If you review the pyramid transactions throughout this book, you will see great flexibility in that technique. The sliding-mortgage technique is much the same, except the mortgage you transfer over to another property isn't made by you. There will be some other mortgagee and the ultimate payments for that mortgage will be paid by you to someone else. However, anytime you are going to sell or exchange a property, you will increase the potential by sliding a mortgage onto that property from a property you are buying, prior to the sale or exchange, removing some of your equity in advance of the sale.

Building Finesse in This Technique

An open mind, wide selection of alternatives, and creative thinking will show you much more variation than you might assume in the first glance at this technique. When you look at any property you are about to buy and see one or more mortgages, you should ask yourself this question: "Is there any benefit to me or to the deal in sliding any of these mortgages to some other property?" You will be better able to answer this question if you understand the five instances in which you should consider mortgage sliding.

When to Consider Sliding a Mortgage

1. *When you need to generate cash for the down payment.* Robin did just this in the earlier example in this chapter. When you move debt from a newly acquired property to another property, you decrease your equity in the newly encumbered property, but you increase it in the newly acquired property. This greater equity and absence of debt now allows you to refinance for additional funds to allow the purchase of that property. In the right situation, you can actually walk away from the deal with cash.

2. *When you are attempting to reduce equity in another property for sale or exchange.* You might own a $70,000 vacant lot and want to sell that lot. If you are buying a home that has a $50,000 second mortgage that you can slide over to the $70,000 lot (now a first mortgage for the mortgagee, so there is some motivation on his part), you have increased your ability to sell that lot. Sliding this mortgage gives you the same benefit as receiving *cash* at the closing.

3. *When you want to refinance the first without changing the second.* Assume that the property you are contemplating has both a first and second mortgage. If you refinance the first mortgage for any reason, you will have to pay off the second (except in the unlikely event that the second is subordinated to permit a new refinance of the first). The payoff of the second mortgage might make the refinancing too costly and not worthwhile—unless you can maintain the total debt level with that second by moving or sliding it over to another property.

4. *When you want to get some other edge from the mortgage.* There are times when you will slide a mortgage for the benefit of the mortgagee. Perhaps the lender has told you, "Jack, if you sell this property, I want you to transfer the security to another of your properties. I don't want to be owed this money by someone else. You are the person I lent the money to." In this kind of situation, you probably had set the loan up this way.

However, there will be times when *you* want to keep the *lender* in your back pocket, so you will go to him and ask if he will transfer over to another property. This will enable you to *sell, exchange, or otherwise dispose* of a property with greater equity if that is both possible and to your benefit. Let's say, for example, a buyer comes to one of your properties and you try to sell him on the advantages of your low-interest second mortgage, but he tells you it doesn't matter as he is going to refinance anyway. This means all the existing mortgages will be paid off. It would be a pity to pay off a low-interest mortgage if you can keep it—and you *can* keep it, by sliding it over to another property. You get the cash out of the sale as your equity has increased in the property you are now selling.

5. *Whenever you want to keep intact a low-interest or favorable-term mortgage.* If you are buying a property that has a 7% mortgage, why not try to transfer it to another property if the alternative is to refinance the property? If the new property is to be turned over fast after a fix-up, always attempt to slide the mortgage to a property you want to keep for a longer time. In this way you can hold new paper at a higher rate of interest on the turnover of the property.

There are some mortgages that are difficult to slide. These will be any institutional mortgages made by banks, insurance companies, savings-and-loans, and the like. The easiest will be purchase-money mortgages where the mortgagee is a former owner of the property. Second-easiest will be convenience loans made by creditors, real-estate brokers (for commissions), and family members.

In the sliding mentioned so far, you have transferred a mortgage from a property you were buying to another of your properties. There will be times when you will cause the *seller* to slide a mortgage to another of *his* own properties. If, for example, the seller had a 20% mortgage on a three-year balloon, you would want that unattractive mortgage removed from a property you were buying and would ask if the seller could slide it over to another of his own properties. If you found that you were going to refinance a property that had a mortgage with penalties for payout, then the seller might move that mortgage for you, getting cash himself rather than paying off the mortgage. If you wanted to make an exchange into a free-and-clear property that was currently encumbered, you could "force" the owner to slide the debt off to other property—if he could possibly do that, of course.

Pitfalls in Using This Technique

There are no pitfalls in this technique other than the potential risk the mortgagee might be taking by removing one security in lieu of another. Your investment risk is highly leveraged, of course, in that you are developing another way to do a cashless deal and you have a greater debt service because of the technique than you would have had otherwise.

However, the use of this technique will astound those around you with its simplicity and function. It will work when you can convince the mortgagees on the "to be purchased" property that the move you contemplate for them is not only safe but good business, in that their position will be improved. And you will have to document their position *is* in fact improved. You can enhance this by adding interest, cutting down the number of years, or just moving them up in rank from a second mortgage to a first mortgage.

Appendix

TABLE A.

Constant Annual Percents Expressing the Sum of 12 Equal Monthly Payments Needed to Amortize a Principal Amount for the Term of Years Shown

% INTEREST	YEARS							
	.5	1	1.5	2	2.5	3	3.5	4
8	204.694	104.387	70.969	54.273	44.266	37.604	32.853	29.296
8.25	204.836	104.523	71.104	54.409	44.403	37.742	32.992	29.436
8.5	204.991	104.666	71.244	54.548	44.542	37.882	33.133	29.578
8.75	205.139	104.805	71.381	54.685	44.680	38.021	33.273	29.720
9	205.287	104.944	71.518	54.823	44.819	38.160	33.414	29.863
9.25	205.433	105.083	71.656	54.960	44.957	38.300	33.555	30.005
9.5	205.578	105.220	71.793	55.098	45.095	38.440	33.696	30.148
9.75	205.729	105.361	71.931	55.236	45.235	38.580	33.838	30.292
10	205.879	105.502	72.070	55.375	45.375	38.722	33.981	30.436
10.25	206.021	105.639	72.207	55.512	45.513	38.862	34.123	30.579
10.5	206.171	105.779	72.345	55.652	45.653	39.003	34.266	30.724
10.75	206.318	105.918	72.484	55.790	45.793	39.145	34.409	30.869
11	206.464	106.057	72.622	55.929	45.933	39.286	34.552	31.015
11.25	206.615	106.199	72.762	56.069	46.075	39.429	34.697	31.161
11.5	206.766	106.340	72.902	56.210	46.216	39.572	34.842	31.307
11.75	206.911	106.479	73.040	56.348	46.357	39.714	34.986	31.454
12	207.060	106.620	73.179	56.489	46.498	39.858	35.131	31.601
12.25	207.204	106.758	73.317	56.628	46.639	40.000	35.276	31.748
12.5	207.356	106.900	73.458	56.769	46.782	40.145	35.422	31.896
12.75	207.503	107.040	73.597	56.909	46.923	40.288	35.568	32.044
13	207.654	107.182	73.738	57.051	47.066	40.433	35.715	32.193
13.25	207.800	107.322	73.877	57.191	47.209	40.578	35.861	32.342
13.5	207.946	107.461	74.017	57.332	47.351	40.722	36.008	32.491
13.75	208.099	107.605	74.158	57.474	47.495	40.868	36.156	32.642
14	208.248	107.746	74.299	57.616	47.639	41.014	36.304	32.792
14.25	208.396	107.887	74.440	57.758	47.782	41.159	36.452	32.943
14.5	208.544	108.028	74.580	57.900	47.926	41.305	36.601	33.094
14.75	208.691	108.168	74.720	58.041	48.070	41.451	36.749	33.245
15	208.841	108.310	74.862	58.184	48.214	41.599	36.899	33.397
15.25	208.991	108.453	75.004	58.327	48.359	41.746	37.049	33.549
15.5	209.141	108.595	75.145	58.470	48.504	41.893	37.199	33.702
15.75	209.287	108.735	75.286	58.612	48.649	42.040	37.349	33.855
16	209.435	108.876	75.427	58.755	48.794	42.188	37.499	34.008
16.25	209.587	109.020	75.570	58.900	48.940	42.337	37.651	34.162
16.5	209.738	109.163	75.713	59.044	49.087	42.486	37.802	34.317
16.75	209.885	109.304	75.854	59.187	49.233	42.634	37.954	34.471
17	210.035	109.447	75.997	59.331	49.379	42.784	38.106	34.626
17.25	210.182	109.588	76.138	59.475	49.525	42.933	38.258	34.781
17.5	210.331	109.731	76.281	59.619	49.672	43.082	38.411	34.937
17.75	210.483	109.874	76.425	59.765	49.820	43.233	38.564	35.094
18	210.632	110.017	76.567	59.909	49.967	43.383	38.717	35.250
18.25	210.780	110.159	76.710	60.054	50.115	43.534	38.871	35.407
18.5	210.931	110.303	76.854	60.200	50.263	43.685	39.025	35.564
18.75	211.078	110.444	76.996	60.344	50.411	43.836	39.179	35.722

TABLE A (*continued*)

% INTEREST	.5	1	1.5	2	2.5	3	3.5	4
				YEARS				
19	211.228	110.588	77.140	60.490	50.559	43.987	39.334	35.880
19.25	211.381	110.732	77.285	60.637	50.709	44.139	39.490	36.039
19.5	211.530	110.875	77.428	60.783	50.857	44.291	39.645	36.198
19.75	211.679	111.018	77.572	60.929	51.006	44.444	39.801	36.357
20	211.827	111.161	77.716	61.075	51.155	44.596	39.957	36.516
20.25	211.976	111.304	77.860	61.221	51.305	44.749	40.113	36.676
20.5	212.129	111.450	78.005	61.369	51.456	44.903	40.270	36.837
20.75	212.279	111.594	78.150	61.516	51.606	45.057	40.428	36.998
21	212.427	111.737	78.294	61.663	51.756	45.210	40.585	37.159
21.25	212.576	111.880	78.439	61.810	51.906	45.364	40.742	37.320
21.5	212.726	112.024	78.583	61.958	52.057	45.518	40.900	37.482
21.75	212.880	112.170	78.730	62.106	52.209	45.674	41.060	37.645
22	213.029	112.314	78.875	62.254	52.360	45.829	41.218	37.807
22.25	213.180	112.459	79.021	62.403	52.512	45.984	41.377	37.971
22.5	213.328	112.602	79.166	62.550	52.663	46.140	41.537	38.134
22.75	213.478	112.747	79.311	62.699	52.815	46.295	41.697	38.298
23	213.628	112.891	79.457	62.848	52.968	46.452	41.857	38.462
23.25	213.780	113.037	79.604	62.997	53.121	46.608	42.017	38.626
23.5	213.930	113.181	79.750	63.146	53.273	46.765	42.178	38.791
23.75	214.081	113.327	79.896	63.296	53.427	46.922	42.339	38.957
24	214.230	113.471	80.042	63.445	53.580	47.079	42.501	39.122
24.25	214.381	113.617	80.189	63.595	53.733	47.237	42.663	39.288
24.5	214.534	113.763	80.337	63.746	53.888	47.395	42.825	39.455
24.75	214.685	113.908	80.484	63.896	54.042	47.554	42.987	39.622
25	214.835	114.053	80.630	64.046	54.196	47.712	43.150	39.789

TABLE A (*continued*)

% INTEREST	YEARS							
	4.5	5	5.5	6	6.5	7	7.5	8
8	26.535	24.332	22.534	21.040	19.780	18.704	17.774	16.964
8.25	26.677	24.475	22.679	21.186	19.928	18.853	17.925	17.117
8.5	26.821	24.620	22.825	21.334	20.077	19.004	18.078	17.271
8.75	26.964	24.765	22.972	21.482	20.227	19.155	18.231	17.425
9	27.108	24.910	23.119	21.631	20.377	19.307	18.384	17.580
9.25	27.252	25.056	23.266	21.780	20.528	19.460	18.538	17.736
9.5	27.396	25.202	23.414	21.930	20.679	19.613	18.693	17.893
9.75	27.542	25.349	23.563	22.080	20.832	19.767	18.849	18.051
10	27.687	25.497	23.712	22.231	20.985	19.922	19.006	18.209
10.25	27.833	25.644	23.861	22.383	21.138	20.077	19.163	18.368
10.5	27.980	25.793	24.012	22.535	21.292	20.233	19.321	18.528
10.75	28.126	25.942	24.162	22.688	21.447	20.390	19.479	18.689
11	28.274	26.091	24.314	22.841	21.602	20.547	19.639	18.850
11.25	28.422	26.241	24.466	22.995	21.758	20.705	19.799	19.012
11.5	28.570	26.392	24.619	23.150	21.915	20.864	19.960	19.176
11.75	28.719	26.542	24.771	23.305	22.072	21.023	20.121	19.339
12	28.868	26.694	24.925	23.460	22.230	21.183	20.284	19.504
12.25	29.017	26.845	25.078	23.616	22.388	21.344	20.447	19.668
12.5	29.168	26.998	25.233	23.774	22.548	21.506	20.610	19.835
12.75	29.318	27.150	25.388	23.931	22.707	21.668	20.775	20.001
13	29.470	27.304	25.544	24.089	22.868	21.831	20.940	20.169
13.25	29.621	27.458	25.700	24.248	23.029	21.994	21.106	20.337
13.5	29.772	27.612	25.857	24.407	23.190	22.158	21.272	20.506
13.75	29.925	27.767	26.015	24.567	23.353	22.323	21.440	20.676
14	30.078	27.922	26.172	24.727	23.516	22.488	21.607	20.846
14.25	30.231	28.078	26.331	24.888	23.679	22.654	21.776	21.017
14.5	30.385	28.234	26.490	25.049	23.843	22.821	21.945	21.189
14.75	30.538	28.391	26.649	25.211	24.008	22.988	22.115	21.361
15	30.693	28.548	26.809	25.374	24.173	23.156	22.286	21.535
15.25	30.848	28.706	26.969	25.537	24.339	23.325	22.457	21.709
15.5	31.004	28.864	27.130	25.701	24.506	23.494	22.629	21.883
15.75	31.159	29.022	27.292	25.865	24.673	23.664	22.802	22.058
16	31.316	29.182	27.454	26.030	24.840	23.834	22.975	22.234
16.25	31.473	29.341	27.616	26.196	25.009	24.006	23.149	22.411
16.5	31.630	29.502	27.780	26.362	25.178	24.178	23.324	22.589
16.75	31.787	29.662	27.943	26.528	25.347	24.350	23.499	22.767
17	31.945	29.823	28.107	26.696	25.518	24.523	23.675	22.946
17.25	32.104	29.985	28.272	26.863	25.688	24.697	23.852	23.125
17.5	32.263	30.147	28.437	27.031	25.859	24.871	24.029	23.305
17.75	32.422	30.309	28.603	27.200	26.031	25.046	24.207	23.486
18	32.582	30.472	28.769	27.369	26.204	25.221	24.385	23.668
18.25	32.742	30.636	28.935	27.539	26.377	25.398	24.565	23.850
18.5	32.903	30.800	29.103	27.710	26.550	25.574	24.744	24.033
18.75	33.063	30.964	29.270	27.881	26.724	25.752	24.925	24.216
19	33.225	31.129	29.438	28.052	26.899	25.930	25.106	24.401
19.25	33.387	31.294	29.607	28.224	27.075	26.108	25.288	24.586
19.5	33.549	31.460	29.776	28.397	27.251	26.287	25.470	24.771
19.75	33.712	31.626	29.946	28.570	27.427	26.467	25.653	24.957
20	33.875	31.793	30.116	28.743	27.604	26.647	25.837	25.144
20.25	34.039	31.960	30.287	28.917	27.781	26.828	26.021	25.331

TABLE A (*continued*)

% INTEREST				YEARS				
	4.5	5	5.5	6	6.5	7	7.5	8
20.5	34.203	32.128	30.458	29.092	27.960	27.010	26.206	25.519
20.75	34.367	32.296	30.630	29.268	28.139	27.192	26.391	25.708
21	34.532	32.464	30.802	29.443	28.318	27.375	26.577	25.897
21.25	34.697	32.633	30.974	29.619	28.497	27.558	26.764	26.087
21.5	34.863	32.802	31.147	29.796	28.678	27.742	26.951	26.278
21.75	35.029	32.973	31.321	29.974	28.859	27.926	27.139	26.469
22	35.196	33.143	31.495	30.151	29.040	28.111	27.327	26.661
22.25	35.363	33.314	31.670	30.330	29.222	28.297	27.516	26.853
22.5	35.530	33.485	31.845	30.509	29.405	28.483	27.706	27.046
22.75	35.698	33.656	32.020	30.688	29.588	28.669	27.896	27.239
23	35.866	33.828	32.197	30.868	29.771	28.857	28.087	27.433
23.25	36.035	34.001	32.373	31.048	29.955	29.044	28.278	27.628
23.5	36.203	34.174	32.550	31.229	30.140	29.233	28.470	27.823
23.75	36.373	34.348	32.728	31.410	30.325	29.422	28.662	28.019
24	36.543	34.521	32.905	31.592	30.511	29.611	28.855	28.216
24.25	36.713	34.696	33.084	31.775	30.697	29.801	29.049	28.413
24.5	36.884	34.871	33.263	31.958	30.884	29.992	29.243	28.610
24.75	37.055	35.046	33.442	32.141	31.071	30.182	29.438	28.809
25	37.226	35.222	33.622	32.325	31.259	30.374	29.633	29.007

TABLE A (continued)

% INTEREST	YEARS							
	8.5	9	9.5	10	10.5	11	11.5	12
8	16.252	15.623	15.062	14.559	14.107	13.699	13.328	12.989
8.25	16.406	15.778	15.219	14.718	14.268	13.860	13.491	13.154
8.5	16.562	15.935	15.378	14.878	14.429	14.024	13.656	13.321
8.75	16.718	16.093	15.537	15.039	14.592	14.188	13.822	13.488
9	16.875	16.252	15.697	15.201	14.756	14.353	13.988	13.657
9.25	17.033	16.411	15.858	15.364	14.920	14.519	14.156	13.826
9.5	17.191	16.571	16.020	15.528	15.085	14.686	14.325	13.997
9.75	17.351	16.733	16.183	15.693	15.252	14.855	14.495	14.168
10	17.511	16.895	16.347	15.858	15.420	15.024	14.666	14.341
10.25	17.672	17.057	16.512	16.025	15.588	15.194	14.838	14.515
10.5	17.834	17.221	16.677	16.192	15.757	15.365	15.011	14.690
10.75	17.996	17.386	16.844	16.361	15.928	15.538	15.185	14.866
11	18.160	17.551	17.011	16.530	16.099	15.711	15.360	15.043
11.25	18.324	17.717	17.180	16.700	16.271	15.885	15.537	15.221
11.5	18.489	17.885	17.349	16.872	16.444	16.060	15.714	15.400
11.75	18.655	18.052	17.519	17.044	16.618	16.236	15.892	15.580
12	18.821	18.221	17.690	17.217	16.794	16.414	16.071	15.761
12.25	18.989	18.391	17.861	17.390	16.969	16.591	16.251	15.943
12.5	19.157	18.561	18.034	17.565	17.146	16.771	16.432	16.126
12.75	19.326	18.732	18.207	17.741	17.324	16.950	16.614	16.310
13	19.496	18.904	18.382	17.917	17.503	17.131	16.797	16.496
13.25	19.666	19.077	18.557	18.095	17.682	17.313	16.981	16.682
13.5	19.837	19.251	18.733	18.273	17.863	17.496	17.166	16.869
13.75	20.010	19.425	18.910	18.452	18.044	17.680	17.352	17.057
14	20.182	19.601	19.087	18.632	18.227	17.864	17.539	17.246
14.25	20.356	19.777	19.266	18.813	18.410	18.049	17.726	17.435
14.5	20.530	19.953	19.445	18.994	18.594	18.236	17.915	17.626
14.75	20.705	20.131	19.625	19.177	18.779	18.423	18.104	17.818
15	20.881	20.309	19.806	19.360	18.964	18.611	18.295	18.011
15.25	21.058	20.488	19.987	19.544	19.151	18.800	18.486	18.204
15.5	21.235	20.668	20.170	19.729	19.338	18.990	18.678	18.399
15.75	21.413	20.849	20.353	19.915	19.526	19.180	18.871	18.594
16	21.592	21.030	20.537	20.102	19.715	19.372	19.065	18.790
16.25	21.771	21.213	20.722	20.289	19.905	19.564	19.260	18.987
16.5	21.952	21.396	20.908	20.477	20.096	19.757	19.455	19.185
16.75	22.133	21.579	21.094	20.666	20.288	19.951	19.652	19.384
17	22.314	21.764	21.281	20.856	20.480	20.146	19.849	19.583
17.25	22.496	21.949	21.469	21.046	20.673	20.342	20.047	19.783
17.5	22.679	22.134	21.657	21.237	20.867	20.538	20.245	19.985
17.75	22.863	22.321	21.847	21.430	21.061	20.735	20.445	20.187
18	23.048	22.508	22.037	21.622	21.257	20.933	20.646	20.389
18.25	23.233	22.696	22.227	21.816	21.453	21.132	20.847	20.593
18.5	23.419	22.885	22.419	22.010	21.650	21.331	21.049	20.797
18.75	23.605	23.074	22.611	22.205	21.847	21.531	21.251	21.002
19	23.792	23.264	22.804	22.401	22.046	21.732	21.455	21.208
19.25	23.980	23.455	22.998	22.597	22.245	21.934	21.659	21.415
19.5	24.169	23.647	23.192	22.794	22.445	22.137	21.864	21.622
19.75	24.358	23.839	23.387	22.992	22.645	22.340	22.070	21.831
20	24.548	24.032	23.583	23.191	22.847	22.544	22.276	22.039
20.25	24.738	24.225	23.779	23.390	23.048	22.748	22.483	22.249

TABLE A (*continued*)

% INTEREST	YEARS							
	8.5	9	9.5	10	10.5	11	11.5	12
20.5	24.929	24.420	23.977	23.590	23.251	22.954	22.691	22.459
20.75	25.121	24.614	24.174	23.791	23.455	23.160	22.900	22.670
21	25.314	24.810	24.373	23.992	23.659	23.366	23.109	22.882
21.25	25.507	25.006	24.572	24.194	23.863	23.573	23.319	23.094
21.5	25.700	25.203	24.772	24.396	24.069	23.781	23.529	23.307
21.75	25.895	25.400	24.972	24.600	24.275	23.990	23.740	23.521
22	26.090	25.598	25.173	24.804	24.481	24.200	23.952	23.735
22.25	26.285	25.797	25.375	25.008	24.689	24.410	24.165	23.950
22.5	26.481	25.996	25.577	25.213	24.897	24.620	24.378	24.165
22.75	26.678	26.196	25.780	25.419	25.105	24.831	24.592	24.381
23	26.876	26.397	25.984	25.626	25.315	25.043	24.806	24.598
23.25	27.074	26.598	26.188	25.833	25.524	25.256	25.021	24.815
23.5	27.272	26.800	26.393	26.041	25.735	25.469	25.237	25.033
23.75	27.471	27.002	26.598	26.249	25.946	25.683	25.453	25.252
24	27.671	27.205	26.804	26.458	26.158	25.897	25.670	25.471
24.25	27.872	27.409	27.011	26.667	26.370	26.112	25.887	25.691
24.5	28.073	27.613	27.218	26.877	26.583	26.327	26.105	25.911
24.75	28.274	27.817	27.426	27.088	26.796	26.543	26.323	26.132
25	28.476	28.023	27.634	27.299	27.010	26.760	26.542	26.353

TABLE A (continued)

% INTEREST	YEARS							
	12.5	13	13.5	14	14.5	15	15.5	16
8	12.680	12.397	12.136	11.896	11.674	11.468	11.277	11.099
8.25	12.847	12.565	12.306	12.067	11.846	11.642	11.452	11.276
8.5	13.015	12.734	12.477	12.239	12.020	11.817	11.629	11.454
8.75	13.184	12.905	12.649	12.413	12.195	11.994	11.807	11.633
9	13.354	13.076	12.822	12.587	12.371	12.171	11.986	11.814
9.25	13.525	13.249	12.996	12.763	12.549	12.350	12.167	11.996
9.5	13.697	13.423	13.172	12.940	12.727	12.531	12.349	12.180
9.75	13.870	13.598	13.348	13.119	12.908	12.712	12.532	12.365
10	14.045	13.774	13.526	13.299	13.089	12.895	12.717	12.551
10.25	14.220	13.952	13.705	13.479	13.271	13.079	12.902	12.738
10.5	14.397	14.130	13.886	13.661	13.455	13.265	13.089	12.927
10.75	14.575	14.310	14.067	13.844	13.640	13.451	13.278	13.117
11	14.754	14.490	14.249	14.029	13.826	13.639	13.467	13.308
11.25	14.934	14.672	14.433	14.214	14.013	13.828	13.658	13.500
11.5	15.115	14.855	14.618	14.401	14.202	14.018	13.850	13.694
11.75	15.297	15.039	14.804	14.588	14.391	14.210	14.043	13.889
12	15.480	15.224	14.991	14.777	14.582	14.402	14.237	14.085
12.25	15.664	15.410	15.179	14.967	14.773	14.596	14.432	14.282
12.5	15.849	15.597	15.368	15.158	14.966	14.790	14.629	14.480
12.75	16.035	15.785	15.558	15.350	15.160	14.986	14.826	14.679
13	16.223	15.975	15.749	15.543	15.355	15.183	15.025	14.880
13.25	16.411	16.165	15.941	15.737	15.551	15.381	15.225	15.081
13.5	16.600	16.356	16.134	15.932	15.748	15.580	15.425	15.284
13.75	16.790	16.548	16.329	16.129	15.946	15.780	15.627	15.488
14	16.981	16.741	16.524	16.326	16.146	15.981	15.830	15.692
14.25	17.173	16.935	16.720	16.524	16.346	16.183	16.034	15.898
14.5	17.366	17.130	16.917	16.723	16.547	16.386	16.239	16.105
14.75	17.560	17.326	17.115	16.923	16.749	16.590	16.445	16.313
15	17.755	17.523	17.314	17.124	16.952	16.795	16.652	16.521
15.25	17.950	17.721	17.514	17.327	17.156	17.001	16.860	16.731
15.5	18.147	17.920	17.715	17.530	17.361	17.208	17.069	16.941
15.75	18.344	18.120	17.917	17.733	17.567	17.416	17.278	17.153
16	18.543	18.320	18.120	17.938	17.774	17.624	17.489	17.365
16.25	18.742	18.522	18.323	18.144	17.981	17.834	17.700	17.579
16.5	18.942	18.724	18.528	18.350	18.190	18.045	17.913	17.793
16.75	19.143	18.928	18.733	18.558	18.399	18.256	18.126	18.008
17	19.345	19.132	18.939	18.766	18.610	18.468	18.340	18.224
17.25	19.548	19.336	19.146	18.975	18.821	18.681	18.555	18.440
17.5	19.751	19.542	19.354	19.185	19.033	18.895	18.770	18.658
17.75	19.956	19.749	19.563	19.396	19.245	19.110	18.987	18.876
18	20.161	19.956	19.772	19.607	19.459	19.325	19.204	19.095
18.25	20.367	20.164	19.983	19.820	19.673	19.541	19.422	19.315
18.5	20.573	20.373	20.194	20.033	19.888	19.758	19.641	19.535
18.75	20.781	20.583	20.406	20.247	20.104	19.976	19.861	19.757
19	20.989	20.793	20.618	20.461	20.321	20.195	20.081	19.979
19.25	21.198	21.004	20.831	20.677	20.538	20.414	20.302	20.201
19.5	21.408	21.216	21.046	20.893	20.756	20.634	20.524	20.425
19.75	21.618	21.429	21.260	21.110	20.975	20.854	20.746	20.649
20	21.829	21.642	21.476	21.327	21.194	21.076	20.969	20.874
20.25	22.041	21.856	21.692	21.545	21.414	21.297	21.193	21.099

TABLE A (*continued*)

% INTEREST	YEARS							
	12.5	13	13.5	14	14.5	15	15.5	16
20.5	22.254	22.071	21.909	21.764	21.635	21.520	21.417	21.325
20.75	22.467	22.287	22.126	21.984	21.857	21.743	21.642	21.552
21	22.681	22.503	22.345	22.204	22.079	21.967	21.868	21.779
21.25	22.895	22.719	22.563	22.425	22.302	22.192	22.094	22.007
21.5	23.111	22.937	22.783	22.646	22.525	22.417	22.321	22.235
21.75	23.327	23.155	23.003	22.869	22.749	22.643	22.548	22.464
22	23.543	23.374	23.224	23.091	22.974	22.869	22.776	22.693
22.25	23.760	23.593	23.445	23.315	23.199	23.096	23.005	22.924
22.5	23.978	23.813	23.667	23.539	23.424	23.323	23.234	23.154
22.75	24.196	24.034	23.890	23.763	23.651	23.551	23.463	23.385
23	24.415	24.255	24.113	23.988	23.878	23.780	23.693	23.617
23.25	24.635	24.476	24.337	24.214	24.105	24.009	23.924	23.849
23.5	24.855	24.699	24.561	24.440	24.333	24.239	24.155	24.081
23.75	25.076	24.922	24.786	24.667	24.561	24.469	24.387	24.314
24	25.297	25.145	25.011	24.894	24.790	24.699	24.619	24.548
24.25	25.519	25.369	25.237	25.122	25.020	24.930	24.851	24.782
24.5	25.742	25.594	25.464	25.350	25.250	25.162	25.085	25.016
24.75	25.965	25.819	25.691	25.579	25.480	25.394	25.318	25.251
25	26.188	26.044	25.918	25.808	25.711	25.626	25.552	25.486

TABLE A (*continued*)

% INTEREST	16.5	17	17.5	18	18.5	19	19.5	20
8	10.934	10.779	10.635	10.500	10.373	10.254	10.142	10.037
8.25	11.112	10.958	10.815	10.682	10.556	10.439	10.328	10.225
8.5	11.291	11.140	10.998	10.866	10.742	10.625	10.516	10.414
8.75	11.472	11.322	11.182	11.051	10.928	10.813	10.706	10.605
9	11.655	11.506	11.367	11.237	11.116	11.003	10.897	10.797
9.25	11.838	11.691	11.554	11.426	11.306	11.194	11.089	10.990
9.5	12.023	11.877	11.742	11.615	11.497	11.386	11.283	11.186
9.75	12.210	12.065	11.931	11.806	11.689	11.580	11.478	11.382
10	12.397	12.255	12.122	11.998	11.883	11.775	11.675	11.580
10.25	12.586	12.445	12.314	12.192	12.078	11.972	11.872	11.780
10.5	12.777	12.637	12.507	12.387	12.274	12.170	12.072	11.981
10.75	12.968	12.830	12.702	12.583	12.472	12.369	12.273	12.183
11	13.161	13.025	12.898	12.781	12.671	12.570	12.475	12.386
11.25	13.355	13.220	13.095	12.979	12.872	12.771	12.678	12.591
11.5	13.550	13.417	13.294	13.180	13.073	12.975	12.883	12.797
11.75	13.747	13.615	13.494	13.381	13.276	13.179	13.089	13.005
12	13.944	13.815	13.695	13.583	13.480	13.385	13.296	13.213
12.25	14.143	14.015	13.897	13.787	13.686	13.591	13.504	13.423
12.5	14.343	14.217	14.100	13.992	13.892	13.799	13.713	13.634
12.75	14.544	14.419	14.304	14.198	14.100	14.009	13.924	13.846
13	14.746	14.623	14.510	14.405	14.308	14.219	14.136	14.059
13.25	14.950	14.828	14.717	14.613	14.518	14.430	14.349	14.273
13.5	15.154	15.034	14.924	14.823	14.729	14.643	14.562	14.488
13.75	15.359	15.242	15.133	15.033	14.941	14.856	14.777	14.705
14	15.566	15.450	15.343	15.245	15.154	15.071	14.993	14.922
14.25	15.773	15.659	15.554	15.457	15.368	15.286	15.210	15.141
14.5	15.982	15.869	15.766	15.671	15.583	15.503	15.428	15.360
14.75	16.191	16.080	15.978	15.885	15.799	15.720	15.647	15.580
15	16.402	16.292	16.192	16.100	16.016	15.938	15.867	15.801
15.25	16.613	16.506	16.407	16.317	16.234	16.158	16.088	16.024
15.5	16.826	16.720	16.623	16.534	16.453	16.378	16.309	16.247
15.75	17.039	16.934	16.839	16.752	16.672	16.599	16.532	16.470
16	17.253	17.150	17.057	16.971	16.893	16.821	16.755	16.695
16.25	17.468	17.367	17.275	17.191	17.114	17.044	16.979	16.921
16.5	17.684	17.585	17.494	17.412	17.336	17.267	17.204	17.147
16.75	17.901	17.803	17.714	17.633	17.559	17.492	17.430	17.374
17	18.118	18.022	17.935	17.855	17.783	17.717	17.657	17.602
17.25	18.336	18.242	18.156	18.078	18.007	17.943	17.884	17.830
17.5	18.556	18.463	18.379	18.302	18.233	18.169	18.112	18.059
17.75	18.776	18.685	18.602	18.527	18.459	18.397	18.341	18.289
18	18.996	18.907	18.826	18.752	18.686	18.625	18.570	18.520
18.25	19.218	19.130	19.050	18.978	18.913	18.854	18.800	18.751
18.5	19.440	19.354	19.276	19.205	19.141	19.083	19.031	18.983
18.75	19.663	19.578	19.502	19.433	19.370	19.313	19.262	19.215
19	19.887	19.803	19.728	19.661	19.599	19.544	19.494	19.448
19.25	20.111	20.029	19.956	19.889	19.829	19.775	19.726	19.682
19.5	20.336	20.256	20.184	20.119	20.060	20.007	19.959	19.916
19.75	20.562	20.483	20.412	20.349	20.291	20.240	20.193	20.151
20	20.788	20.711	20.642	20.579	20.523	20.473	20.427	20.386
20.25	21.015	20.939	20.871	20.810	20.755	20.706	20.662	20.622

TABLE A (*continued*)

% INTEREST	YEARS							
	16.5	17	17.5	18	18.5	19	19.5	20
20.5	21.242	21.168	21.102	21.042	20.988	20.940	20.897	20.858
20.75	21.471	21.398	21.333	21.274	21.222	21.175	21.133	21.095
21	21.699	21.628	21.564	21.507	21.456	21.410	21.369	21.332
21.25	21.929	21.859	21.796	21.740	21.690	21.646	21.605	21.569
21.5	22.158	22.090	22.029	21.974	21.925	21.882	21.842	21.807
21.75	22.389	22.322	22.262	22.209	22.161	22.118	22.080	22.046
22	22.620	22.554	22.496	22.443	22.397	22.355	22.318	22.285
22.25	22.851	22.787	22.730	22.679	22.633	22.593	22.556	22.524
22.5	23.083	23.020	22.964	22.914	22.870	22.830	22.795	22.764
22.75	23.316	23.254	23.199	23.151	23.107	23.069	23.034	23.004
23	23.549	23.488	23.435	23.387	23.345	23.307	23.274	23.244
23.25	23.782	23.723	23.671	23.624	23.583	23.546	23.514	23.485
23.5	24.016	23.958	23.907	23.862	23.821	23.786	23.754	23.726
23.75	24.251	24.194	24.144	24.100	24.060	24.025	23.995	23.967
24	24.485	24.430	24.381	24.338	24.299	24.266	24.235	24.209
24.25	24.721	24.666	24.619	24.576	24.539	24.506	24.477	24.451
24.5	24.956	24.903	24.857	24.815	24.779	24.747	24.718	24.693
24.75	25.192	25.141	25.095	25.055	25.019	24.988	24.960	24.936
25	25.429	25.378	25.334	25.294	25.260	25.229	25.202	25.179

Appendix

TABLE A (*continued*)

% INTEREST	20.5	21	21.5	22	22.5	23	23.5	24
8	9.938	9.845	9.757	9.674	9.596	9.521	9.451	9.385
8.25	10.127	10.035	9.948	9.867	9.789	9.716	9.647	9.582
8.5	10.318	10.227	10.142	10.061	9.985	9.913	9.845	9.781
8.75	10.510	10.420	10.336	10.257	10.182	10.111	10.045	9.982
9	10.703	10.615	10.532	10.454	10.381	10.311	10.246	10.184
9.25	10.898	10.811	10.730	10.653	10.581	10.513	10.449	10.388
9.5	11.095	11.009	10.929	10.854	10.783	10.716	10.653	10.593
9.75	11.293	11.209	11.130	11.056	10.986	10.920	10.858	10.800
10	11.492	11.409	11.332	11.259	11.191	11.126	11.066	11.009
10.25	11.693	11.612	11.535	11.464	11.397	11.334	11.274	11.219
10.5	11.895	11.815	11.740	11.670	11.604	11.542	11.484	11.430
10.75	12.099	12.020	11.947	11.878	11.813	11.753	11.696	11.642
11	12.304	12.226	12.154	12.087	12.023	11.964	11.908	11.856
11.25	12.510	12.434	12.363	12.297	12.235	12.177	12.123	12.072
11.5	12.717	12.643	12.573	12.509	12.448	12.391	12.338	12.288
11.75	12.926	12.853	12.785	12.721	12.662	12.606	12.554	12.506
12	13.136	13.064	12.998	12.935	12.877	12.823	12.772	12.725
12.25	13.347	13.277	13.211	13.150	13.093	13.040	12.991	12.945
12.5	13.560	13.491	13.426	13.367	13.311	13.259	13.211	13.166
12.75	13.773	13.705	13.643	13.584	13.530	13.479	13.432	13.388
13	13.988	13.921	13.860	13.803	13.750	13.700	13.654	13.611
13.25	14.203	14.138	14.078	14.022	13.970	13.922	13.877	13.835
13.5	14.420	14.356	14.298	14.243	14.192	14.145	14.101	14.061
13.75	14.638	14.576	14.518	14.465	14.415	14.369	14.327	14.287
14	14.856	14.796	14.739	14.687	14.639	14.594	14.553	14.514
14.25	15.076	15.017	14.962	14.911	14.864	14.820	14.780	14.742
14.5	15.297	15.239	15.185	15.135	15.089	15.047	15.007	14.971
14.75	15.519	15.462	15.409	15.361	15.316	15.274	15.236	15.201
15	15.741	15.685	15.634	15.587	15.543	15.503	15.466	15.431
15.25	15.965	15.910	15.860	15.814	15.771	15.732	15.696	15.662
15.5	16.189	16.136	16.087	16.042	16.000	15.962	15.927	15.894
15.75	16.414	16.362	16.314	16.270	16.230	16.193	16.159	16.127
16	16.640	16.589	16.543	16.500	16.461	16.424	16.391	16.361
16.25	16.867	16.817	16.772	16.730	16.692	16.657	16.624	16.595
16.5	17.094	17.046	17.002	16.961	16.924	16.890	16.858	16.830
16.75	17.322	17.275	17.232	17.193	17.156	17.123	17.093	17.065
17	17.551	17.505	17.463	17.425	17.390	17.358	17.328	17.301
17.25	17.781	17.736	17.695	17.658	17.624	17.592	17.564	17.538
17.5	18.011	17.968	17.928	17.891	17.858	17.828	17.800	17.775
17.75	18.242	18.200	18.161	18.126	18.093	18.064	18.037	18.012
18	18.474	18.433	18.395	18.360	18.329	18.300	18.274	18.251
18.25	18.706	18.666	18.629	18.596	18.565	18.538	18.512	18.489
18.5	18.939	18.900	18.864	18.832	18.802	18.775	18.751	18.729
18.75	19.173	19.135	19.100	19.068	19.039	19.013	18.990	18.968
19	19.407	19.370	19.336	19.305	19.277	19.252	19.229	19.208
19.25	19.642	19.605	19.572	19.543	19.516	19.491	19.469	19.449
19.5	19.877	19.842	19.810	19.781	19.754	19.731	19.709	19.690
19.75	20.113	20.078	20.047	20.019	19.994	19.971	19.950	19.931
20	20.349	20.315	20.285	20.258	20.233	20.211	20.191	20.173
20.25	20.586	20.553	20.524	20.497	20.473	20.452	20.432	20.415

TABLE A (*continued*)

% INTEREST	20.5	21	21.5	22	22.5	23	23.5	24
				YEARS				
20.5	20.823	20.791	20.763	20.737	20.714	20.693	20.674	20.657
20.75	21.060	21.030	21.002	20.977	20.955	20.934	20.916	20.900
21	21.298	21.269	21.242	21.218	21.196	21.176	21.159	21.143
21.25	21.537	21.508	21.482	21.458	21.437	21.419	21.402	21.386
21.5	21.776	21.748	21.722	21.700	21.679	21.661	21.645	21.630
21.75	22.015	21.988	21.963	21.941	21.922	21.904	21.888	21.874
22	22.255	22.228	22.205	22.183	22.164	22.147	22.132	22.118
22.25	22.495	22.469	22.446	22.426	22.407	22.391	22.376	22.363
22.5	22.736	22.710	22.688	22.668	22.650	22.634	22.620	22.607
22.75	22.976	22.952	22.930	22.911	22.894	22.878	22.865	22.852
23	23.217	23.194	23.173	23.154	23.137	23.123	23.109	23.097
23.25	23.459	23.436	23.416	23.398	23.381	23.367	23.354	23.343
23.5	23.701	23.679	23.659	23.641	23.626	23.612	23.599	23.588
23.75	23.943	23.921	23.902	23.885	23.870	23.857	23.845	23.834
24	24.185	24.164	24.146	24.129	24.115	24.102	24.090	24.080
24.25	24.428	24.408	24.390	24.374	24.360	24.347	24.336	24.326
24.5	24.671	24.651	24.634	24.619	24.605	24.593	24.582	24.573
24.75	24.914	24.895	24.878	24.863	24.850	24.839	24.828	24.819
25	25.158	25.139	25.123	25.109	25.096	25.085	25.075	25.066

TABLE A (*continued*)

% INTEREST	YEARS							
	24.5	25	25.5	26	26.5	27	27.5	28
8	9.322	9.262	9.205	9.151	9.100	9.051	9.005	8.961
8.25	9.520	9.461	9.406	9.353	9.303	9.255	9.210	9.167
8.5	9.720	9.663	9.608	9.557	9.508	9.461	9.417	9.375
8.75	9.922	9.866	9.812	9.762	9.714	9.669	9.625	9.585
9	10.126	10.070	10.018	9.969	9.922	9.878	9.836	9.796
9.25	10.331	10.277	10.226	10.177	10.131	10.088	10.047	10.008
9.5	10.537	10.484	10.434	10.387	10.343	10.300	10.260	10.223
9.75	10.745	10.694	10.645	10.599	10.555	10.514	10.475	10.438
10	10.955	10.904	10.857	10.812	10.769	10.729	10.691	10.656
10.25	11.166	11.117	11.070	11.026	10.985	10.946	10.909	10.874
10.5	11.378	11.330	11.285	11.242	11.202	11.164	11.128	11.094
10.75	11.592	11.545	11.501	11.459	11.420	11.383	11.348	11.315
11	11.807	11.761	11.718	11.678	11.639	11.603	11.570	11.538
11.25	12.024	11.979	11.937	11.897	11.860	11.825	11.792	11.761
11.5	12.241	12.198	12.157	12.118	12.082	12.048	12.016	11.986
11.75	12.460	12.418	12.378	12.340	12.305	12.272	12.241	12.212
12	12.680	12.639	12.600	12.563	12.529	12.497	12.467	12.439
12.25	12.901	12.861	12.823	12.788	12.755	12.724	12.695	12.667
12.5	13.124	13.084	13.047	13.013	12.981	12.951	12.923	12.897
12.75	13.347	13.309	13.273	13.240	13.208	13.179	13.152	13.127
13	13.571	13.534	13.499	13.467	13.437	13.409	13.382	13.358
13.25	13.797	13.760	13.727	13.695	13.666	13.639	13.613	13.589
13.5	14.023	13.988	13.955	13.925	13.896	13.870	13.845	13.822
13.75	14.250	14.216	14.184	14.155	14.127	14.102	14.078	14.056
14	14.478	14.445	14.414	14.386	14.359	14.334	14.311	14.290
14.25	14.707	14.675	14.645	14.618	14.592	14.568	14.546	14.525
14.5	14.937	14.906	14.877	14.850	14.825	14.802	14.781	14.761
14.75	15.168	15.138	15.110	15.084	15.059	15.037	15.016	14.997
15	15.399	15.370	15.343	15.318	15.294	15.273	15.253	15.234
15.25	15.632	15.603	15.577	15.552	15.530	15.509	15.490	15.472
15.5	15.865	15.837	15.811	15.788	15.766	15.746	15.728	15.711
15.75	16.098	16.071	16.047	16.024	16.003	15.984	15.966	15.950
16	16.333	16.307	16.283	16.261	16.241	16.222	16.205	16.189
16.25	16.568	16.542	16.519	16.498	16.479	16.461	16.444	16.429
16.5	16.803	16.779	16.757	16.736	16.717	16.700	16.684	16.669
16.75	17.039	17.016	16.994	16.975	16.957	16.940	16.925	16.910
17	17.276	17.254	17.233	17.214	17.196	17.180	17.165	17.152
17.25	17.514	17.492	17.472	17.453	17.436	17.421	17.407	17.394
17.5	17.752	17.730	17.711	17.693	17.677	17.662	17.649	17.636
17.75	17.990	17.970	17.951	17.934	17.918	17.904	17.891	17.879
18	18.229	18.209	18.191	18.175	18.160	18.146	18.133	18.122
18.25	18.468	18.449	18.432	18.416	18.401	18.388	18.376	18.365
18.5	18.708	18.690	18.673	18.658	18.644	18.631	18.619	18.609
18.75	18.949	18.931	18.915	18.900	18.886	18.874	18.863	18.853
19	19.189	19.172	19.157	19.142	19.129	19.118	19.107	19.097
19.25	19.431	19.414	19.399	19.385	19.373	19.362	19.351	19.342
19.5	19.672	19.656	19.642	19.628	19.617	19.606	19.596	19.587
19.75	19.914	19.899	19.885	19.872	19.861	19.850	19.841	19.832
20	20.156	20.141	20.128	20.116	20.105	20.095	20.086	20.078
20.25	20.399	20.385	20.372	20.360	20.349	20.340	20.331	20.323

TABLE A (*continued*)

% INTEREST	YEARS							
	24.5	25	25.5	26	26.5	27	27.5	28
20.5	20.642	20.628	20.616	20.604	20.594	20.585	20.577	20.569
20.75	20.885	20.872	20.860	20.849	20.839	20.831	20.823	20.816
21	21.129	21.116	21.104	21.094	21.085	21.076	21.069	21.062
21.25	21.373	21.360	21.349	21.339	21.330	21.322	21.315	21.308
21.5	21.617	21.605	21.594	21.585	21.576	21.568	21.561	21.555
21.75	21.861	21.850	21.840	21.830	21.822	21.815	21.808	21.802
22	22.106	22.095	22.085	22.076	22.068	22.061	22.055	22.049
22.25	22.351	22.340	22.331	22.322	22.315	22.308	22.302	22.296
22.5	22.596	22.586	22.577	22.569	22.561	22.555	22.549	22.544
22.75	22.841	22.832	22.823	22.815	22.808	22.802	22.796	22.791
23	23.087	23.078	23.069	23.062	23.055	23.049	23.044	23.039
23.25	23.333	23.324	23.316	23.309	23.302	23.296	23.291	23.287
23.5	23.579	23.570	23.562	23.555	23.549	23.544	23.539	23.535
23.75	23.825	23.817	23.809	23.803	23.797	23.792	23.787	23.783
24	24.071	24.063	24.056	24.050	24.044	24.039	24.035	24.031
24.25	24.318	24.310	24.303	24.297	24.292	24.287	24.283	24.279
24.5	24.565	24.557	24.551	24.545	24.540	24.535	24.531	24.528
24.75	24.811	24.804	24.798	24.792	24.788	24.783	24.779	24.776
25	25.058	25.052	25.046	25.040	25.036	25.031	25.028	25.025

TABLE A (*continued*)

% INTEREST	YEARS							
	28.5	29	29.5	30	30.5	31	31.5	32
8	8.919	8.879	8.841	8.805	8.771	8.738	8.706	8.676
8.25	9.126	9.087	9.050	9.015	8.982	8.950	8.919	8.890
8.5	9.335	9.297	9.261	9.227	9.194	9.163	9.134	9.106
8.75	9.546	9.509	9.474	9.440	9.409	9.379	9.350	9.323
9	9.758	9.722	9.688	9.656	9.625	9.596	9.568	9.541
9.25	9.972	9.937	9.904	9.872	9.842	9.814	9.787	9.762
9.5	10.187	10.153	10.121	10.090	10.061	10.034	10.008	9.983
9.75	10.404	10.371	10.339	10.310	10.282	10.255	10.230	10.206
10	10.622	10.590	10.560	10.531	10.504	10.478	10.454	10.431
10.25	10.841	10.810	10.781	10.753	10.727	10.702	10.679	10.657
10.5	11.062	11.032	11.004	10.977	10.952	10.928	10.905	10.884
10.75	11.284	11.255	11.228	11.202	11.177	11.154	11.132	11.112
11	11.508	11.480	11.453	11.428	11.404	11.382	11.361	11.341
11.25	11.732	11.705	11.679	11.655	11.632	11.611	11.591	11.572
11.5	11.958	11.932	11.907	11.884	11.862	11.841	11.821	11.803
11.75	12.185	12.160	12.135	12.113	12.092	12.072	12.053	12.035
12	12.413	12.388	12.365	12.343	12.323	12.304	12.286	12.269
12.25	12.642	12.618	12.596	12.575	12.555	12.537	12.519	12.503
12.5	12.872	12.849	12.827	12.807	12.788	12.770	12.754	12.738
12.75	13.103	13.081	13.060	13.040	13.022	13.005	12.989	12.974
13	13.335	13.313	13.293	13.274	13.257	13.241	13.225	13.211
13.25	13.567	13.547	13.527	13.509	13.492	13.477	13.462	13.448
13.5	13.801	13.781	13.762	13.745	13.729	13.714	13.700	13.686
13.75	14.035	14.016	13.998	13.981	13.966	13.951	13.938	13.925
14	14.270	14.252	14.234	14.218	14.204	14.190	14.177	14.165
14.25	14.506	14.488	14.472	14.456	14.442	14.429	14.416	14.405
14.5	14.742	14.725	14.709	14.695	14.681	14.668	14.656	14.645
14.75	14.980	14.963	14.948	14.934	14.921	14.908	14.897	14.887
15	15.217	15.202	15.187	15.173	15.161	15.149	15.138	15.128
15.25	15.456	15.441	15.427	15.414	15.401	15.390	15.380	15.370
15.5	15.695	15.680	15.667	15.654	15.643	15.632	15.622	15.613
15.75	15.934	15.920	15.907	15.895	15.884	15.874	15.865	15.856
16	16.174	16.161	16.149	16.137	16.127	16.117	16.108	16.100
16.25	16.415	16.402	16.390	16.379	16.369	16.360	16.351	16.343
16.5	16.656	16.644	16.632	16.622	16.612	16.603	16.595	16.588
16.75	16.898	16.886	16.875	16.865	16.856	16.847	16.839	16.832
17	17.140	17.128	17.118	17.108	17.099	17.091	17.084	17.077
17.25	17.382	17.371	17.361	17.352	17.343	17.336	17.329	17.322
17.5	17.625	17.614	17.605	17.596	17.588	17.581	17.574	17.568
17.75	17.868	17.858	17.849	17.840	17.833	17.826	17.819	17.813
18	18.111	18.102	18.093	18.085	18.078	18.071	18.065	18.059
18.25	18.355	18.346	18.338	18.330	18.323	18.317	18.311	18.306
18.5	18.599	18.591	18.583	18.575	18.569	18.563	18.557	18.552
18.75	18.844	18.835	18.828	18.821	18.815	18.809	18.804	18.799
19	19.089	19.081	19.073	19.067	19.061	19.055	19.050	19.046
19.25	19.334	19.326	19.319	19.313	19.307	19.302	19.297	19.293
19.5	19.579	19.572	19.565	19.559	19.554	19.549	19.544	19.540
19.75	19.825	19.818	19.811	19.806	19.800	19.796	19.791	19.787
20	20.070	20.064	20.058	20.052	20.047	20.043	20.039	20.035
20.25	20.316	20.310	20.304	20.299	20.294	20.290	20.286	20.283

TABLE A (*continued*)

% Interest	28.5	29	29.5	30	30.5	31	31.5	32
				Years				
20.5	20.563	20.557	20.551	20.546	20.542	20.538	20.534	20.531
20.75	20.809	20.803	20.798	20.793	20.789	20.785	20.782	20.779
21	21.056	21.050	21.045	21.041	21.037	21.033	21.030	21.027
21.25	21.303	21.297	21.293	21.288	21.284	21.281	21.278	21.275
21.5	21.550	21.545	21.540	21.536	21.532	21.529	21.526	21.524
21.75	21.797	21.792	21.788	21.784	21.780	21.777	21.774	21.772
22	22.044	22.040	22.035	22.032	22.029	22.026	22.023	22.021
22.25	22.292	22.287	22.283	22.280	22.277	22.274	22.271	22.269
22.5	22.539	22.535	22.531	22.528	22.525	22.522	22.520	22.518
22.75	22.787	22.783	22.780	22.776	22.774	22.771	22.769	22.767
23	23.035	23.031	23.028	23.025	23.022	23.020	23.018	23.016
23.25	23.283	23.279	23.276	23.273	23.271	23.268	23.266	23.265
23.5	23.531	23.528	23.525	23.522	23.519	23.517	23.515	23.514
23.75	23.779	23.776	23.773	23.770	23.768	23.766	23.764	23.763
24	24.027	24.024	24.022	24.019	24.017	24.015	24.013	24.012
24.25	24.276	24.273	24.270	24.268	24.266	24.264	24.263	24.261
24.5	24.524	24.522	24.519	24.517	24.515	24.513	24.512	24.510
24.75	24.773	24.770	24.768	24.766	24.764	24.762	24.761	24.760
25	25.022	25.019	25.017	25.015	25.013	25.012	25.010	25.009

TABLE A (*continued*)

% INTEREST	YEARS							
	32.5	33	33.5	34	34.5	35	35.5	36
8	8.648	8.621	8.595	8.570	8.546	8.523	8.501	8.481
8.25	8.862	8.836	8.811	8.787	8.764	8.742	8.721	8.701
8.5	9.079	9.053	9.029	9.006	8.983	8.962	8.942	8.923
8.75	9.297	9.272	9.249	9.226	9.205	9.184	9.165	9.146
9	9.516	9.492	9.470	9.448	9.428	9.408	9.389	9.372
9.25	9.737	9.714	9.692	9.672	9.652	9.633	9.615	9.598
9.5	9.960	9.938	9.917	9.896	9.877	9.859	9.842	9.826
9.75	10.184	10.162	10.142	10.123	10.104	10.087	10.071	10.055
10	10.409	10.388	10.369	10.350	10.333	10.316	10.300	10.285
10.25	10.636	10.616	10.597	10.579	10.562	10.546	10.531	10.517
10.5	10.863	10.844	10.826	10.809	10.793	10.778	10.763	10.749
10.75	11.092	11.074	11.057	11.040	11.025	11.010	10.996	10.983
11	11.322	11.305	11.288	11.272	11.258	11.243	11.230	11.218
11.25	11.554	11.537	11.521	11.506	11.491	11.478	11.465	11.453
11.5	11.786	11.769	11.754	11.740	11.726	11.713	11.701	11.690
11.75	12.019	12.003	11.989	11.975	11.962	11.950	11.938	11.927
12	12.253	12.238	12.224	12.211	12.198	12.187	12.176	12.165
12.25	12.488	12.473	12.460	12.447	12.436	12.424	12.414	12.404
12.5	12.724	12.710	12.697	12.685	12.674	12.663	12.653	12.644
12.75	12.960	12.947	12.935	12.923	12.912	12.902	12.893	12.884
13	13.197	13.185	13.173	13.162	13.152	13.142	13.133	13.125
13.25	13.435	13.424	13.412	13.402	13.392	13.383	13.374	13.366
13.5	13.674	13.663	13.652	13.642	13.633	13.624	13.616	13.608
13.75	13.914	13.903	13.892	13.883	13.874	13.866	13.858	13.851
14	14.154	14.143	14.133	14.124	14.116	14.108	14.101	14.094
14.25	14.394	14.384	14.375	14.366	14.358	14.351	14.344	14.337
14.5	14.635	14.626	14.617	14.609	14.601	14.594	14.587	14.581
14.75	14.877	14.868	14.859	14.852	14.844	14.838	14.831	14.826
15	15.119	15.110	15.102	15.095	15.088	15.082	15.076	15.070
15.25	15.362	15.353	15.346	15.339	15.332	15.326	15.321	15.315
15.5	15.605	15.597	15.590	15.583	15.577	15.571	15.566	15.561
15.75	15.848	15.841	15.834	15.827	15.822	15.816	15.811	15.807
16	16.092	16.085	16.078	16.072	16.067	16.062	16.057	16.053
16.25	16.336	16.329	16.323	16.317	16.312	16.307	16.303	16.299
16.5	16.581	16.574	16.568	16.563	16.558	16.553	16.549	16.545
16.75	16.826	16.819	16.814	16.809	16.804	16.800	16.796	16.792
17	17.071	17.065	17.060	17.055	17.050	17.046	17.043	17.039
17.25	17.316	17.311	17.306	17.301	17.297	17.293	17.290	17.286
17.5	17.562	17.557	17.552	17.548	17.544	17.540	17.537	17.534
17.75	17.808	17.803	17.799	17.795	17.791	17.787	17.784	17.781
18	18.054	18.050	18.045	18.042	18.038	18.035	18.032	18.029
18.25	18.301	18.296	18.292	18.289	18.285	18.282	18.279	18.277
18.5	18.548	18.543	18.540	18.536	18.533	18.530	18.527	18.525
18.75	18.794	18.790	18.787	18.784	18.781	18.778	18.775	18.773
19	19.042	19.038	19.034	19.031	19.028	19.026	19.024	19.021
19.25	19.289	19.285	19.282	19.279	19.277	19.274	19.272	19.270
19.5	19.536	19.533	19.530	19.527	19.525	19.522	19.520	19.518
19.75	19.784	19.781	19.778	19.775	19.773	19.771	19.769	19.767
20	20.032	20.029	20.026	20.024	20.021	20.019	20.017	20.016
20.25	20.280	20.277	20.274	20.272	20.270	20.268	20.266	20.265

TABLE A (*continued*)

% INTEREST				YEARS				
	32.5	33	33.5	34	34.5	35	35.5	36
20.5	20.528	20.525	20.523	20.520	20.518	20.517	20.515	20.514
20.75	20.776	20.773	20.771	20.769	20.767	20.765	20.764	20.763
21	21.024	21.022	21.020	21.018	21.016	21.014	21.013	21.012
21.25	21.273	21.270	21.268	21.266	21.265	21.263	21.262	21.261
21.5	21.521	21.519	21.517	21.515	21.514	21.512	21.511	21.510
21.75	21.770	21.768	21.766	21.764	21.763	21.762	21.760	21.759
22	22.018	22.017	22.015	22.013	22.012	22.011	22.010	22.009
22.25	22.267	22.265	22.264	22.262	22.261	22.260	22.259	22.258
22.5	22.516	22.514	22.513	22.511	22.510	22.509	22.508	22.507
22.75	22.765	22.763	22.762	22.761	22.760	22.759	22.758	22.757
23	23.014	23.012	23.011	23.010	23.009	23.008	23.007	23.006
23.25	23.263	23.262	23.260	23.259	23.258	23.257	23.257	23.256
23.5	23.512	23.511	23.510	23.509	23.508	23.507	23.506	23.505
23.75	23.761	23.760	23.759	23.758	23.757	23.756	23.756	23.755
24	24.011	24.009	24.008	24.007	24.007	24.006	24.005	24.005
24.25	24.260	24.259	24.258	24.257	24.256	24.255	24.255	24.254
24.5	24.509	24.508	24.507	24.506	24.506	24.505	24.504	24.504
24.75	24.759	24.758	24.757	24.756	24.755	24.755	24.754	24.754
25	25.008	25.007	25.006	25.006	25.005	25.004	25.004	25.003

Appendix

TABLE A (*continued*)

% INTEREST	36.5	37	37.5	38	38.5	39	39.5	40
				YEARS				
8	8.461	8.442	8.424	8.406	8.390	8.374	8.358	8.344
8.25	8.682	8.664	8.646	8.629	8.613	8.598	8.584	8.570
8.5	8.905	8.887	8.870	8.854	8.839	8.824	8.810	8.797
8.75	9.129	9.112	9.096	9.081	9.066	9.052	9.039	9.026
9	9.355	9.338	9.323	9.308	9.294	9.281	9.268	9.256
9.25	9.582	9.566	9.552	9.538	9.524	9.512	9.499	9.488
9.5	9.810	9.795	9.781	9.768	9.755	9.743	9.732	9.721
9.75	10.040	10.026	10.012	10.000	9.988	9.976	9.965	9.955
10	10.271	10.258	10.245	10.233	10.221	10.210	10.200	10.190
10.25	10.503	10.490	10.478	10.466	10.455	10.445	10.435	10.426
10.5	10.736	10.724	10.712	10.701	10.691	10.681	10.672	10.663
10.75	10.971	10.959	10.948	10.937	10.927	10.918	10.909	10.901
11	11.206	11.195	11.184	11.174	11.165	11.156	11.147	11.140
11.25	11.442	11.431	11.421	11.412	11.403	11.395	11.387	11.379
11.5	11.679	11.669	11.659	11.651	11.642	11.634	11.627	11.619
11.75	11.917	11.907	11.898	11.890	11.882	11.874	11.867	11.860
12	12.156	12.146	12.138	12.130	12.122	12.115	12.108	12.102
12.25	12.395	12.386	12.378	12.370	12.363	12.357	12.350	12.344
12.5	12.635	12.627	12.619	12.612	12.605	12.599	12.593	12.587
12.75	12.876	12.868	12.861	12.854	12.847	12.841	12.836	12.830
13	13.117	13.110	13.103	13.096	13.090	13.084	13.079	13.074
13.25	13.359	13.352	13.345	13.339	13.333	13.328	13.323	13.318
13.5	13.601	13.595	13.588	13.583	13.577	13.572	13.568	13.563
13.75	13.844	13.838	13.832	13.827	13.822	13.817	13.812	13.808
14	14.088	14.082	14.076	14.071	14.066	14.062	14.058	14.054
14.25	14.331	14.326	14.321	14.316	14.311	14.307	14.303	14.299
14.5	14.576	14.570	14.565	14.561	14.557	14.553	14.549	14.546
14.75	14.820	14.815	14.811	14.806	14.802	14.799	14.795	14.792
15	15.065	15.061	15.056	15.052	15.048	15.045	15.042	15.039
15.25	15.311	15.306	15.302	15.298	15.295	15.291	15.288	15.286
15.5	15.556	15.552	15.548	15.545	15.541	15.538	15.535	15.533
15.75	15.802	15.798	15.795	15.791	15.788	15.785	15.783	15.780
16	16.049	16.045	16.041	16.038	16.035	16.033	16.030	16.028
16.25	16.295	16.292	16.288	16.285	16.283	16.280	16.278	16.276
16.5	16.542	16.538	16.535	16.533	16.530	16.528	16.526	16.524
16.75	16.789	16.786	16.783	16.780	16.778	16.776	16.773	16.772
17	17.036	17.033	17.030	17.028	17.026	17.024	17.022	17.020
17.25	17.283	17.281	17.278	17.276	17.274	17.272	17.270	17.268
17.5	17.531	17.528	17.526	17.524	17.522	17.520	17.518	17.517
17.75	17.779	17.776	17.774	17.772	17.770	17.768	17.767	17.765
18	18.027	18.024	18.022	18.020	18.019	18.017	18.016	18.014
18.25	18.275	18.272	18.270	18.269	18.267	18.266	18.264	18.263
18.5	18.523	18.521	18.519	18.517	18.516	18.514	18.513	18.512
18.75	18.771	18.769	18.768	18.766	18.765	18.763	18.762	18.761
19	19.020	19.018	19.016	19.015	19.013	19.012	19.011	19.010
19.25	19.268	19.266	19.265	19.264	19.262	19.261	19.260	19.259
19.5	19.517	19.515	19.514	19.513	19.511	19.510	19.509	19.508
19.75	19.766	19.764	19.763	19.762	19.760	19.759	19.759	19.758
20	20.014	20.013	20.012	20.011	20.010	20.009	20.008	20.007
20.25	20.263	20.262	20.261	20.260	20.259	20.258	20.257	20.257

TABLE A (*continued*)

% INTEREST	YEARS							
	36.5	37	37.5	38	38.5	39	39.5	40
20.5	20.512	20.511	20.510	20.509	20.508	20.507	20.507	20.506
20.75	20.761	20.760	20.759	20.758	20.758	20.757	20.756	20.756
21	21.011	21.009	21.009	21.008	21.007	21.006	21.006	21.005
21.25	21.260	21.259	21.258	21.257	21.256	21.256	21.255	21.255
21.5	21.509	21.508	21.507	21.507	21.506	21.505	21.505	21.504
21.75	21.758	21.757	21.757	21.756	21.755	21.755	21.754	21.754
22	22.008	22.007	22.006	22.006	22.005	22.004	22.004	22.004
22.25	22.257	22.256	22.256	22.255	22.255	22.254	22.254	22.253
22.5	22.507	22.506	22.505	22.505	22.504	22.504	22.503	22.503
22.75	22.756	22.755	22.755	22.754	22.754	22.753	22.753	22.753
23	23.006	23.005	23.004	23.004	23.004	23.003	23.003	23.003
23.25	23.255	23.255	23.254	23.254	23.253	23.253	23.253	23.252
23.5	23.505	23.504	23.504	23.503	23.503	23.503	23.502	23.502
23.75	23.754	23.754	23.753	23.753	23.753	23.752	23.752	23.752
24	24.004	24.004	24.003	24.003	24.003	24.002	24.002	24.002
24.25	24.254	24.253	24.253	24.253	24.252	24.252	24.252	24.252
24.5	24.503	24.503	24.503	24.502	24.502	24.502	24.502	24.501
24.75	24.753	24.753	24.753	24.752	24.752	24.752	24.752	24.751
25	25.003	25.003	25.002	25.002	25.002	25.002	25.001	25.001

Appendix

TABLE B.

Constant Annual Percents for Loans with Annual Payments

*To be used only in the event of 1 payment
made annually or semiannually.*

% INTEREST	YEARS							
	1	1.5	2	2.5	3	3.5	4	4.5
6	106.001	71.692	54.544	44.261	37.411	32.522	28.859	26.014
6.25	106.250	71.901	54.735	44.441	37.584	32.691	29.025	26.177
6.5	106.501	72.112	54.926	44.622	37.758	32.860	29.190	26.340
6.75	106.751	72.323	55.118	44.803	37.932	33.029	29.357	26.504
7	107.001	72.533	55.309	44.983	38.105	33.198	29.523	26.669
7.25	107.251	72.744	55.501	45.164	38.280	33.368	29.690	26.834
7.5	107.500	72.954	55.693	45.345	38.454	33.538	29.857	26.999
7.75	107.751	73.166	55.885	45.526	38.629	33.709	30.024	27.164
8	108.000	73.376	56.077	45.708	38.803	33.879	30.192	27.330
8.25	108.251	73.588	56.270	45.890	38.979	34.050	30.360	27.497
8.5	108.501	73.799	56.462	46.072	39.154	34.221	30.529	27.664
8.75	108.750	74.010	56.654	46.254	39.330	34.393	30.698	27.831
9	109.001	74.221	56.847	46.436	39.506	34.565	30.867	27.998
9.25	109.250	74.432	57.040	46.618	39.682	34.737	31.036	28.166
9.5	109.501	74.644	57.233	46.801	39.858	34.909	31.206	28.334
9.75	109.750	74.855	57.426	46.984	40.035	35.082	31.377	28.503
10	110.001	75.067	57.619	47.167	40.212	35.255	31.547	28.672
10.25	110.250	75.278	57.812	47.350	40.389	35.428	31.718	28.841

TABLE B (*continued*)

% INTEREST	YEARS							
	5	5.5	6	6.5	7	7.5	8	8.5
6	23.740	21.882	20.336	19.031	17.914	16.947	16.104	15.361
6.25	23.901	22.043	20.496	19.190	18.073	17.107	16.263	15.521
6.5	24.064	22.204	20.657	19.351	18.233	17.267	16.424	15.682
6.75	24.226	22.366	20.818	19.511	18.394	17.428	16.585	15.843
7	24.389	22.528	20.980	19.673	18.555	17.590	16.747	16.006
7.25	24.553	22.690	21.142	19.835	18.718	17.752	16.910	16.169
7.5	24.717	22.853	21.305	19.997	18.880	17.915	17.073	16.332
7.75	24.881	23.017	21.468	20.161	19.043	18.078	17.237	16.497
8	25.046	23.181	21.632	20.324	19.207	18.243	17.401	16.662
8.25	25.211	23.346	21.796	20.489	19.372	18.408	17.567	16.828
8.5	25.377	23.511	21.961	20.654	19.537	18.573	17.733	16.995
8.75	25.543	23.676	22.126	20.819	19.703	18.739	17.900	17.163
9	25.709	23.843	22.292	20.985	19.869	18.906	18.068	17.331
9.25	25.876	24.009	22.458	21.152	20.036	19.074	18.236	17.500
9.5	26.044	24.176	22.625	21.319	20.204	19.242	18.405	17.670
9.75	26.211	24.343	22.793	21.486	20.372	19.411	18.574	17.840
10	26.380	24.511	22.961	21.655	20.541	19.580	18.744	18.012
10.25	26.548	24.680	23.129	21.823	20.710	19.750	18.915	18.183

TABLE B (*continued*)

% INTEREST	9	9.5	10	10.5	11	11.5	12	12.5
6	14.702	14.115	13.587	13.111	12.679	12.287	11.928	11.599
6.25	14.863	14.275	13.748	13.273	12.842	12.450	12.092	11.763
6.5	15.024	14.437	13.911	13.436	13.006	12.614	12.257	11.929
6.75	15.186	14.600	14.074	13.600	13.170	12.780	12.423	12.096
7	15.349	14.763	14.238	13.764	13.336	12.946	12.590	12.264
7.25	15.512	14.927	14.403	13.930	13.502	13.113	12.759	12.434
7.5	15.677	15.092	14.569	14.097	13.670	13.282	12.928	12.604
7.75	15.842	15.258	14.735	14.264	13.838	13.451	13.098	12.775
8	16.008	15.425	14.903	14.433	14.008	13.621	13.270	12.948
8.25	16.175	15.593	15.071	14.602	14.178	13.793	13.442	13.121
8.5	16.342	15.761	15.241	14.773	14.349	13.965	13.615	13.296
8.75	16.511	15.930	15.411	14.944	14.522	14.139	13.790	13.471
9	16.680	16.101	15.582	15.116	14.695	14.313	13.965	13.648
9.25	16.850	16.271	15.754	15.285	14.869	14.488	14.141	13.825
9.5	17.021	16.443	15.927	15.463	15.044	14.664	14.319	14.004
9.75	17.192	16.615	16.100	15.637	15.220	14.841	14.497	14.183
10	17.364	16.789	16.275	15.813	15.396	15.019	14.676	14.364
10.25	17.537	16.963	16.450	15.989	15.574	15.198	14.857	14.545

TABLE B (*continued*)

% INTEREST	13	13.5	14	14.5	15	15.5	16	16.5
6	11.296	11.017	10.759	10.519	10.296	10.089	9.895	9.714
6.25	11.462	11.183	10.926	10.687	10.465	10.259	10.066	9.886
6.5	11.628	11.351	11.094	10.856	10.635	10.430	10.238	10.059
6.75	11.796	11.519	11.264	11.027	10.807	10.602	10.411	10.233
7	11.965	11.689	11.435	11.199	10.979	10.776	10.586	10.408
7.25	12.135	11.860	11.607	11.372	11.154	10.951	10.762	10.586
7.5	12.306	12.033	11.780	11.546	11.329	11.127	10.939	10.764
7.75	12.479	12.206	11.954	11.721	11.505	11.305	11.118	10.944
8	12.652	12.380	12.130	11.898	11.683	11.483	11.298	11.125
8.25	12.827	12.556	12.306	12.076	11.862	11.663	11.479	11.307
8.5	13.002	12.733	12.484	12.255	12.042	11.845	11.661	11.491
8.75	13.179	12.911	12.663	12.435	12.223	12.027	11.845	11.675
9	13.357	13.089	12.843	12.616	12.406	12.211	12.030	11.862
9.25	13.535	13.269	13.025	12.799	12.590	12.396	12.216	12.049
9.5	13.715	13.450	13.207	12.982	12.774	12.582	12.404	12.238
9.75	13.896	13.633	13.390	13.167	12.960	12.769	12.592	12.427
10	14.078	13.816	13.575	13.353	13.147	12.958	12.782	12.618
10.25	14.261	14.000	13.760	13.539	13.336	13.147	12.972	12.810

TABLE B (*continued*)

% INTEREST	17	17.5	18	18.5	19	19.5	20	20.5
6	9.545	9.385	9.236	9.095	8.962	8.837	8.718	8.607
6.25	9.717	9.559	9.410	9.270	9.138	9.014	8.896	8.785
6.5	9.891	9.733	9.585	9.446	9.316	9.192	9.076	8.966
6.75	10.066	9.910	9.763	9.625	9.495	9.372	9.257	9.148
7	10.243	10.087	9.941	9.804	9.675	9.554	9.439	9.331
7.25	10.421	10.266	10.121	9.985	9.857	9.737	9.624	9.516
7.5	10.600	10.447	10.303	10.168	10.041	9.922	9.809	9.703
7.75	10.781	10.629	10.486	10.352	10.226	10.108	9.997	9.891
8	10.963	10.812	10.670	10.537	10.413	10.296	10.185	10.081
8.25	11.146	10.996	10.856	10.724	10.601	10.485	10.375	10.273
8.5	11.331	11.182	11.043	10.913	10.790	10.675	10.567	10.465
8.75	11.517	11.370	11.231	11.102	10.981	10.867	10.760	10.660
9	11.705	11.558	11.421	11.293	11.173	11.060	10.955	10.855
9.25	11.893	11.748	11.612	11.485	11.367	11.255	11.150	11.052
9.5	12.083	11.939	11.805	11.679	11.561	11.451	11.348	11.251
9.75	12.274	12.131	11.998	11.874	11.757	11.648	11.546	11.450
10	12.466	12.325	12.193	12.070	11.955	11.847	11.746	11.651
10.25	12.660	12.520	12.389	12.267	12.153	12.047	11.947	11.854

TABLE B (*continued*)

% INTEREST	21	21.5	22	22.5	23	23.5	24	24.5
6	8.500	8.400	8.305	8.214	8.128	8.046	7.968	7.894
6.25	8.680	8.580	8.486	8.396	8.311	8.230	8.153	8.079
6.5	8.861	8.763	8.669	8.580	8.496	8.416	8.340	8.267
6.75	9.044	8.947	8.854	8.766	8.683	8.604	8.528	8.457
7	9.229	9.132	9.041	8.954	8.871	8.793	8.719	8.648
7.25	9.415	9.319	9.229	9.143	9.062	8.984	8.911	8.841
7.5	9.603	9.508	9.419	9.334	9.254	9.177	9.105	9.036
7.75	9.792	9.699	9.610	9.526	9.447	9.372	9.301	9.233
8	9.983	9.891	9.803	9.721	9.642	9.568	9.498	9.431
8.25	10.176	10.084	9.998	9.916	9.839	9.766	9.697	9.631
8.5	10.370	10.279	10.194	10.113	10.037	9.965	9.897	9.832
8.75	10.565	10.476	10.391	10.312	10.237	10.166	10.099	10.035
9	10.762	10.674	10.591	10.512	10.438	10.368	10.302	10.240
9.25	10.960	10.873	10.791	10.714	10.641	10.572	10.507	10.446
9.5	11.159	11.074	10.993	10.917	10.845	10.777	10.713	10.653
9.75	11.360	11.276	11.196	11.121	11.050	10.984	10.921	10.862
10	11.562	11.479	11.401	11.327	11.257	11.192	11.130	11.072
10.25	11.766	11.684	11.606	11.534	11.465	11.401	11.340	11.283

TABLE B (*continued*)

% INTEREST	YEARS							
	25	25.5	26	26.5	27	27.5	28	28.5
6	7.823	7.755	7.690	7.629	7.570	7.513	7.459	7.408
6.25	8.009	7.943	7.879	7.818	7.760	7.704	7.651	7.600
6.5	8.198	8.132	8.069	8.010	7.952	7.898	7.845	7.795
6.75	8.389	8.324	8.262	8.203	8.147	8.093	8.041	7.992
7	8.581	8.517	8.456	8.398	8.343	8.290	8.239	8.191
7.25	8.775	8.712	8.652	8.595	8.541	8.489	8.439	8.392
7.5	8.971	8.909	8.850	8.794	8.740	8.689	8.641	8.594
7.75	9.169	9.108	9.050	8.994	8.942	8.892	8.844	8.798
8	9.368	9.308	9.251	9.196	9.145	9.096	9.049	9.004
8.25	9.569	9.510	9.454	9.400	9.350	9.301	9.256	9.212
8.5	9.771	9.713	9.658	9.606	9.556	9.509	9.464	9.421
8.75	9.975	9.918	9.864	9.813	9.764	9.718	9.674	9.632
9	10.181	10.125	10.072	10.021	9.974	9.928	9.885	9.844
9.25	10.388	10.333	10.281	10.231	10.184	10.140	10.098	10.058
9.5	10.596	10.542	10.491	10.443	10.397	10.354	10.312	10.273
9.75	10.806	10.753	10.703	10.655	10.611	10.568	10.528	10.490
10	11.017	10.965	10.916	10.870	10.826	10.784	10.745	10.708
10.25	11.229	11.178	11.130	11.085	11.042	11.002	10.963	10.927

TABLE B (*continued*)

% INTEREST	YEARS				
	29	29.5	30	35	40
6	7.358	7.310	7.265	6.897	6.646
6.25	7.552	7.505	7.460	7.101	6.857
6.5	7.747	7.702	7.658	7.306	7.069
6.75	7.945	7.900	7.857	7.514	7.284
7	8.145	8.101	8.059	7.723	7.501
7.25	8.346	8.303	8.262	7.935	7.720
7.5	8.550	8.508	8.467	8.148	7.940
7.75	8.755	8.714	8.674	8.363	8.162
8	8.962	8.921	8.883	8.580	8.386
8.25	9.170	9.131	9.093	8.799	8.611
8.5	9.381	9.342	9.305	9.019	8.838
8.75	9.592	9.555	9.519	9.241	9.066
9	9.806	9.769	9.734	9.464	9.296
9.25	10.020	9.984	9.950	9.688	9.527
9.5	10.236	10.201	10.168	9.914	9.759
9.75	10.454	10.420	10.387	10.141	9.992
10	10.673	10.640	10.608	10.369	10.226
10.25	10.893	10.860	10.830	10.598	10.461